"It's about time a sociologist wrote an amazing and accessible book for a non-specialist audience. *Everything Is Obvious*: Once You Know the Answer* by Duncan J. Watts is that amazing book."

—*Inside Higher Ed*

"Watts is clearly a gifted educator; he makes complex concepts and opaque disciplines accessible and pertinent, resulting in a readable, entertaining, and useful book."

—*Publishers Weekly*

"This clever and amusing assault on conventional wisdom ought to become a popular science hit."

—*Management Today*

"A brilliant account of why, for every hard question, there's a common sense answer that's simple, seductive, and spectacularly wrong. If you are suspicious of pop sociology, rogue economics, and didactic history—or, more importantly, if you aren't!—*Everything is Obvious* is necessary reading. It will literally change the way you think."

—Eric Klinenberg, Professor of Sociology, New York University

"You have to take notice when common sense, the bedrock thing we've always counted on, is challenged brilliantly. Especially when something better than common sense is suggested. As we increasingly experience the world as a maddeningly complex blur, we need a new way of seeing. The fresh ideas in this book, like the invention of spectacles, help bring things into better focus."

—Alan Alda

"Watts brings science to life. A complicated, global, inter-connected world, one which often overwhelms, is tamed by wit, skepticism, and the power to challenge conventional wisdom. The book will help you see patterns, where you might have thought chaos ruled."

—Sudhir Venkatesh, William B. Ransford Professor of Sociology, Columbia University

"A truly important work that's bound to rattle the cages of pseudo- and self-proclaimed experts in every field. If this book doesn't force you to re-examine what you're doing, something is wrong with you."

—Guy Kawasaki, author of *Enchantment: The Art of Changing Hearts, Minds, and Actions,* and cofounder of Alltop.com

EVERYTHING
IS OBVIOUS

EVERYTHING IS OBVIOUS*

*Once You Know the Answer

Duncan J. Watts

CROWN
BUSINESS
NEW YORK

Library of Congress Cataloging-in-Publication Data
Watts, Duncan J., 1971–
Everything is obvious : once you know the answer /
Duncan Watts.
p. cm.
1. Thought and thinking.   2. Common sense.   3. Reasoning.
I. Title.

BF441.W347 2011
153.4–dc22
2010031550

ISBN 978-0-307-95179-3
eISBN 978-0-385-53169-6

Book design by R. Bull
Cover design by Jessie Bright
Cover photograph by Keenan

First Paperback Edition

146122990

For Jack and Lily

CONTENTS

PREFACE

A Sociologist's Apology

In January 1998, about halfway through my first year out of graduate school, my housemate at the time handed me a copy of *New Scientist* magazine containing a book review by the physicist and science writer John Gribbin. The book Gribbin was reviewing was called *Tricks of the Trade,* by the Chicago sociologist Howard Becker, and was mostly a collection of Becker's musings on how to do productive social science research. Gribbin clearly hated it, judging Becker's insights to be the kind of self-evident checks that "real scientists learn in the cradle." But he didn't stop there. He went on to note that the book had merely reinforced his opinion that all of social science was "something of an oxymoron" and that "any physicist threatened by cuts in funding ought to consider a career in the social sciences, where it ought to be possible to solve the problems the social scientists are worked up about in a trice."[1]

There was a reason my roommate had given me this particular review to read and why that particular line stuck in my head. I had majored in physics at college, and at the time when I read Gribbin's review I had just finished my PhD in engineering; I had written my dissertation on the mathematics of what are now called small-world networks.[2] But although my training had been in physics and mathematics, my interests had turned increasingly toward the social sciences and I was just beginning what turned out to be a career in sociology. So I felt that in a sense I was embarking on a miniature version of Gribbin's proposed experiment. And to be honest, I might have suspected that he was right.

Twelve years later, however, I think I can say that the problems sociologists, economists, and other social scientists are "worked up about" are not going to be solved in a trice, by me or even by a legion of physicists. I say this because since the late 1990s many hundreds, if not thousands of physicists, computer scientists, mathematicians, and other "hard" scientists have taken an increasing interest in questions that have traditionally been the province of the social sciences—questions about the structure of social networks, the dynamics of group formation, the spread of information and influence, or the evolution of cities and markets. Whole fields have arisen over the past decade with ambitious names like "network science" and "econophysics." Datasets of immense proportions have been analyzed, countless new theoretical models have been proposed, and thousands of papers have been published, many of them in the world's leading science journals, such as *Science, Nature,* and *Physical Review Letters.* Entire new funding programs have come into existence to support these new research directions. Conferences on topics such as "computational social science" increasingly provide forums for scientists to interact across old disciplinary boundaries. And yes, many new jobs have appeared that offer young physicists the chance to explore problems that once would have been deemed beneath them.

The sum total of this activity has far exceeded the level of effort that Gribbin's offhand remark implied was required. So what have we learned about those problems that social scientists were so worked up about back in 1998? What do we really know about the nature of deviant behavior or the origins of social practices or the forces that shift cultural norms—

the kinds of problems that Becker talks about in his book—that we didn't know then? What new solutions has this new science provided to real-world problems, like helping relief agencies respond more effectively to humanitarian disasters in places like Haiti or New Orleans, or helping law enforcement agencies stop terrorist attacks, or helping financial regulatory agencies police Wall Street and reduce systemic risk? And for all the thousands of papers that have been published by physicists in the past decade, how much closer are we to answering the really big questions of social science, like the economic development of nations, the globalization of the economy, or the relationship between immigration, inequality, and intolerance? Pick up the newspaper and judge for yourself, but I would say not much.[3]

If there's a lesson here, you might think it would be that the problems of social science are hard not just for social scientists, but for everyone, even physicists. But this lesson, it seems, has not been learned. Quite to the contrary, in fact, in 2006 Senator Kay Bailey Hutchison, a Republican from Texas, proposed that Congress cut the entire social and behavioral sciences budget of the National Science Foundation. Bailey Hutchison, it should be noted, is not antiscience—in 2005 she proposed doubling funds for medical science. Rather, it was exclusively *social* science research that she felt "is not where we should be directing [NSF] resources at this time." Ultimately the proposal was defeated, but one might still wonder what the good senator was thinking. Presumably she doesn't think that social *problems* are unimportant—surely no one would argue that immigration, economic development, and inequality are problems that are somehow unworthy of attention. Rather it appears that, like Gribbin, she doesn't consider social problems to be *scientific* problems, requiring the prolonged attention of serious scientists. Or as

Hutchinson's colleague from Oklahoma, Senator Tom Coburn, put it three years later in a similar proposal, "Theories on political behavior are best left to CNN, pollsters, pundits, historians, candidates, political parties, and the voters."[4]

Senators Hutchinson and Coburn are not alone in their skepticism of what social science has to offer. Since becoming a sociologist, I have frequently been asked by curious outsiders what sociology has to say about the world that an intelligent person couldn't have figured out on their own. It's a reasonable question, but as the sociologist Paul Lazarsfeld pointed out nearly sixty years ago, it also reveals a common misconception about the nature of social science. Lazarsfeld was writing about *The American Soldier,* a then-recently published study of more than 600,000 servicemen that had been conducted by the research branch of the war department during and immediately after the Second World War. To make his point, Lazarsfeld listed six findings from the study that he claimed were representative of the report. For example, number two was that "Men from rural backgrounds were usually in better spirits during their Army life than soldiers from city backgrounds." "Aha," says Lazarsfeld's imagined reader, "that makes perfect sense. Rural men in the 1940s were accustomed to harsher living standards and more physical labor than city men, so naturally they had an easier time adjusting. Why did we need such a vast and expensive study to tell me what I could have figured out on my own?"

Why indeed.... But Lazarsfeld then reveals that all six of the "findings" were in fact the exact opposite of what the study actually found. It was city men, not rural men, who were happier during their Army life. Of course, had the reader been told the real answers in the first place she could just as easily have reconciled them with other things that she already thought she knew: "City men are more used to working in crowded conditions and in corporations, with chains of command, strict standards of clothing and social etiquette, and so on. That's obvious!" But that's exactly the point that Lazarsfeld was making. When every answer *and its opposite* appears equally obvious, then, as Lazarsfeld put it, "something is wrong with the entire argument of 'obviousness.' "[5]

Lazarsfeld was talking about social science, but what I will argue in this book is that his point is equally relevant to any activity—whether politics, business, marketing, philanthropy—that involves understanding, predicting, changing, or responding to the behavior of people. Politicians trying to decide how to deal with urban poverty already feel that they have a pretty good idea why people are poor. Marketers planning an advertising campaign already feel that they have a decent sense of what consumers want and how to make them want more of it. And policy makers designing new schemes to drive down healthcare costs or to improve teaching quality in public schools or to reduce smoking or to improve energy conservation already feel that they can do a reasonable job of getting the incentives right. Typically people in these positions do not expect to get everything right all the time. But they also feel that the problems they are contemplating are mostly within their ability to solve—that "it's not rocket science," as it were.[6] Well, I'm no rocket scientist, and I have immense respect for the people who can land a machine the size of a small car on another planet. But the sad fact is that we're actually much better at planning the flight path of an interplanetary rocket than we are at managing the economy, merging two corporations, or even predicting how many copies of a book will sell. So why is it that rocket science *seems* hard, whereas problems having to do with people—which arguably are much harder—*seem* like they ought to be just a matter of common sense? In this book, I argue that the key to the paradox is common sense itself.

Criticizing common sense, it must be said, is a tricky business, if only because it's almost universally regarded as a good thing—when was the last time you were told *not* to use it? Well, I'm going to tell you that a lot. As we'll see, common sense is indeed exquisitely adapted to handling the kind of complexity that arises in everyday situations. And for those situations, it's every bit as good as advertised. But "situations" involving corporations, cultures, markets, nation-states, and global institutions exhibit a very different kind of complexity from everyday situations. And under these circumstances, common sense turns out to suffer from a number of errors that systematically mislead us. Yet because of the way we learn from experience—even experiences that are never repeated, or that take place in other times and places—the failings of commonsense reasoning are rarely apparent to us. Rather, they manifest themselves to us simply as "things we didn't know at the time" but which seem obvious in hindsight. The paradox of common sense, therefore, is that even as it helps us make sense of the world, it can actively undermine our ability to understand it. If you don't quite understand what that last sentence means, that's OK, because explaining it, along with its implications for policy, planning, forecasting, business strategy, marketing, and social science is what the rest of this book is about.

Before I start, though, I would like to make one related point: that in talking with friends and colleagues about this book, I've noticed an interesting pattern. When I describe the argument *in the abstract*—that the way we make sense of the world can actually prevent us from understanding it—they nod their heads in vigorous agreement. "Yes," they say, "I've always thought that people believe all sorts of silly things in order to make themselves feel like they understand things that in fact they don't understand at all." Yet when the very same argument calls into question some particular belief of their own, they invariably change their tune. "Everything you are saying about the pitfalls of common sense and intuition may be right," they are in effect saying, "but it doesn't undermine my own confidence in the particular beliefs I happen to hold." It's as if the failure of commonsense reasoning is only the failure of other people's reasoning, not their own.

People, of course, make this sort of error all the time. Around 90 percent of Americans believe they are better-than-average drivers, and a similarly impossible number of people claim that they are happier, more popular, or more likely to succeed than the average person. In one study, an incredible 25 percent of respondents rated themselves in the top 1 percent in terms of leadership ability.[7] This "illusory superiority" effect is so common and so well known that it even has a colloquial catchphrase—the Lake Wobegone effect, named for *Prairie Home Companion* host Garrison Keillor's fictitious town where "all the children are above average." It's probably not surprising, therefore, that people are much more willing to believe that others have misguided beliefs about the world than that their own beliefs are misguided. Nevertheless, the uncomfortable reality is that what applies to "everyone" necessarily applies to us, too. That is, the fallacies embedded in our everyday thinking and explanations, which I will be discussing in more detail later, *must* apply to many of our own, possibly deeply held, beliefs.

None of this is to say that we should abandon all our beliefs and start over from scratch—only that we should hold them up to a spotlight and regard with suspicion. For example, I *do* think that I'm an above-average driver—even though I know that statistically speaking, nearly half the people who think the same thing as I do are wrong. I just can't help it. Knowing this, however, I can at least consider the possibility that I might be deluding myself, and so try to pay attention to when I make mistakes as well as when others do. Possibly I can begin to accept that not every altercation is necessarily the other guy's fault, even if I'm still inclined to think it is. And perhaps I can learn from these experiences to determine what I should do differently as well as what others should be doing differently. Even after doing all this, I can't be sure that I'm a better-than-average driver. But I can at least become a better driver.

In the same way, when we challenge our assumptions about the world—or even more important, when we realize we're making an assumption that we didn't even know we were making—we may or may not change our views. But even if we don't, the exercise of challenging them should at least force us to notice our own stubbornness, which in turn should give us pause. Questioning our own beliefs in this way isn't easy, but it is the first step in forming new, hopefully more accurate, beliefs. Because the chances that we're already correct in everything we believe are essentially zero. In fact, the argument that Howard Becker was really making in the book that I read about all those years ago—an argument that was obviously lost on his reviewer, and at the time would have been lost on me, too—was that learning to think like a sociologist means learning to question precisely your instincts about how things work, and possibly to unlearn them altogether. So if reading this book only confirms what you already thought you knew about the world, then I apologize. As a sociologist, I will not have done my job.

EVERYTHING
IS OBVIOUS

PART ONE

COMMON SENSE

CHAPTER 1

The Myth of Common Sense

Every day in New York City five million people ride the subways. Starting from their homes throughout the boroughs of Manhattan, Brooklyn, Queens, and the Bronx, they pour themselves in through hundreds of stations, pack themselves into thousands of cars that barrel though the dark labyrinth of the Metropolitan Transportation Authority's tunnel system, and then once again flood the platforms and stairwells—a subterranean river of humanity urgently seeking the nearest exit and the open air beyond. As anyone who has ever participated in this daily ritual can attest, the New York subway system is something between a miracle and nightmare, a Rube Goldberg contraption of machines, concrete, and people that in spite of innumerable breakdowns, inexplicable delays, and indecipherable public announcements, more or less gets everyone where they're going, but not without exacting a certain amount of wear and tear on their psyche. Rush hour in particular verges on a citywide mosh pit—of tired workers, frazzled mothers, and shouting, shoving teenagers, all scrabbling over finite increments of space, time, and oxygen. It's not the kind of place you go in search of the milk of human kindness. It's not the kind of place where you'd expect a perfectly healthy, physically able young man to walk up to you and ask you for your seat.

And yet that's precisely what happened one day in the early 1970s when a group of psychology students went out into the subway system on the suggestion of their teacher, the social psychologist Stanley Milgram. Milgram was already famous for his controversial "obedience" studies, conducted some years earlier at Yale, in which he had shown that ordinary people brought into a lab would apply what they thought were deadly electrical shocks to a human subject (really an actor who was pretending to be shocked) simply because they were told to do so by a white-coated researcher who claimed to be running an experiment on learning. The finding that otherwise respectable citizens could, under relatively unexceptional circumstances, perform what seemed like morally incomprehensible acts was deeply disturbing to many people—and the phrase "obedience to authority" has carried a negative connotation ever since.[1]

What people appreciated less, however, is that following the instructions of authority figures is, as a general rule, indispensable to the proper functioning of society. Imagine if students argued with their teachers, workers challenged their bosses, and drivers ignored traffic cops anytime they asked them to do something they didn't like. The world would descend into chaos in about five minutes. Clearly there are moments when it's appropriate to resist authority, and most people would agree that the situation Milgram created in the lab would qualify as such a moment. But what the experiment also illustrated was that the social order that we take for granted in everyday life is maintained in part by hidden rules that we don't even realize exist until we try to break them.

Based on this experience, and having subsequently moved to New York, Milgram had begun to wonder if there was a similar "rule" about asking people for seats on the subway. Like the rule about obeying authority figures, this rule is never really articulated, nor would a typical rider be likely to mention it if asked to describe the rules of subway riding. And yet it exists, as Milgram's students quickly discovered when they went about their little field experiment. Although more than half of the riders asked eventually surrendered their seats, many of them reacted angrily or demanded some explanation for the request. Everyone reacted with surprise, even amazement, and onlookers often made disparaging remarks. But more interesting than the response of the riders was that of the experimenters themselves, who found it extremely difficult to perform the experiment in the first place. Their reluctance was so great, in fact, that they had to go out in pairs, with one of them acting as moral support for the other. When the students reported their discomfort to Milgram, he scoffed at them. But when he tried to do the experiment himself, the simple act of walking up to a complete stranger and asking for his or her seat left him feeling physically nauseated. As trivial as it seemed, in other words, this rule was no more easily violated than the obedience-to-authority "rule" that Milgram had exposed years earlier.[2]

As it turns out, a big city like New York is full of these sorts of rules. On a crowded train, for example, it's no big deal if you're squeezed in against other people. But if someone stands right next to you when the train is empty, it's actually kind of repellant. Whether it's acknowledged or not, there's clearly some rule that encourages us to spread out as much as we can in the available space, and violations of the rule can generate extreme discomfort. In the same way, imagine how uncomfortable you'd feel if someone got on your elevator and stood facing you instead of turning around to face the door. People face each other all the time in enclosed spaces, including on subway trains, and nobody thinks twice about it. But on an elevator it would feel completely weird, just as if the other person had violated some rule—even though it might not have occurred to you until that moment that any such rule existed. Or how about all the rules we follow for passing one another on the sidewalk, holding open doors, getting in line at the deli, acknowledging someone else's right to a cab, making just the right amount of eye contact with drivers as you cross the street at a busy intersection, and generally being considerate of our fellow human beings while still asserting our own right to take up a certain amount of space and time?

No matter where we live, our lives are guided and shaped by unwritten rules—so many of them, in fact, that we couldn't write them all down if we tried. Nevertheless, we expect reasonable people to know them all. Complicating matters, we also expect reasonable people to know which of the many rules that *have* been written down are OK to ignore. When I graduated from high school, for example, I joined the Navy and spent the next four years completing my officer training at the Australian Defence Force Academy. The academy back then was an intense place, replete with barking drill instructors, predawn push-ups, running around in the pouring rain with rifles, and of course lots and lots of rules. At first this new life seemed bizarrely complicated and confusing. However, we quickly learned that although some of the rules were important, to be ignored at your peril, many were enforced with something like a wink and a nod. Not that the punishments couldn't be severe. You could easily get sentenced to seven days of marching around a parade ground for some minor infraction like being late to a meeting or having a wrinkled bedcover. But what you were supposed to understand (although of course you weren't supposed to admit that you understood it) was that life at the academy was more like a game than real life. Sometimes you won, and sometimes you lost, and that was when you ended up on the drill square; but whatever happened, you weren't supposed to take it personally. And sure enough, after about six months of acclimation, situations that would have terrified us on our arrival seemed entirely natural—it was now the rest of the world that seemed odd.

We've all had experiences like this. Maybe not quite as extreme as a military academy—which, twenty years later, sometimes strikes me as having happened in another life. But whether it's learning to fit in at a new school, or learning the ropes in a new job, or learning to live in a foreign country, we've all had to learn to negotiate new environments that at first seem strange and intimidating and filled with rules that we don't understand but eventually become familiar. Very often the formal rules—the ones that are written down—are less important than the informal rules, which just like the rule about subway seats may not even be articulated until we break them. Conversely, rules that we do know about may not be enforced, or may be enforced only sometimes depending on some other rule that we don't know about. When you think about how complex these games of life can be, it seems kind of amazing that we're capable of playing them at all. Yet in the way that young children learn a new language seemingly by osmosis, we learn to navigate even the most novel social environments more or less without even knowing that we're doing it.

COMMON SENSE

The miraculous piece of human intelligence that enables us to solve these problems is what we call common sense. Common sense is so ordinary that we tend to notice it only when it's missing, but it is absolutely essential to functioning in everyday life. Common sense is how we know what to wear when we go to work in the morning, how to behave on the street or the subway, and how to maintain harmonious relationships with our friends and coworkers. It tells us when to obey the rules, when to quietly ignore them, and when to stand up and challenge the rules themselves. It is the essence of social intelligence, and is also deeply embedded in our legal system, in political philosophy, and in professional training.

For something we refer to so often, however, common sense is surprisingly hard to pin down.[3] Roughly speaking, it is the loosely organized set of facts, observations, experiences, insights, and pieces of received wisdom that each of us accumulates over a lifetime, in the course of encountering, dealing with, and learning from, everyday situations. Beyond that, however, it tends to resist easy classification. Some common-sense knowledge is very general in nature—what the American anthropologist Clifford Geertz called an "ancient tangle of received practices, accepted beliefs, habitual judgments, and untaught emotions."[4] But common sense can also refer to more specialized knowledge, as with the everyday working knowledge of a professional, such as a doctor, a lawyer, or an engineer, that develops over years of training and experience. In his address to the annual meeting of the American Sociological Society in Chicago in 1946, Carl Taylor, then president of the association, put it as well as anyone:

> By common sense I mean the knowledge possessed by those who live in the midst and are a part of the social situations and processes which sociologists seek to understand. The term thus used may be synonymous with folk knowledge, or it may be the knowledge possessed

by engineers, by the practical politicians, by those who gather and publish news, or by others who handle or work with and must interpret and predict the behavior or persons and groups.[5]

Taylor's definition highlights two defining features of common sense that seem to differentiate it from other kinds of human knowledge, like science or mathematics. The first of these features is that unlike formal systems of knowledge, which are fundamentally theoretical, common sense is overwhelmingly *practical,* meaning that it is more concerned with providing answers to questions than in worrying about how it came by the answers. From the perspective of common sense, it is good enough to know that something is true, or that it is the way of things. One does not need to know why in order to benefit from the knowledge, and arguably one is better off not worrying about it too much. In contrast with theoretical knowledge, in other words, common sense does not reflect on the world, but instead attempts to deal with it simply "as it is."[6]

The second feature that differentiates common sense from formal knowledge is that while the power of formal systems resides in their ability to organize their specific findings into logical categories described by general principles, the power of common sense lies in its ability to deal with every concrete situation on its own terms. For example, it is a matter of common sense that what we wear or do or say in front of our boss will be different from how we behave in front of our friends, our parents, our parents' friends, or our friends' parents. But whereas a formal system of knowledge would try to derive the appropriate behavior in all these situations from a single, more general "law," common sense just "knows" what the appropriate thing to do is in any particular situation, without knowing how it knows it.[7] It is largely for this reason, in fact, that commonsense knowledge has proven so hard to replicate in computers—because, in contrast with theoretical knowledge, it requires a relatively large number of rules to deal with even a small number of special cases. Let's say, for example, that you wanted to program a robot to navigate the subway. It seems like a relatively simple task. But as you would quickly discover, even a single component of this task such as the "rule" against asking for another person's subway seat turns out to depend on a complex variety of other rules—about seating arrangements on subways in particular, about polite behavior in public in general, about life in crowded cities, and about general-purpose norms of courteousness, sharing, fairness, and ownership—that at first glance seem to have little to do with the rule in question.

Attempts to formalize commonsense knowledge have all encountered versions of this problem—that in order to teach a robot to imitate even a limited range of human behavior, you would have to, in a sense, teach it *everything* about the world. Short of that, the endless subtle distinctions between the things that matter, the things that are supposed to matter but don't, and the things that may or may not matter depending on other things, would always eventually trip up even the most sophisticated robot. As soon as it encountered a situation that was slightly different from those you had programmed it to handle, it would have no idea how to behave. It would stick out like a sore thumb. It would always be screwing up.[8]

People who lack common sense are a bit like the hapless robot in that they never seem to understand what it is that they should be paying attention to, and they never seem to understand what it is that they don't understand. And for exactly the same reason that programming robots is hard, it's surprisingly hard to explain to someone lacking in common sense what it is that they're doing wrong. You can take them back through various examples of when they said or did the wrong thing, and perhaps they'll be able to avoid making exactly those errors again. But as soon as anything is different, they're effectively back to square one. We had a few cadets like that at the academy: otherwise perfectly intelligent, competent people who just couldn't seem to figure out how to play the game. Everyone knew who they were, and everyone could see that they just didn't get it. But because it wasn't exactly clear what it was that they didn't get, we were unable to help them. Bewildered and overwhelmed, most of them eventually left.

NOT COMMON AT ALL

As remarkable as it is, common sense exhibits some mysterious quirks, one of the most striking of which is how much it varies over time, and across cultures. Several years ago, for example, an enterprising group of economists and anthropologists set out to test how different cultures play a particular kind of game, called an ultimatum game. The game goes something like this: First, pick two people and give one of them $100. That person then has to propose a split of the money between himself and the other player, ranging from offering them the whole amount to nothing at all. The other player then gets to accept the deal or reject it. If the second player accepts the deal, they get what they were offered and both players go on their merry way. But if they reject the offer, neither player gets anything; hence the "ultimatum."

In hundreds of these experiments conducted in industrialized societies, researchers had already demonstrated that most players propose a fifty-fifty split, and offers of less than $30 are typically rejected. Economists find this behavior surprising because it conflicts with their standard notion of economic rationality. Even a single dollar, the reasoning goes, is better than nothing at all, so from a strictly rational perspective, recipients ought to accept any offer above zero. And knowing this, rational "proposers" ought to offer the least they can get away with—namely, one dollar. Of course, a moment's thought quickly suggests why people play the way they do—namely that it doesn't seem fair to exploit a situation just because you can. Recipients being offered less than a third therefore feel taken advantage of and so opt to walk away from even a substantial sum of money in order to teach miserly proposers a lesson. And anticipating this response, proposers tend to offer what they assume the recipient will consider a fair split.

If your reaction to this breakthrough insight is that economists need to get out a little more, then you're not alone. If anything seems like common sense, it's that people care about fairness as well as money—sometimes even more so. But when the experimenters replicated the game in fifteen small-scale preindustrial societies across five continents, they found that people in different societies have very different ideas about what counts as fair. At one extreme, the Machiguenga tribe of Peru tended to offer only about a quarter of the total amount, and virtually no offers were refused. At the other extreme, the Au and Gnau tribes of Papua New Guinea tended to make offers that were even better than fifty-fifty, but surprisingly these "hyperfair" offers tended to get rejected just as frequently as unfair offers.[9]

What explains these differences? As it turns out, the Au and Gnau tribes had long-established customs of gift exchange, according to which receiving a gift obligates the receiver to reciprocate at some point in the future. Because there was no equivalent of the ultimatum game in the Au or Gnau societies, they simply "mapped" the unfamiliar interaction onto the most similar social exchange they could think of—which happened to be gift exchange—and responded accordingly. Thus what might have seemed like free money to a Western participant looked to an Au or Gnau participant very much like an unwanted obligation. The Machiguenga, by contrast, live in a society in which the only relationship bonds that carry any expectation of loyalty are with immediate family members. When playing the ultimatum game with a stranger, therefore, Machiguenga participants—again mapping the unfamiliar onto the familiar—saw little obligation to make fair offers, and experienced very little of the resentment that would well up in a Western player upon being presented with a split that was patently unequal. To them, even low offers were seen as a good deal.

Once you understand these features of Au, Gnau, and Machiguenga cultures, their puzzling behavior starts to seem entirely reasonable—commonsense even. And that's exactly what it was. Just as we reflexively regard fairness and reciprocity as commonsense principles in our world that should be respected in general, and should be defended when violated without good reason, so the people of the fifteen preindustrial societies have their own implicit set of understandings about how the world is supposed to work. Those understandings might be different from ours. But once they have been accepted, their commonsense logic works in exactly the same way as ours does. It is simply what any reasonable person would do if they had grown up in that culture.

What these results reveal is that common sense is "common" only to the extent that two people share sufficiently similar social and cultural experiences. Common sense, in other words, depends on what the sociologist Harry Collins calls collective tacit knowledge, meaning that it is encoded in the social norms, customs, and practices of the world.[10] According to Collins, the acquisition of this type of knowledge can be learned only by participating in society itself— and that's why it is so hard to teach to machines. But it also means that even among humans, what seems reasonable to one might seem curious, bizarre, or even repugnant to another. For example, as Clifford Geertz, the anthropologist, has described, the treatment of hermaphroditic children has varied dramatically across different times and cultures. The Romans abhorred and killed them; the Greeks tolerated them; the Navajo revered them; and the east African Pokot tribe regarded them simply as "mistakes," to be kept around or discarded in the same way they might keep or throw out a flawed pot.[11] Likewise, practices including human slavery, sacrifice, cannibalism, foot binding, and female genital mutilation that are reviled in most contemporary cultures have all been (and in some cases, still are) considered entirely legitimate in different times and places.

Another important consequence of the socially embedded nature of common sense is that disagreements over matters of common sense can be surprisingly difficult to resolve. For example, it may seem remarkable to people who have grown up with the impression that New York is a crime-ridden cesspool, or at the very least a cold, hard-edged city full of people you can't trust, that, according to a recent news story, there is a small cadre of Manhattan residents who don't lock their doors. As the article makes clear, most people in the city think that the "no lock people" are crazy. As one woman said, "I live in a high-rise with a doorman, I've been there fifteen years, and I've never heard of a burglary in the building. But that has absolutely nothing to do with it—it's common sense [to lock your door]." Yet the only thing that seems shocking to the people who don't lock their doors is that anyone else would be shocked by it.[12]

What's curious about this story is that the language of the people involved almost precisely mirrors the experiences of Geertz, who noted in his study of witchcraft in Java that "when the whole family of a Javanese boy tells me that the reason he has fallen out of a tree and broken his leg is that the spirit of his deceased grandfather pushed him out because some ritual duty toward the grandfather has been inadvertently overlooked, that, so far as they are concerned, is the beginning, the middle, and the end of the matter: it is precisely what they think has occurred, it is all they think has occurred, and they are puzzled only at my puzzlement at their lack of puzzlement." Disagreements over matters of common sense, in other words, are hard to resolve because it's unclear to either side on what grounds one can even conduct a reasonable argument. Whether the issue is a Western anthropologist discussing witchcraft with preindustrial tribes in Indonesia, New Yorkers disagreeing about door locks, or the NRA disagreeing with the Brady Campaign over the sorts of guns that Americans ought to be able to buy, whatever it is that people believe to be a matter of common sense, they believe it with absolute certainty. They are puzzled only at the fact that others disagree.[13]

SOME RESERVATIONS

That what is self-evident to one person can be seen as silly by another should give us pause about the reliability of common sense as a basis for understanding the world. How can we be confident that what we believe is right when someone else feels equally strongly that it's wrong—especially when we can't articulate why we think we're right in the first place? Of course, we can always write them off as crazy or ignorant or something and therefore not worth paying attention to. But once you go down that road, it gets increasingly hard to account for why we ourselves believe what we do. Consider, for example, that since 1996 support among the general public for allowing same-sex couples to marry has almost doubled, from 25 percent to 45 percent.[14] Presumably those of us who changed our minds over this period do not think that we were crazy fourteen years ago, but we obviously think that we were wrong. So if something that seemed so obvious turned out to be wrong, what else that we believe to be self-evident now will seem wrong to us in the future?

Once we start to examine our own beliefs, in fact, it becomes increasingly unclear even how the various beliefs we espouse at any given time fit together. Most people, for example, consider their own views about politics to be derived from a single coherent worldview: "I'm a moderate liberal" or "I'm a diehard conservative," and so on. If that were true, however, then one would expect that people who identify as liberals would tend to espouse the "liberal" perspective on most matters, and that conservatives would espouse a consistently different view. Yet research finds that regardless of whether people identify themselves as liberals or conservatives, what they think about any one issue, like, say, abortion, has relatively little relation to what they believe about other issues, such as the death penalty or illegal immigration. In other words, we have the impression that our particular beliefs are all derived from some overarching philosophy, but the reality is that we arrive at them quite independently, and often haphazardly.[15]

The same difficulty of reconciling what, individually, appear to be self-evident beliefs shows up even more clearly in the aphorisms that we invoke to make sense of the world. As sociologists are fond of pointing out, many of these aphorisms appear to be direct contradictions of each other. Birds of a feather flock together, but opposites attract. Absence indeed makes the heart grow fonder, but out of sight is out of mind. Look before you leap, but he who hesitates is lost. Of course, it is not necessarily the case that these beliefs are contradictory—because we invoke different aphorisms in different circumstances. But because we never specify the conditions under which one aphorism applies versus another, we have no way of describing what it is that we really think or why we think it. Common sense, in other words, is not so much a worldview as a grab bag of logically inconsistent, often contradictory beliefs, each of which seems right at the time but carries no guarantee of being right any other time.

THE MISUSE OF COMMON SENSE

The fragmented, inconsistent, and even self-contradictory nature of common sense does not generally present a problem in our everyday lives. The reason is that everyday life is effectively broken up into small problems, grounded in very specific contexts that we can solve more or less independently of one another. Under these circumstances, being able to connect our thought processes in a logical manner isn't really the point. It doesn't really matter that absence makes the heart grow fonder in one situation, and that out of sight is out of mind in the next. In any given situation we know the point we're trying to make, or the decision we want to support, and we choose the appropriate piece of commonsense wisdom to apply to it. If we had to explain how all our explanations, attitudes, and commonsense beliefs fit together, we would encounter all kinds of inconsistencies and contradictions. But because our experience of life rarely forces us to perform this task, it doesn't really matter how difficult it would be.

Where it does start to matter, however, is when we use common sense to solve problems that are *not* grounded in the immediate here and now of everyday life—problems that involve anticipating or managing the behavior of large numbers of people, in situations that are distant from us either in time or space. This may sound like an unlikely thing to do, but in fact we do it all the time. Whenever we read a newspaper and try to understand events playing out in some foreign country—the Israel-Palestine conflict, the unfolding insurgency in Iraq, or the seemingly endless conflict in Afghanistan—we are implicitly using our commonsense reasoning to infer the causes and explanations of the events we're reading about. Whenever we form an opinion about financial reform or healthcare policy, we are implicitly using our commonsense reasoning to speculate about how different rules and incentives will affect the various parties' behavior. And whenever we argue about politics or economics or the law, we are implicitly using our commonsense reasoning to reach conclusions about how society will be affected by whatever policy or proposal is being debated.

In none of these cases are we using our common sense to reason about how we should behave in the here and now. Rather, we are using it to reason about how other people behaved—or will behave—in circumstances about which we have at best an incomplete understanding. At some level we understand that the world is complicated, and that everything is somehow connected to everything else. But when we read some story about reforming the healthcare system, or about banker bonuses, or about the Israel-Palestine conflict, we don't try to understand how all these different problems fit together. We just focus on the one little piece of the huge underlying tapestry of the world that's being presented to us at that moment, and form our opinion accordingly. In this way, we can flip through the newspaper while drinking our morning cup of coffee and develop twenty different opinions about twenty different topics without breaking a sweat. It's all just common sense.

It may not matter much, of course, what conclusions ordinary citizens reach about the state of the world in the privacy of their own homes, based on what they're reading in the newspaper or arguing about with their friends. So it may not matter much that the way we reason about the problems of the world is poorly suited to the nature of the problems themselves. But ordinary citizens are not the only ones who apply commonsense reasoning to social problems. When policy makers sit down, say, to design some scheme to alleviate poverty, they invariably rely on their own commonsense ideas about why it is that poor people are poor, and therefore how best to help them. As with all commonsense explanations, it is likely that everyone will have his or her own views, and that these views will be logically inconsistent or even contradictory. Some may believe that people are poor because they lack certain necessary values of hard work and thrift, while others may think they are genetically inferior, and others still may attribute their lack of wealth to lack of opportunities, inferior systems of social support, or other environmental factors. All these beliefs will lead to different proposed solutions, not all of which can be right. Yet policy makers empowered to enact sweeping plans that will affect thousands or millions of people are no less tempted to trust their intuition about the causes of poverty than ordinary citizens reading the newspaper.

A quick look at history suggests that when common sense is used for purposes beyond the everyday, it can fail spectacularly. As the political scientist James Scott writes in *Seeing Like a State,* the late nineteenth and early twentieth centuries were characterized by pervasive optimism among engineers, architects, scientists, and government technocrats that the problems of society could be solved in the same way that the problems of science and engineering had been solved during the Enlightenment and the industrial revolution. According to these "high modernists," the design of cities, the management of natural resources, even the business of running an entire economy were all within the scope of "scientific" planning. As one of the undisputed high priests of modernism, the architect Le Corbusier, wrote in 1923, "the plan is generator; without it poverty, disorder, willfulness reign supreme."[16]

Naturally, the high modernists didn't describe what they were doing as an exercise in using their common sense, preferring instead to clothe their ambitions in the language of science. But as Scott points out, this scientific aura was a mirage. In reality there was no science of planning—just the opinions of individual planners who relied on their intuition to speculate about how their plans would play out in the real world. No one doubts that men like Le Corbusier were brilliant and original thinkers. Nevertheless, the outcomes of their plans, like Soviet collectivization or the Le Corbusier inspired Brasilia, were often disastrous; and some of them, like the social engineering of Nazism or apartheid in South Africa, are now regarded among the great evils of the twentieth century. Moreover, even when these plans did succeed, they often did so in spite of themselves, as individuals on the ground figured out ways to create a reasonable outcome by ignoring, circumventing, or even undermining the plan itself.[17]

Looking back, it may seem as if the failures of high modernism—whether centrally planned economies or centrally designed cities—are a thing of the past, a product of a naïve and simplistic belief in science that we have since outgrown. Yet politicians, bureaucrats, architects, and regulators continue to make essentially the same mistake all the time. As the economist William Easterly has argued, the foreign aid community has been dominated for the past fifty years by large, bureaucratic organizations that are in turn run by powerful individuals whose ideas about what should and should not work inevitably play a large role in determining how resources will be devoted. Just as with the high modernists before them, these "planners," as Easterly calls them, are well-meaning and intelligent people who are often passionately devoted to the task of helping the people of the developing world. Yet in spite of the trillions of dollars of aid that planners have devoted to economic development, there is shockingly little evidence that the recipients are better off for it.[18]

Closer to home, and over roughly the same period of time, urban planners in the United States have repeatedly set out to "solve" the problem of urban poverty and have repeatedly failed. As the journalist and urban activist Jane Jacobs put it fifty years ago, "There is a wistful myth that if only we had enough money to spend—the figure is usually put at a hundred billion dollars—we could wipe out all our slums in ten years. . . . But look what we have built with the first several billions: Low-income projects that have become worse centers of delinquency, vandalism and general social hopelessness than the slums they were supposed to replace."[19] It is ironic that around the same time that Jacobs reached this conclusion, work began on the Robert Taylor Homes in Chicago, the largest public housing project ever built. And sure enough, as the sociologist Sudhir Venkatesh describes in *American Project,* what started out as a high-minded and carefully thought-out plan to help inner-city, largely African American families rise

up into the middle class became a debacle of dilapidated buildings, overcrowded apartments and playgrounds, concentrated
poverty, and eventually gang violence.[20]

The large scale and disruptive nature of economic and
urban development plans make them especially prone to failure, but many of the same criticisms have been leveled at government plans to improve public education, reform healthcare
services, manage public resources, design local regulations, or
decide foreign policy.[21] Nor are governments alone in suffering from extreme planning failures. Corporations are rarely
as large as governments, so their failures tend not to attract
the same kind of scrutiny—although the near collapse of the
financial system in 2008–2009 comes close. There are also so
many more corporations than governments that it's always
possible to find success stories, thereby perpetuating the view
that the private sector is better at planning than the government sector. But as a number of management scholars have
shown in recent years, corporate plans—whether strategic
bets, mergers and acquisitions, or marketing campaigns—
also fail frequently, and for much the same reasons that government plans do.[22] In all these cases, that is, a small number
of people sitting in conference rooms are using their own
commonsense intuition to predict, manage, or manipulate
the behavior of thousands or millions of distant and diverse
people whose motivations and circumstances are very different from their own.[23]

The irony of all this is that even as we observe the mistakes
of politicians, planners, and others, our reaction is not to
criticize common sense, but instead to demand more of it. At
the World Economic Forum meeting in Davos in early 2009,
for example, in the darkest depths of the global financial crisis,
one indignant audience member announced to the audience,

"What we need now is a return to common sense!" It's an appealing notion, and drew loud applause at the time, but I couldn't help wondering what it was that he meant by it. After all, two years earlier at the 2007 Davos meeting, much the same mix of businesspeople, politicians, and economists were congratulating one another on having generated astonishing levels of wealth and unprecedented stability of the financial sector. Did anyone suspect that they had somehow taken leave of their common sense? And if not, then how exactly would it help to return to it? If anything, in fact, what the history of financial crises, both before and after the advent of high-technology trading, ought to teach us is that—like truth in war—it is common sense, not computer models, that is the first casualty of a financial mania.[24] And much the same is true of failures in politics, business, and marketing. Bad things happen not because we forget to use our common sense, but rather because the incredible effectiveness of common sense in solving the problems of everyday life causes us to put more faith in it than it can bear.

TOO MUCH INTUITION

But if common sense is so bad at dealing with complex social phenomena like political conflicts, healthcare economics, or marketing campaigns, why are its shortcomings not more obvious to us? After all, when it comes to the physical world, we also have plenty of intuition that we use to solve everyday problems—think of all the intuitive physics that is required to chase down and catch a fly baseball. But unlike in the social world, we have learned over time that our "commonsense physics" is easily tripped up. For example, common sense tells us that heavy objects fall under the force of gravity. But consider the following: A man stands on a perfectly flat plain holding a bullet in his left hand and a pistol, loaded with an identical bullet, in his right. Holding both pistol and bullet at the same height, he simultaneously fires the gun and drops the bullet. Which bullet will hit the ground first? Elementary high school physics will tell you that in fact the two bullets will hit the ground at exactly the *same* time. But even knowing this, it is hard not to think that the bullet from the gun is somehow kept up for longer by its velocity.

The physical world is filled with examples like this that defy commonsense reasoning. Why does water spiral down the toilet in opposite directions in the northern and southern hemispheres? Why do you see more shooting stars after midnight? And when floating ice melts in a glass, does the water level go up or down? Even if you really do understand the physics behind some of these questions, it is still easy to get them wrong, and they're nothing compared to the really strange phenomena of quantum mechanics and relativity. But as frustrating as it can be for physics students, the consistency with which our commonsense physics fails us has one great advantage for human civilization: It forces us to do science. In science, we accept that if we want to learn how the world works, we need to test our theories with careful observations and experiments, and then trust the data no matter what our intuition says. And as laborious as it can be, the scientific method is responsible for essentially all the gains in understanding the natural world that humanity has made over the past few centuries.

But when it comes to the human world, where our unaided intuition is so much better than it is in physics, we rarely feel the need to use the scientific method. Why is it, for example, that most social groups are so homogeneous in terms of race, education level, and even gender? Why do some things become popular and not others? How much does the media influence society? Is more choice better or worse? Do taxes stimulate the economy? Social scientists are endlessly perplexed by these questions, yet many people feel as though they could come up with perfectly satisfactory explanations themselves. We all have friends, most of us work, and we generally buy things, vote, and watch TV. We are constantly immersed in markets, politics, and culture, and so are intimately familiar with how they work—or at least that is how it seems to us. Unlike problems in physics, biology, and so on, therefore, when the topic is human or social behavior, the idea of running expensive, time-consuming "scientific" studies to figure out what we're pretty sure we already know seems largely unnecessary.

HOW COMMON SENSE FAILS US

Without a doubt, the experience of participating in the social world greatly facilitates our ability to understand it. Were it not for the intimate knowledge of our own thought processes, along with countless observations of the words, actions, and explanations of others—both experienced in person and also learned remotely—the vast intricacies of human behavior might well be inscrutable. Nevertheless, the combination of intuition, experience, and received wisdom on which we rely to generate commonsense explanations of the social world also disguises certain errors of reasoning that are every bit as systematic and pervasive as the errors of commonsense physics. Part One of this book is devoted to exploring these errors, which fall into three broad categories.

The first type of error is that when we think about why people do what they do, we invariably focus on factors like incentives, motivations, and beliefs, of which we are consciously aware. As sensible as it sounds, decades of research in psychology and cognitive science have shown that this view of human behavior encompasses just the tip of the proverbial iceberg. It doesn't occur to us, for example, that the music playing in the background can influence our choice of wine in the liquor store, or that the font in which a statement is written may make it more or less believable; so we don't factor these details into our anticipation of how people will react. But they do matter, as do many other apparently trivial or seemingly irrelevant factors. In fact, as we'll see, it is probably impossible to anticipate everything that might be relevant to a given situation. The result is that no matter how carefully we try to put ourselves in someone else's shoes, we are likely to make serious mistakes when predicting how they'll behave anywhere outside of the immediate here and now.

If the first type of commonsense error is that our mental model of individual behavior is systematically flawed, the second type is that our mental model of collective behavior is even worse. The basic problem here is that whenever people get together in groups—whether at social events, workplaces, volunteer organizations, markets, political parties, or even as entire societies—they interact with one another, sharing information, spreading rumors, passing along recommendations, comparing themselves to their friends, rewarding and punishing each other's behaviors, learning from the experience of others, and generally influencing one another's perspectives about what is good and bad, cheap and expensive, right and wrong. As sociologists have long argued, these influences pile up in unexpected ways, generating collective behavior that is "emergent" in the sense that it cannot be understood solely in terms of its component parts. Faced with such complexity, however, commonsense explanations instinctively fall back on the logic of individual action. Sometimes we invoke fictitious "representative individuals" like "the crowd," "the market," "the workers," or "the electorate," whose actions stand in for the actions and interactions of the many. And sometimes we single out "special people," like leaders, visionaries, or "influencers" to whom we attribute all the agency. Regardless of which trick we use, however, the result is that our explanations of collective behavior paper over most of what is actually happening.

The third and final type of problem with commonsense reasoning is that we learn less from history than we think we do, and that this misperception in turn skews our perception of the future. Whenever something interesting, dramatic, or terrible happens—Hush Puppies become popular again, a book by an unknown author becomes an international best seller, the housing bubble bursts, or terrorists crash planes into the World Trade Center—we instinctively look for explanations. Yet because we seek to explain these events only after the fact, our explanations place far too much emphasis on what actually happened relative to what might have happened but didn't. Moreover, because we only try to explain events that strike us as sufficiently interesting, our explanations account only for a tiny fraction even of the things that do happen. The result is that what appear to us to be causal explanations are in fact just stories—descriptions of what happened that tell us little, if anything, about the mechanisms at work. Nevertheless, because these stories have the form of causal explanations, we treat them as if they have predictive power. In this way, we deceive ourselves into believing that we can make predictions that are impossible, even in principle.

Commonsense reasoning, therefore, does not suffer from a single overriding limitation but rather from a combination of limitations, all of which reinforce and even disguise one another. The net result is that common sense is wonderful at *making sense* of the world, but not necessarily at understanding it. By analogy, in ancient times, when our ancestors were startled by lightning bolts descending from the heavens, accompanied by claps of thunder, they assuaged their fears with elaborate stories about the gods, whose all-too-human struggles were held responsible for what we now understand to be entirely natural processes. In explaining away otherwise strange and frightening phenomena in terms of stories they did understand, they were able to make sense of them, effectively creating an illusion of understanding about the world that was enough to get them out of bed in the morning. All of which is fine. But we would not say that our ancestors "understood" what was going on, in the sense of having a successful scientific theory. Indeed, we tend to regard the ancient mythologies as vaguely amusing.

What we don't realize, however, is that common sense often works just like mythology. By providing ready explanations for whatever particular circumstances the world throws at us, commonsense explanations give us the confidence to navigate from day to day and relieve us of the burden of worrying about whether what we think we know is really true, or is just something we happen to believe. The cost, however, is that we think we have understood things that in fact we have simply papered over with a plausible-sounding story. And because this illusion of understanding in turn undercuts our motivation to treat social problems the way we treat problems in medicine, engineering, and science, the unfortunate result is that common sense actually inhibits our understanding of the world. Addressing this problem is not easy, although in Part Two of the book I will offer some suggestions, along with examples of approaches that are already being tried in the worlds of business, policy, and science. The main point, though, is that just as an unquestioning belief in the correspondence between natural events and godly affairs had to give way in order for "real" explanations to be developed, so too, real explanations of the social world will require us to examine what it is about our common sense that misleads us into thinking that we know more than we do.[25]

CHAPTER 2

Thinking About Thinking

In many countries around the world, it is common for the state to ask its citizens if they will volunteer to be organ donors. Now, organ donation is one of those issues that elicit strong feelings from many people. On the one hand, it's an opportunity to turn one person's loss into another person's salvation. But on the other hand, it's more than a little unsettling to be making plans for your organs that don't involve you. It's not surprising, therefore, that different people make different decisions, nor is it surprising that rates of organ donation vary considerably from country to country. It might surprise you to learn, however, how much cross-national variation there is. In a study conducted a few years ago, two psychologists, Eric Johnson and Dan Goldstein, found that rates at which citizens consented to donate their organs varied across different European countries, from as low as 4.25 percent to as high as 99.98 percent. What was even more striking about these differences is that they weren't scattered all over the spectrum, but rather were clustered into two distinct groups—one group that had organ-donation rates in the single digits and teens, and one group that had rates in the high nineties—with almost nothing in between.[1]

What could explain such a huge difference? That's the question I put to a classroom of bright Columbia undergraduates not long after the study was published. Actually, what I asked them to consider was two anonymous countries, A and B.

In country A, roughly 12 percent of citizens agree to be organ donors, while in country B 99.9 percent do. So what did they think was different about these two countries that could account for the choices of their citizens? Being smart and creative students, they came up with lots of possibilities. Perhaps one country was secular while the other was highly religious. Perhaps one had more advanced medical care, and better success rates at organ transplants, than the other. Perhaps the rate of accidental death was higher in one than another, resulting in more available organs. Or perhaps one had a highly socialist culture, emphasizing the importance of community, while the other prized the rights of individuals.

All were good explanations. But then came the curveball. Country A was in fact Germany, and country B was...Austria. My poor students were stumped—*what on earth could be so different about Germany and Austria?* But they weren't giving up yet. Maybe there was some difference in the legal or education systems that they didn't know about? Or perhaps there had been some important event or media campaign in Austria that had galvanized support for organ donation. Was it something to do with World War II? Or maybe Austrians and Germans are more different than they seem. My students didn't know what the reason for the difference was, but they were sure it was *something* big—you don't see extreme differences like that by accident. Well, no—but you can get differences like that for reasons that you'd never expect. And for all their creativity, my students never pegged the real reason, which is actually absurdly simple: *In Austria, the default choice is to be an organ donor, whereas in Germany the default is not to be.* The difference in policies seems trivial—it's just the difference between having to mail in a simple form and not having to—but it's enough to push the donor rate from 12 percent to 99.9 percent. And what was true for Austria and Germany was true across all of Europe—all the countries with very high rates of organ donation had opt-out policies, while the countries with low rates were all opt-in.

DECISIONS, DECISIONS

Understanding the influence of default settings on the choices we make is important, because our beliefs about what people choose and why they choose it affect virtually all our explanations of social, economic, and political outcomes. Read the op-ed section of any newspaper, watch any pundit on TV, or listen to any late-night talk radio, and you will be bombarded with theories of why we choose this over that. And although we often decry these experts, the broader truth is that all of us—from politicians and bureaucrats, to newspaper columnists, to corporate executives and ordinary citizens—are equally willing to espouse our own theory of human choice. Indeed, virtually *every* argument of social consequence— whether about politics, economic policy, taxes, education, healthcare, free markets, global warming, energy policy, foreign policy, immigration policy, sexual behavior, the death penalty, abortion rights, or consumer demand—is either explicitly or implicitly an argument about why people make the choices they make. And, of course, how they can be encouraged, educated, legislated, or coerced into making different ones.

Given the ubiquity of choice in the world and its relevance to virtually every aspect of life—from everyday decisions to the grand events of history—it should come as little surprise that theories about how people make choices are also central to most of the social sciences. Commenting on an early paper by the Nobel laureate Gary Becker, the economist James Duesenberry famously quipped that "economics is all about choice, while sociology is about why people have no choices."[2] But the truth is that sociologists are every bit as interested in how people make choices as economists are—not to mention political scientists, anthropologists, psychologists, and legal, business, and management scholars. Nevertheless, Duesenberry had a point in that for much of the last century, social and behavioral scientists of different stripes have tended to view the matter of choice in strikingly different ways. More than anything, they have differed, sometimes acrimoniously, over the nature and importance of human rationality.

COMMON SENSE AND RATIONALITY

To many sociologists, the phrase "rational choice" evokes the image of a cold, calculating individual who cares only for himself and who relentlessly seeks to maximize his economic well-being. Nor is this reaction entirely unjustified. For many years, economists seeking to understand market behavior invoked something like this notion of rationality—sometimes referred to as "homo economicus"—in large part because it lends itself naturally to mathematical models that are simple enough to be written down and solved. And yet, as countless examples like the ultimatum game from the previous chapter show, real people care not only about their own welfare, economic or otherwise, but also the welfare of others for whom they will often make considerable sacrifices. We also care about upholding social norms and conventions, and frequently punish others who violate them—even when doing so is costly.[3] And finally, we often care about intangible benefits, like our reputation, belonging to a group, and "doing the right thing," sometimes as much as or even more than we care about wealth, comfort, and worldly possessions.

Critics of homo economicus have raised all these objections, and many more, over the years. In response, advocates of what is often called rational choice theory have expanded the scope of what is considered rational behavior dramatically to include not just self-interested economic behavior, but also more realistic social and political behavior as well.[4] These days, in fact, rational choice theory is not so much a single theory at all as it is a family of theories that make often rather different assumptions depending on the application in question. Nevertheless, all such theories tend to include variations on two fundamental insights—first, that people have preferences for some outcomes over others; and second, that given these preferences they select among the means available to them as best they can to realize the outcomes that they prefer. To take a simple example, if my preference for ice cream exceeds my preference for the money I have in my pocket, and there is an available course of action that allows me to exchange my money for the ice cream, then that's what I'll choose to do. But if, for example, the weather is cold, or the ice cream is expensive, my preferred course of action may instead be to keep the money for a sunnier day. Similarly, if buying the ice cream requires a lengthy detour, my preference to get where I am going may also cause me to wait for another time. Regardless of what I end up choosing—the money, the ice cream, the walk followed by the ice cream, or some other alternative—I am always doing what is "best" for me, given the preferences I have at the time I make the decision.

What is so appealing about this way of thinking is its implication that *all* human behavior can be understood in terms of individuals' attempts to satisfy their preferences. I watch TV shows because I enjoy the experience enough to devote the time to them rather than doing something else. I vote because I care about participating in politics, and when I vote,

I choose the candidate I think will best serve my interests. I apply to the colleges that I think I can get into, and of those I get accepted to, I attend the one that offers the best combination of status, financial aid, and student life. When I get there, I study what is most interesting to me, and when I graduate, I take the best job I can get. I make friends with people I like, and keep those friends whose company I continue to enjoy. I get married when the benefits of stability and security outweigh the excitement of dating. We have children when the benefits of a family (the joy of having children who we can love unconditionally, as well as having someone to care for us in our old age) outweigh the costs of increased responsibility, diminished freedom, and extra mouths to feed.[5]

In *Freakonomics,* Steven Levitt and Stephen Dubner illustrate the explanatory power of rational choice theory in a series of stories about initially puzzling behavior that, upon closer examination, turns out to be perfectly rational. You might think, for example, that because your real estate agent works on commission, she will try to get you the highest price possible for your house. But as it turns out, real estate agents keep their own houses on the market longer, and sell them for higher prices, than the houses of their clients. Why? Because when it's your house they're selling, they make only a small percentage of the difference of the higher price, whereas when it's their house, they get the whole difference. The latter is enough money to hold out for, but the former isn't. Once you understand the incentives that real estate agents face, in other words, their true preferences, and hence their actions, become instantly clear.

Likewise, it might at first surprise you to learn that parents at an Israeli day school, when fined for picking up their children late, actually arrived late more often than they did before any fine was imposed. But once you understand that the fine assuaged the pangs of guilt they were feeling at inconveniencing the school staff—essentially, they felt they were paying for the right to be late—it makes perfect sense. So does the initially surprising observation that most gang members live with their mothers. Once you do the math, it turns out that gang members don't make nearly as much money as you would think; thus it makes perfect economic sense for them to live at home. Similarly, one can explain the troubling behavior of a number of high-school teachers who, in response to the new accountability standards introduced by the Bush Administration's 2002 No Child Left Behind legislation, actually altered the test responses of their students. Even though cheating could cost them their jobs, the risk of getting caught seemed small enough that the cost of being stuck with a low-performing class outweighed the potential for being punished for cheating.[6]

Regardless of the person and the context, in other words— sex, politics, religion, families, crime, cheating, trading, and even editing Wikipedia entries—the point that Levitt and Dubner keep returning to is that if we want to understand why people do what they do, we must understand the incentives that they face, and hence their preference for one outcome versus another. When someone does something that seems strange or puzzling to us, rather than writing them off as crazy or irrational, we should instead seek to analyze their situation in hopes of finding a rational incentive. It is precisely this sort of exercise, in fact, that we went through in the last chapter with the ultimatum game experiments. Once we discover that the Au and Gnau tradition of gift exchange effectively transforms what to us looks like free money into something that to them resembles an unwelcome future obligation, what was previously puzzling behavior suddenly seems as rational as our own. It is just rational according to a different set of premises than we were familiar with before. The central claim of *Freakonomics* is that we can almost always perform this exercise, no matter how weird or wonderful is the behavior in question.

As intriguing and occasionally controversial as Levitt and Dubner's explanations are, in principle they are no different from the vast majority of social scientific explanations. However much sociologists and economists might argue about the details, that is, until they have succeeded in accounting for a given behavior in terms of some combination of motivations, incentives, perceptions, and opportunities—until they have, in a word, *rationalized* the behavior—they do not feel that they have really understood it.[7] And it is not only social scientists who feel this way. When we try to understand why an ordinary Iraqi citizen would wake up one morning and decide to turn himself into a living bomb, we are implicitly rationalizing his behavior. When we attempt to explain the origins of the recent financial crisis, we are effectively searching for rational financial incentives that led bankers to create and market high-risk assets. And when we blame soaring medical costs on malpractice legislation or procedure-based payments, we are instinctively invoking a model of rational action to understand why doctors do what they do. When we think about how we think, in other words, we reflexively adopt a framework of rational behavior.[8]

THINKING IS ABOUT MORE THAN THOUGHT

The implicit assumption that people are rational until proven otherwise is a hopeful, even enlightened, one that in general ought to be encouraged. Nevertheless, the exercise of rationalizing behavior glosses over an important difference between what we mean when we talk about "understanding" human behavior, as opposed to the behavior of electrons, proteins, or planets. When trying to understand the behavior of electrons, for example, the physicist does not start by imagining himself in the circumstances of the electrons in question. He may have intuitions concerning theories about electrons, which in turn help him to understand their behavior. But at no point would he expect to understand what it is actually like to *be* an electron—indeed, the very notion of such intuition is laughable. Rationalizing human behavior, however, is precisely an exercise in simulating, in our mind's eye, what it would be like to be the person whose behavior we are trying to understand. Only when we can imagine this simulated version of ourselves responding in the manner of the individual in question do we really feel that we have understood the behavior in question.

So effortlessly can we perform this exercise of "understanding by simulation" that it rarely occurs to us to wonder how reliable it is. And yet, as the earlier example of the organ donors illustrates, our mental simulations have a tendency to ignore certain types of factors that turn out to be important. The reason is that when we think about how we think, we instinctively emphasize consciously accessible costs and benefits such as those associated with motivations, preferences, and beliefs—the kinds of factors that predominate in social scientists' models of rationality. Defaults, by contrast, are a part of the environment in which the decision maker operates, and so affect behavior in a way that is largely invisible to the conscious mind, and therefore largely absent from our commonsense explanations of behavior.[9] And defaults are just the proverbial tip of the iceberg. For several decades, psychologists and, more recently, behavioral economists have been examining human decision-making, often in controlled laboratory settings. Their findings not only undermine even the most basic assumptions of rationality but also require a whole new way of thinking about human behavior.[10]

In countless experiments, for example, psychologists have shown that an individual's choices and behavior can be influenced by "priming" them with particular words, sounds, or other stimuli. Subjects in experiments who read words like "old" and "frail" walk more slowly down the corridor when they leave the lab. Consumers in wine stores are more likely to buy German wine when German music is playing in the background, and French wine when French music is playing. Survey respondents asked about energy drinks are more likely to name Gatorade when they are given a green pen in order to fill out the survey. And shoppers looking to buy a couch online are more likely to opt for an expensive, comfortable-looking couch when the background of the website is of fluffy white clouds, and more likely to buy the harder, cheaper option when the background consists of dollar coins.[11]

Our responses can also be skewed by the presence of irrelevant numerical information. In one experiment, for example, participants in a wine auction were asked to write down the last two digits of their social security numbers before bidding. Although these numbers were essentially random and certainly had nothing to do with the value a buyer should place on the wine, researchers nevertheless found that the higher the numbers, the more people were willing to bid. This effect, which psychologists call anchoring, affects all sorts of estimates that we make, from estimating the number of countries in the African Union to how much money we consider to be a fair tip or donation. Whenever you receive a solicitation from a charity with a "suggested" donation amount, in fact, or a bill with precomputed tip percentages, you should suspect that your anchoring bias is being exploited—because by suggesting amounts on the high side, the requestor is anchoring your initial estimate of what is fair. Even if you subsequently adjust your estimate downward—because, say, a 25 percent tip seems like too much—you will probably end up giving more than you would have without the initial suggestion.[12]

Individual preferences can also be influenced dramatically simply by changing the way a situation is presented. Emphasizing one's potential to lose money on a bet, for example, makes people more risk averse while emphasizing one's potential to win has the opposite effect, even when the bet itself is identical. Even more puzzling, an individual's preferences between two items can be effectively reversed by introducing a third alternative. Say, for example, that option A is a high-quality, expensive camera while B is both much lower quality and also much cheaper. In isolation, this could be a difficult comparison to make. But if, as shown in the figure below, I introduce a third option, C1, that is clearly more expensive than A and around the same quality, the choice between A and C1 becomes unambiguous. In these situations people tend to pick A, which seems perfectly reasonable until you consider what happens if I introduce instead of C1 a third option, C2, that is about as expensive as B yet significantly lower quality. Now the choice between B and C2 is clear, and so people tend to pick B. Depending on which third option is introduced, in other words, the preference of the decision maker can effectively be reversed between A and B, even though nothing about either has changed. What's even stranger is that the third option—the one that causes the switch in preferences—is never itself chosen.[13]

Illustration of preference reversal

Continuing this litany of irrationality, psychologists have found that human judgments are often affected by the ease with which different kinds of information can be accessed or recalled. People generally overestimate the likelihood of dying in a terrorist attack on a plane relative to dying on a plane from *any* cause, even though the former is strictly less likely than the latter, simply because terrorist attacks are such vivid events. Paradoxically, people rate themselves as less assertive when they are asked to recall instances where they have acted assertively—not because the information contradicts their beliefs, but rather because of the effort required to recall it. They also systematically remember their own past behavior and beliefs to be more similar to their current behavior and beliefs than they really were. And they are more likely to believe a written statement if the font is easy to read, or if they have read it before—even if the last time they read it, it was explicitly labeled as false.[14]

Finally, people digest new information in ways that tend to reinforce what they already think. In part, we do this by noticing information that confirms our existing beliefs more readily than information that does not. And in part, we do it by subjecting disconfirming information to greater scrutiny and skepticism than confirming information. Together, these two closely related tendencies—known as confirmation bias and motivated reasoning respectively—greatly impede our ability to resolve disputes, from petty disagreements over domestic duties to long-running political conflicts like those in Northern Ireland or Israel-Palestine, in which the different parties look at the same set of "facts" and come away with completely different impressions of reality. Even in science, confirmation bias and motivated reasoning play pernicious roles. Scientists, that is, are supposed to follow the evidence, even if it contradicts their own preexisting beliefs; and yet, more often than they should, they question the evidence instead. The result, as the physicist Max Planck famously acknowledged, is often that "A new scientific truth does not triumph by convincing its opponents and making them see the light, but rather because its opponents eventually die."[15]

WHAT IS RELEVANT?

Taken together, the evidence from psychological experiments makes clear that there are a great many potentially relevant factors that affect our behavior in very real and tangible ways but that operate largely outside of our conscious awareness. Unfortunately, psychologists have identified so many of these effects—priming, framing, anchoring, availability, motivated reasoning, loss aversion, and so on—that it's hard to see how they all fit together. By design, experiments emphasize one potentially relevant factor at a time in order to isolate its effects. In real life, however, many such factors may be present to varying extents in any given situation; thus it's critical to understand how they interact with one another. It may be true, in other words, that holding a green pen makes you think of Gatorade, or that listening to German music predisposes you to German wine, or that thinking of your social security number affects how much you will bid for something. But what will you buy, and how much will you pay for it, when you are exposed to many, possibly conflicting, subconscious influences at once?

It simply isn't clear. Nor is the profusion of unconscious psychological biases the only problem. To return to the ice cream example from before, although it may be true that I like ice cream as a general rule, how much I like it at a particular point in time might vary considerably, depending on the time of day, the weather, how hungry I am, and how good the ice cream is that I expect to get. My decision, moreover, doesn't depend just on how much I like ice cream, or even just the relation between how much I like it versus how much it costs. It also depends on whether or not I know the location of the nearest ice cream shop, whether or not I have been there before, how much of a rush I'm in, who I'm with and what they want, whether or not I have to go to the bank to get money, where the nearest bank is, whether or not I just saw someone else eating an ice cream, or just heard a song that reminded me of a pleasurable time when I happened to be eating an ice cream, and so on. Even in the simplest situations, the list of factors that might turn out to be relevant can get very long very quickly. And with so many factors to worry about, even very similar situations may differ in subtle ways that turn out to be important. When trying to understand—or better yet predict—individual decisions, how are we to know which of these many factors are the ones to pay attention to, and which can be safely ignored?

The ability to know what is relevant to a given situation

is of course the hallmark of commonsense knowledge that I discussed in the previous chapter. And in practice, it rarely occurs to us that the ease with which we make decisions disguises any sort of complexity. As the philosopher Daniel Dennett points out, when he gets up in the middle of the night to make himself a midnight snack, all he needs to know is that there is bread, ham, mayonnaise, and beer in the fridge, and the rest of the plan pretty much works itself out. Of course he also knows that "mayonnaise doesn't dissolve knives on contact, that a slice of bread is smaller than Mount Everest, that opening the refrigerator doesn't cause a nuclear holocaust in the kitchen" and probably trillions of other irrelevant facts and logical relations. But somehow he is able to ignore all these things, without even being aware of what it is that he's ignoring, and focus on the few things that matter.[16]

But as Dennett argues, there is a big difference between knowing what is relevant in practice and being able to explain how it is that we know it. To begin with, it seems clear that what is relevant about a situation is just those features that it shares with other comparable situations—for example, we know that how much something costs is relevant to a purchase decision because cost is something that generally matters whenever people buy something. But how do we know which situations are comparable to the one we're in? Well, that also seems clear: Comparable situations are those that share the same features. All "purchase" decisions are comparable in the sense that they involve a decision maker contemplating a number of options, such as cost, quality, availability, and so on. But now we encounter the problem. Determining which features are relevant about a situation requires us to associate it with some set of comparable situations. Yet determining which situations are comparable depends on knowing which features are relevant.

This inherent circularity poses what philosophers and cognitive scientists call the frame problem, and they have been beating their heads against it for decades. The frame problem was first noticed in the field of artificial intelligence, when researchers started trying to program computers and robots to solve relatively simple everyday tasks like, say, cleaning a messy room. At first they assumed that it couldn't be *that* hard to write down everything that was relevant to a situation like this. After all, people manage to clean their rooms every day without even really thinking about it. How hard could it be to teach a robot? Very hard indeed, as it turned out. As I discussed in the last chapter, even the relatively straightforward activity of navigating the subway system requires a surprising amount of knowledge about the world—not just about subway doors and platforms but also about maintaining personal distance, avoiding eye contact, and getting out of the way of pushy New Yorkers. Very quickly AI researchers realized that virtually *every* everyday task is difficult for essentially the same reason—that the list of potentially relevant facts and rules is staggeringly long. Nor does it help that most of this list can be safely ignored most of the time—because it's generally impossible to know in advance which things can be ignored and which cannot. So in practice, the researchers found that they had to wildly overprogram their creations in order to perform even the most trivial tasks.[17]

The intractability of the frame problem effectively sank the original vision of AI, which was to replicate human intelligence more or less as we experience it ourselves. And yet there was a silver lining to this defeat. Because AI researchers had to program *every* fact, rule, and learning process into their creations from scratch, and because their creations failed to behave as expected in obvious and often catastrophic ways—like driving off a cliff or trying to walk through a wall—the frame problem was impossible to ignore. Rather than trying to crack the problem, therefore, AI researchers took a different approach entirely—one that emphasized statistical models of data rather than thought processes. This approach, which nowadays is called machine learning, was far less intuitive than the original cognitive approach, but it has proved to be much more productive, leading to all kinds of impressive breakthroughs, from the almost magical ability of search engines to complete queries as you type them to building autonomous robot cars, and even a computer that can play *Jeopardy!*[18]

WE DON'T THINK THE WAY
WE THINK WE THINK

The frame problem, however, isn't just a problem for artificial intelligence—it's a problem for human intelligence as well. As the psychologist Daniel Gilbert describes in *Stumbling on Happiness,* when we imagine ourselves, or someone else, confronting a particular situation, our brains do not generate a long list of questions about all the possible details that might be relevant. Rather, just as an industrious assistant might use stock footage to flesh out a drab PowerPoint presentation, our "mental simulation" of the event or the individual in question simply plumbs our extensive database of memories, images, experiences, cultural norms, and imagined outcomes, and seamlessly inserts whatever details are necessary in order to complete the picture. Survey respondents leaving restaurants, for example, readily described the outfits of the waiters inside, even in cases where the waitstaff had been entirely female. Students asked about the color of a classroom blackboard recalled it as being green—the normal color—even though the board in question was blue. In general, people systematically overestimate both the pain they will experience as a consequence of anticipated losses and the joy they will garner from anticipated gains. And when matched online with prospective dates, subjects report greater levels of liking for their matches when they are given *less* information about them. In all of these cases, a careful person ought to respond that he can't answer the question accurately without being given more information. But because the "filling in" process happens instantaneously and effortlessly, we are typically unaware that it is even taking place; thus it doesn't occur to us that anything is missing.[19]

The frame problem should warn us that when we do this, we are bound to make mistakes. And we do, all the time. But unlike the creations of the AI researchers, humans do not surprise us in ways that force us to rewrite our whole mental model of how we think. Rather, just as Paul Lazarsfeld's imagined reader of the *American Soldier* found every result and opposite is equally obvious, once we know the outcome we can almost always identify previously overlooked aspects of the situation that *then* seem relevant. Perhaps we expected to be happy after winning the lottery, and instead find ourselves depressed—obviously a bad prediction. But by the time we realize our mistake, we also have new information, say about all the relatives who suddenly appeared wanting financial support. It will then seem to us that if we had only had *that* information earlier, we would have anticipated our future state of happiness correctly, and maybe never bought the lottery ticket. Rather than questioning our ability to make predictions about our future happiness, therefore, we simply conclude that we missed something important—a mistake we surely won't make again. And yet we do make the mistake again. In fact, no matter how many times we fail to predict someone's behavior correctly, we can always explain away our mistakes in terms of things that we didn't know at the time. In this way, we manage to sweep the frame problem under the carpet—always convincing ourselves that this time we are going to get it right, without ever learning what it is that we are doing wrong.

Nowhere is this pattern more evident, and more difficult to expunge, than in the relationship between financial rewards and incentives. It seems obvious, for example, that employee performance can be improved through the application of financial incentives, and in recent decades performance-based pay schemes have proliferated in the workplace, most notably in terms of executive compensation tied to stock price.[20] Of course, it's also obvious that workers care about more than just money—factors like intrinsic enjoyment, recognition, and a feeling of advancement in one's career might all affect performance as well. All else equal, however, it seems obvious that one can improve performance with the proper application of financial rewards. And yet, the actual relationship between pay and performance turns out to be surprisingly complicated, as a number of studies have shown over the years.

Recently, for example, my Yahoo! colleague Winter Mason and I conducted a series of Web-based experiments in which subjects were paid at different rates to perform a variety of simple repetitive tasks, like placing a series of photographs of moving traffic into the correct temporal sequence, or uncovering words hidden in a rectangular grid of letters. All our participants were recruited from a website called Amazon's Mechanical Turk, which Amazon launched in 2005 as a way to identify duplicate listings among its own inventory. Nowadays, Mechanical Turk is used by hundreds of businesses looking to "crowd-source" a wide range of tasks, from labeling objects in an image to characterizing the sentiment of a newspaper article or deciding which of two explanations is clearer. However, it is also an extremely effective way to recruit subjects for psychology experiments—much as psychologists have done over the years by posting flyers around college campuses—except that because workers (or "turkers") are usually paid on the order of a few cents per task, it can be done for a fraction of the usual cost.[21]

In total, our experiments involved hundreds of participants who completed tens of thousands of tasks. In some cases they were paid as little as one cent per task—for example, sorting a single set of images or finding a single word—while in other cases they were paid five or even ten cents to do the same thing. A factor of ten is a pretty big difference in pay—by comparison, the average hourly rate of a computer engineer in the United States is only six times the federal minimum wage—so you'd expect it to have a pretty big effect on how people behave. And indeed it did. The more we paid people, the more tasks they completed before leaving the experiment. We also found that for any given pay rate, workers who were assigned "easy" tasks—like sorting sets of two images—completed more tasks than workers assigned medium or hard tasks (three and four images per set respectively). All of this, in other words, is consistent with common sense. But then the kicker: in spite of these differences, we found that the *quality* of their work—meaning the accuracy with which they sorted images—did not change with pay level at all, even though they were paid only for the tasks they completed correctly.[22]

What could explain this result? It's not completely clear; however, after the subjects had finished their work we asked them some questions, including how much they thought they ought to have been paid for what they had just done. Interestingly, their responses depended less on the difficulty of the task than on how much they had been paid to do it. On average, subjects who were paid one cent per task thought they should have been paid five cents; subjects who were paid five cents thought they should have been paid eight cents; and subjects who were paid ten cents thought they should have been paid thirteen cents. In other words, no matter what they were actually paid—and remember that some of them were getting paid ten times as much as others—everyone thought they had been underpaid. What this finding suggested to us is that even for very simple tasks, the extra motivation to perform that we intuitively expect workers to experience with increased financial incentives is largely undermined by their increased sense of entitlement.

It's hard to test this effect outside of a laboratory setting, because workers in most real environments have expectations about what they should be paid that are hard to manipulate. But consider, for example, that in the United States women get paid on average only 90 percent as much as men who do exactly the same jobs, or that European CEOs get paid considerably less than their US counterparts.[23] In either case, could you really argue that the lower-paid group works less hard or does a worse job than the higher-paid group? Or imagine if next year, your boss unexpectedly doubled your annual pay—how much harder would you actually work? Or imagine a parallel universe in which bankers got paid half of what they get in ours. No doubt some of them might have chosen to go into other professions, but for those who remained in banking, would they really work less hard or do a worse job? The outcome of our experiment suggests that they would not. But if so, then you have to wonder how much influence employers can have on worker performance simply by changing financial incentives.

A number of studies, in fact, have found that financial incentives can actually undermine performance. When a task is multifaceted or hard to measure, for example, workers tend to focus only on those aspects of their jobs that are actively measured, thereby overlooking other important aspects of the job—like teachers emphasizing the material that will be covered in standardized tests at the expense of overall learning. Financial rewards can also generate a "choking" effect, when the psychological pressure of the reward cancels out the increased desire to perform. Finally, in environments where individual contributions are hard to separate from those of the team, financial rewards can encourage workers to ride on the coattails of the efforts of others, or to avoid taking risks, thereby hampering innovation. The upshot of all these confusing and often contradictory findings is that although virtually everyone agrees that people respond to financial incentives in some manner, it's unclear how to use them in practice to elicit the desired result. Some management scholars have even concluded after decades of studies that financial incentives are largely irrelevant to performance.[24]

No matter how many times this lesson is pointed out, however, managers, economists, and politicians continue to act as if they can direct human behavior via the application of incentives. As Levitt and Dubner write, "The typical economist believes that the world has not yet invented a problem that he cannot fix if given a free hand to design the proper incentive scheme.... An incentive is a bullet, a lever, a key: an often tiny object with astonishing power to change a situation."[25] Well, maybe, but that doesn't mean that the incentives we create will bring about the changes we intended. Indeed, one of Levitt and Dubner's own vignettes—of the high-school teachers cheating on the tests—was an attempt by policy makers to improve teaching through explicit performance-based incentives. That it backfired, producing outright cheating and all manner of lesser gaming, like "teaching to the test," and focusing exclusively on marginal students for whom a small improvement could generate an additional passing grade, should give one pause about the feasibility of designing incentive schemes to elicit desired behavior.[26]

And yet common sense does not pause. Rather, once we realize that some particular incentive scheme did not work, we conclude simply that it got the incentives wrong. Once they know the answer, in other words, policy makers can always persuade themselves that all they need to do is to design the *correct* incentive scheme—overlooking, of course, that this was precisely what they thought they were doing previously as well. Nor are policy makers uniquely susceptible to this particular oversight—we all are. For example, a recent news story about the perennial problem of politicians failing to take long-term fiscal responsibility seriously concluded blithely, "Like bankers, politicians respond to incentives." The article's solution? "To align the interests of the country with those of the politicians who are guiding it." It all sounds so simple. But as the article itself concedes, the history of previous attempts to "fix" politics has been disappointing.[27]

Like rational choice theory, in other words, common sense insists that people have reasons for what they do—and this may be true. But it doesn't necessarily allow us to predict in advance either what they will do or what their reasons will be for doing it.[28] Once they do it, of course, the reasons will appear obvious, and we will conclude that had we only known about some particular factor that turned out to be important, we could have predicted the outcome. After the fact, it will always seem as if the right incentive system could have produced the desired result. But this appearance of after-the-fact predictability is deeply deceptive, for two reasons. First, the frame problem tells us that we can never know everything that could be relevant to a situation. And second, a huge psychological literature tells us that much of what could be relevant lies beyond the reach of our conscious minds. This is not to say that humans are completely unpredictable, either. As I'll argue later (in Chapter 8), human behavior displays all sorts of regularities that can be predicted, often to useful ends. Nor is it to say that we shouldn't try to identify the incentives that individuals respond to when making decisions. If nothing else, our inclination to rationalize the behavior of others probably helps us to get along with one another—a worthy goal in itself—and it may also help us to learn from our mistakes. What it does say, however, is that our impressive ability to make sense of behavior that we have observed does not imply a corresponding ability to predict it, or even that the predictions we can make reliably are best arrived at on the basis of intuition and experience alone. It is this difference between making sense of behavior and predicting it that is responsible for many of the failures of commonsense reasoning. And if this difference poses difficulties for dealing with individual behavior, the problem gets only more pronounced when dealing with the behavior of groups.

CHAPTER 3

The Wisdom (and Madness)
of Crowds

In 1519, shortly before he died, the Italian artist, scientist, and inventor Leonardo da Vinci put the finishing touches on a portrait of a young Florentine woman, Lisa Gherardini del Giocondo, whose husband, a wealthy silk merchant, had commissioned the painting sixteen years earlier to celebrate the birth of their son. By the time he finished it, Leonardo had moved to France at the invitation of King François I, who eventually purchased the painting; thus apparently neither Ms. del Giocondo nor her husband ever got the chance to view Leonardo's handiwork. Which is a pity really, because five hundred years later that painting has made her face about the most famous face in all of history.

The painting, of course, is the *Mona Lisa,* and for those who have lived their entire lives in a cave, it now hangs in a bulletproof, climate-controlled case on a wall all by itself in the Musée du Louvre in Paris. Louvre officials estimate that nearly 80 percent of their six million visitors each year come primarily to see it. Its current insurance value is estimated at nearly $700 million—far in excess of any painting ever sold—but it is unclear that any price could be meaningfully assigned to it. The *Mona Lisa,* it seems fair to say, is more than just a painting—it is a touchstone of Western culture. It has been copied, parodied, praised, mocked, co-opted, analyzed, and speculated upon more than any other work of art. Its origins, for centuries shrouded in mystery, have captivated scholars, and its name has leant itself to operas, movies, songs, people, ships—even a crater on Venus.[1]

Knowing all this, a naïve visitor to the Louvre might be forgiven for experiencing a sense of, well, disappointment upon first laying eyes on the *most famous painting in the world*. To start with, it is surprisingly small. And being enclosed in that bulletproof box, and invariably surrounded by mobs of picture-snapping tourists, it is irritatingly difficult to see. So when you do finally get up close, you're really expecting something special—what the art critic Kenneth Clark called "the supreme example of perfection," which causes viewers to "forget all our misgivings in admiration of perfect mastery."[2] Well, as they say, I'm no art critic. But when, on my first visit to the Louvre several years ago, I finally got my chance to bask in the glow of perfect mastery, I couldn't help wondering about the three other da Vinci paintings I had just walked by in the previous chamber, and to which nobody seemed to be paying the slightest attention. As far as I could tell, the *Mona Lisa* looked like an amazing accomplishment of artistic talent, but no more so than those other three. In fact, if I hadn't already known which painting was the famous one, I doubt that I could have picked it out of a lineup. For that matter, if you had put it in with any number of the other great works of art on display at the Louvre, I'm quite positive it wouldn't have jumped out at me as the obvious contender for most-famous-painting award.

Now, Kenneth Clark might well reply that that's why he's the art critic and I'm not—that there are attributes of mastery that are evident only to the trained eye, and that neophytes like me would do better simply to accept what we're told. OK, fair enough. But if that's true, you would expect that the same perfection that is obvious to Clark would have been obvious to other art experts throughout history. And yet, as the historian Donald Sassoon relates in his illuminating biography of the *Mona Lisa,* nothing could be further from the case.[3] For centuries, the *Mona Lisa* was a relatively obscure painting languishing in the private residences of kings—still a masterpiece, to be sure, but only one among many. Even when it was moved to the Louvre, after the French Revolution, it did not attract as much attention as the works of other artists, like Esteban Murillo, Antonio da Correggio, Paolo Veronese, Jean-Baptiste Greuze, and Pierre Paul Prud'hon, names that for the most part are virtually unheard of today outside of art history classes. And admired as he was, up until the 1850s, da Vinci was considered no match for the true greats of painting, like Titian and Rafael, some of whose works were worth almost ten times as much as the *Mona Lisa.* In fact, it wasn't until the twentieth century that the *Mona Lisa* began its meteoric rise to global brand name. And even then it wasn't the result of art critics suddenly appreciating the genius that had sat among them for so long, nor was it due to the efforts of museum curators, socialites, wealthy patrons, politicians, or kings. Rather, it all began with a burglary.

On August 21, 1911, a disgruntled Louvre employee named Vincenzo Peruggia hid in a broom closet until closing time and then walked out of the museum with the *Mona Lisa* tucked under his coat. A proud Italian, Peruggia apparently believed that the *Mona Lisa* ought rightly to be displayed in Italy, not France, and he was determined to repatriate the long-lost treasure personally. Like many art thieves, however, Peruggia discovered that it was much easier to steal a famous work of art than to dispose of it. After hiding it in his apartment for two years, he was arrested while attempting to sell it to the Uffizi Gallery in Florence. But although he failed in his mission, Peruggia succeeded in catapulting the *Mona Lisa* into a new category of fame. The French public was captivated by the bold theft and electrified by the painting's unexpected recovery. The Italians, too, were thrilled by the patriotism of their countryman, and treated Peruggia more like a hero than a criminal—before the *Mona Lisa* was returned to its French owner, it was shown all over Italy.

From that point on, the *Mona Lisa* never looked back. The painting was to be the object of criminal activity twice more—first, when a vandal threw acid on it, and then when a young Bolivian, Ugo Ungaza Villegas, threw a rock at it. But primarily it became a reference point for other artists—most famously in 1919, when the Dadaist Marcel Duchamp parodied the painting and poked fun at its creator by adorning a commercial reproduction with a mustache, a goatee, and an obscene inscription. Salvador Dalí and Andy Warhol followed suit with their own interpretations, and so did many others—in all, it has been copied hundreds of times and incorporated into thousands of advertisements. As Sassoon points out, all these different people—thieves, vandals, artists, and advertisers, not to mention musicians, moviemakers, and even NASA (remember the crater on Venus?)—were using the *Mona Lisa* for their own purposes: to make a point, to increase their own fame, or simply to use a label they felt would convey meaning to other people. But every time they used the *Mona Lisa,* it used them back, insinuating itself deeper into the fabric of Western culture and the awareness of billions of people. It is impossible now to imagine the history of Western art without the *Mona Lisa,* and in that sense it truly is the greatest of paintings. But it is also impossible to attribute its unique status to anything about the painting itself.

This last point presents a problem because when we try

to explain the success of the *Mona Lisa,* it is precisely its attributes on which we focus our attention. If you're Kenneth Clark, you don't need to know anything about the circumstances of the *Mona Lisa*'s rise to fame to know why it happened—everything you need to know is right there in front of you. To oversimplify only slightly, the *Mona Lisa* is the most famous painting in the world because it is *the best,* and although it might have taken us a while to figure this out, it was inevitable that we would. And that's why so many people are puzzled when they first actually set eyes on the *Mona Lisa.* They're expecting these intrinsic qualities to be apparent, and they're not. Of course, most of us, when faced with this moment of dissonance, simply shrug our shoulders and assume that somebody wiser than us has seen things we can't see. And yet as Sassoon deftly but relentlessly lays out, whatever attributes the experts cite as evidence—the novel painting technique that Leonardo employed to produce so gauzy a finish, the mysterious subject, her enigmatic smile, even da Vinci's own fame—one can always find numerous other works of art that would seem as good, or even better.

Of course, one can always get around this problem by pointing out that it's not any one attribute of the *Mona Lisa* that makes it so special, but rather the combination of *all* its attributes—the smile, *and* the use of light, *and* the fantastical background, and so on. There's actually no way to beat this argument, because the *Mona Lisa* is of course a unique object. No matter how many similar portraits or paintings some pesky skeptic drags out of the dustbin of history, one can always find *some* difference between them and the one that we all know is the deserving winner. Unfortunately, however, this argument wins only at the cost of eviscerating itself. It sounds as if we're assessing the quality of a work of art in terms of its attributes, but in fact we're doing the opposite—

deciding first which painting is the best, and only then inferring from its attributes the metrics of quality. Subsequently, we can invoke these metrics to justify the known outcome in a way that seems rational and objective. But the result is circular reasoning. We claim to be saying that the *Mona Lisa* is the most famous painting in the world because it has attributes X, Y, and Z. But really what we're saying is that the *Mona Lisa* is famous because it's more like the *Mona Lisa* than anything else.

CIRCULAR REASONING

Not everybody appreciates this conclusion. When I explained the argument to an English literature professor at a party once, she practically shouted, "Are you suggesting that Shakespeare might just be a fluke of history?" Well, as a matter of fact, that's exactly what I was suggesting. Don't get me wrong: I enjoy Shakespeare as much as any normal person. But I also know that I didn't acquire my appreciation in a vacuum. Like just about everyone else in the Western world, I spent years of high school laboring over his plays and sonnets. And presumably, like many others, it wasn't immediately obvious to me what all the fuss was about. Try reading *Midsummer Night's Dream* and forget for a moment that you know it's a work of genius. Right about the point where Titania is fawning over a man with the head of a donkey, you might just start to wonder what on earth Shakespeare was thinking. But I digress. The point is that no matter what my schoolboy brain thought of what it was reading, I was determined to appreciate the genius that my teachers assured us was there. And if I hadn't, it would have been my failing, not Shakespeare's—because Shakespeare, like da Vinci, *defines* genius. As with the *Mona Lisa*, this outcome may be perfectly justified. Nevertheless, the point remains that locating the source of his genius in the particular attributes of his work invariably leads us in circles: Shakespeare is a genius because he is more like Shakespeare than anyone else.

Although it is rarely presented as such, this kind of circular reasoning—X succeeded because X had the attributes of X—pervades commonsense explanations for why some things succeed and others fail. For example, an article on the success of the *Harry Potter* books explained it this way: "A Cinderella plot set in a novel type of boarding school peopled by jolly pupils already has a lot going for it. Add in some easy stereotypes illustrating meanness, gluttony, envy, or black-hearted evil to raise the tension, round off with a sound, unchallenging moral statement about the value of courage, friendship, and the power of love, and there already are some of the important ingredients necessary for a match-winning formula." In other words, *Harry Potter* was successful because it had exactly the attributes of *Harry Potter,* and not something else.

Likewise, when Facebook first became popular, conventional wisdom held that its success lay in its exclusivity to college students. Yet by 2009, long after Facebook had opened itself to everyone, a report by Nielsen, the ratings company, attributed its success to its broad appeal, along with its "simple design" and "focus on connecting." Facebook, in other words, was successful because it had exactly the attributes of Facebook, even as the attributes themselves changed completely. Or consider a news story reviewing 2009 movies that inferred from the success of *The Hangover* that "relatable, non-thinking comedies…are the perfect balm for the recession," implying in effect that *The Hangover* succeeded because moviegoers wanted to see a movie like *The Hangover,* and not something else. In all these cases, we want to believe that X succeeded because it had just the right attributes, but the only attributes we know about are the attributes that X possesses; thus we conclude that these attributes must have been responsible for X's success.[4]

Even when we are not explaining success, we still rely on circular reasoning to make sense of why certain things happen. For example, in another recent news story about an apparent downshift in postrecession consumer behavior, one expert explained the change with the helpful observation that "It's simply less fun pulling up to the stoplight in a Hummer than it used to be. It's a change in norms." People do X, in other words, because X is the norm, and it is normal to follow norms. OK, great, but how do we know that something is a norm? We know because people are following it. Again we are going in circles, and this is no isolated example. Once you start to pay attention, it's amazing how often explanations contain this circularity. Whether it is women getting the vote, gay and lesbian couples being allowed to marry, or a black man being elected president, we routinely explain social trends in terms of what society "is ready for." But the only way we know society is ready for something is because it happened. Thus, in effect, all we are really saying is that "X happened because that's what people wanted; and we know that X is what they wanted because X is what happened."[5]

THE MICRO-MACRO PROBLEM

The circularity evident in commonsense explanations is important to address because it derives from what is arguably the central intellectual problem of sociology—which sociologists call the micro-macro problem. The problem, in a nutshell, is that the outcomes that sociologists seek to explain are intrinsically "macro" in nature, meaning that they involve large numbers of people. Paintings, books, and celebrities can only be popular or unpopular to the extent that large numbers of people care about them. Firms, markets, governments, and other forms of political and economic organization all require large numbers of people to abide by their rules in order for anything to actually happen. And cultural institutions such as marriage, social norms, and even legal principles have relevance only to the extent that large numbers of people believe that they do. At the same time, however, it is necessarily the case that all these outcomes are driven in some way by the "micro" actions of individual humans, who are making the kinds of choices that I discussed in the previous chapter. So how do we get from the micro choices of individuals to the macro phenomena of the social world? Where, in other words, do families, firms, markets, cultures, and societies come from, and why do they exhibit the particular features that they exhibit? This is the micro-macro problem.

As it turns out, something like the micro-macro problem comes up in every realm of science, often under the label "emergence." How is it, for example, that one can lump together a collection of atoms and somehow get a molecule? How is it that one can lump together a collection of molecules and somehow get amino acids? How is it that one can lump together a collection of amino acids and other chemicals and somehow get a living cell? How is it that one can lump together a collection of living cells and somehow get complex organs like the brain? And how is it that one can lump together a collection of organs and somehow get a sentient being that wonders about its eternal self? Seen in this light, sociology is merely at the tip of the pyramid of complexity that begins with subatomic particles and ends with global society. And at each level of the pyramid, we have essentially the same problem—how do you get from one "scale" of reality to the next?

Historically, science has done its best to dodge this question, opting instead for a division of labor across the scales. Physics, therefore, is its own subject with its own set of facts, laws, and regularities, while chemistry is a different subject altogether, with an entirely different set of facts, laws, and regularities, and biology is a whole new ballgame all over again. At some level the laws that apply at different scales must be consistent—one cannot have chemistry that violates the laws of physics—but it is not generally possible to derive the laws that apply at one scale from those that govern the scale below it. Knowing everything about the behavior of individual neurons, for example, would be of little help in understanding human psychology, just as a complete knowledge of particle physics would be of little use in explaining the chemistry of synapses.[6]

Increasingly, however, the questions that scientists find most interesting—from the genomics revolution to the preservation of ecosystems to cascading failures in power grids—are forcing them to consider more than one scale at a time, and so to confront the problem of emergence head-on. Individual genes interact with each other in complex chains of activation and suppression to express phenotypic traits that are not reducible to the properties of any one gene. Individual plants and animals interact with each other in complex ways, via prey-predator relations, symbiosis, competition, and cooperation, to produce ecosystem-level properties that cannot be understood in terms of any individual species. And individual power generators and substations interact with each other via high-voltage transmission cables to produce system-level dynamics that cannot be understood in terms of any individual component.

Social systems are also replete with interactions—between individual people, between individuals and firms, between firms and other firms, between individuals, firms, and markets, and between everyone and the government. Individual people are influenced by what other people are doing or saying or wearing. Firms are affected by what individual consumers want and also by what their competitors are producing, or what their debt holders require of them. Markets are affected by government regulations as well as by the actions of individual firms, and sometimes even of individual people (think Warren Buffett or Ben Bernanke). And governments are swayed by all manner of influences, from corporate lobbyists to opinion polls to stock market indices. In the kinds of systems that sociologists study, in fact, the interactions come in so many forms and carry such consequence, that our own version of emergence—the micro-macro problem— is arguably more complex and intractable than in any other discipline.

Common sense, however, has a remarkable knack for papering over this complexity. Emergence, remember, is a hard problem precisely because the behavior of the whole cannot easily be related to the behavior of its parts, and in the natural sciences we implicitly acknowledge this difficulty. For example, we do not speak of the genome as if it behaves like a single gene, nor do we speak of brains as if they behave like individual neurons, or ecosystems like individual creatures. That would be ridiculous. When it comes to social phenomena, however, we *do* speak of "social actors" like families, firms, markets, political parties, demographic segments, and nation-states as if they act in more or less the same way as the individuals that comprise them. Families, that is, "decide" where to go on vacation, firms "choose" between business strategies, and political parties "pursue" legislative agendas. Likewise, advertisers speak of appealing to their "target demographic," Wall Street traders dissect the sentiment of "the market," politicians speak about "the will of the people," and historians describe a revolution as a "fever gripping society."

Everyone understands, of course, that corporations and political parties, even families, do not literally have feelings, form beliefs, or imagine the future the way individual people do. Nor are they subject to the same psychological quirks and biases that I discussed in the previous chapter. At some level, we know that the "behavior" of social actors is really a convenient shorthand for the aggregate behavior of large numbers of individuals. Nevertheless, it is so natural to talk this way that the shorthand has become indispensible to our ability to explain things. Imagine trying to recount the history of World War II without talking about the actions of the Allies or the Nazis. Imagine trying to understand the Internet without talking about the behavior of large Internet companies like Microsoft or Yahoo! or Google. Or imagine trying to analyze the debate over healthcare reform in the United States without talking about the interests of Democrats or Republicans, or "special interests." Margaret Thatcher was famous for having said "There is no such thing as society. There are individual men and women, and there are families."[7] But if we actually tried to apply Thatcher's doctrine to explaining the world, we wouldn't even know where to start.

In social science, Thatcher's philosophical position goes by the name of methodological individualism, which claims that until one has succeeded in explaining some social phenomenon—the popularity of the *Mona Lisa* or the relation between interest rates and economic growth—exclusively in terms of the thoughts, actions, and intentions of individual people, one has not fully succeeded in explaining it at all. Explanations that ascribe individual psychological motivations to aggregate entities like firms, markets, and governments might be convenient, but they are not, as the philosopher John Watkins put it, "rock bottom" explanations.[8]

Unfortunately, attempts to construct the kind of rock-bottom explanations that methodological individualists imagined have all run smack into the micro-macro problem. In practice, therefore, social scientists invoke what is called a representative agent, a fictitious individual whose decisions stand in for the behavior of the collective. To take a single example, albeit an important one, the economy is composed of many thousands of firms and millions of individuals all making decisions about what to buy, what to sell, and what to invest in. The end result of all this activity is what economists call the business cycle—in effect, a time series of aggregate economic activity that seems to exhibit periodic ups and downs. Understanding the dynamics of the business cycle is one of the central problems of macroeconomics, in no small part because it affects how policy makers deal with events like recessions. Yet the mathematical models that economists rely on do not attempt to represent the vast complexity of the economy at all. Rather, they specify a single "representative firm" and ask how that firm would rationally allocate its resources given certain information about the rest of the economy. Roughly speaking, the response of that firm is then interpreted as the response of the economy as a whole.[9]

By ignoring the interactions between thousands or millions of individual actors, the representative agent simplifies the analysis of business cycles enormously. It assumes, in effect, that as long as economists have a good model of how individuals behave, they effectively have a good model for how the economy behaves as well. In eliminating the complexity, however, the representative-agent approach effectively ignores the crux of the micro-macro problem—the very core of what makes macroeconomic phenomena "macro" in the first place. It was for precisely this reason, in fact, that the economist Joseph Schumpeter, who is often regarded as the founding father of methodological individualism, attacked the representative-agent approach as flawed and misleading.[10]

In practice, however, methodological individualists have lost the battle, and not just in economics. Pick up any work of history, sociology, or political science that deals with "macro" phenomena, like class, race, business, war, wealth, innovation, politics, law, or government, and you will find a world populated with representative agents. So common is their use in social science, in fact, that the substitution of a fictitious individual for what is in reality a collective typically happens without so much as an acknowledgment, like the magician placing the rabbit in the hat while the audience is looking elsewhere. No matter how it is done, however, the representative agent is only and always a convenient fiction. And no matter how we try to dress them up in mathematics or other finery, explanations that invoke representative agents are making essentially the same error as commonsense explanations that talk about firms, markets, and societies in the same terms that we use to describe individual people.[11]

GRANOVETTER'S RIOT MODEL

The sociologist Mark Granovetter highlighted this problem using a very simple mathematical model of a crowd poised on the brink of a riot. Say a crowd of a hundred students is gathered in a town square, protesting the government's proposed increase in student fees. The students are angry about the new policy and frustrated with their lack of input to the political process. There's a possibility of things getting out of hand. But being educated, civilized people, they also understand that reason and dialogue are preferable to violence. To oversimplify somewhat, each individual in the crowd is torn between two instincts—one to go berserk and smash things up, and the other to remain calm and protest peacefully. Everyone, whether they are conscious of it or not, has to make a choice between these two actions. But they are not making a choice between violence and peaceful protest independently—they are doing so, at least in part, in response to what other people are doing. The greater the number of individuals who engage in a riot, the more likely their efforts will force the politicians to pay attention, and the less likely that any one of them will be caught and punished. Also, riots have a primal energy of their own that can undermine otherwise strong social conventions against physical destruction, even skewing our psychological estimation of risk. In a riot, even sensible people can go crazy. For all these reasons, the choice about whether to remain calm or to engage in violence is subject to the general rule that the more other people are rioting, the more likely any particular individual is to join in.

Nevertheless, in this crowd, as everywhere, individual people have different tendencies toward violence. Perhaps those who are better off or who are less affected financially by the new policy are less inclined to risk jail time to make a point. Others are more persuaded that violence, although regrettable, is a useful political device. Some may have an unrelated gripe against the police or the politicians or society, and this event is giving them an excuse to vent. And perhaps some of them are just crazier than others. Whatever the reason—

and the reasons can be as many and as complicated as you can imagine—each individual in the crowd can be thought of as having a "threshold," a point at which, if enough other people join in the riot, they will too, but below which they will refrain. Some people—the "rabble rousers"—have very low thresholds, while others, like the president of the student society, have very high thresholds. But everyone has a threshold of social influence, above which they will "tip" from calm to violence. This might seem like a strange way to characterize individual behavior. But the benefit of describing people in the crowd in terms of their threshold is that the distribution of thresholds over the whole crowd, from crazy ("I will riot even if no one else does") to Gandhi ("I will not riot even if everyone else does") turns out to capture some interesting and surprising lessons about crowd behavior.[12]

To illustrate what could happen, Granovetter posited a very simple distribution in which each of the hundred people has a unique threshold. Exactly one person that is, has a threshold of zero, while another has a threshold of one other person, another has a threshold of two other people, and so on all the way up to the most conservative person, who will join in only after all ninety-nine others have. What will happen? Well, first Mr. Crazy—the one with the threshold of zero—will start throwing things, apropos of nothing. Then, his sidekick with the threshold of one (who needs only one other person to riot before joining in) joins him. Together, these two troublemakers prompt a third person—the guy with the threshold of two—to join in as well, and that's enough to get the threshold-three person going, which is enough to… well, you get the idea: Given this particular threshold distribution, the entire crowd ends up joining the riot, one after the other. Chaos reigns.

Imagine, however, that in the next town over, a second

crowd of students, of exactly the same size, has gathered for exactly the same reason. As unlikely as it may sound, let's imagine that this crowd has almost exactly the same distribution of thresholds as the first one. So closely matched are these two crowds, in fact, that they differ with respect to just one person: Whereas in the first crowd each person had a unique threshold, in this one nobody has a threshold of three, and two people have a threshold of four. To an outside observer, this difference is so minute as to be undetectable. We know they're different because we're playing God here, but no feasible psychological test or statistical model could tell these two crowds apart. So what happens now to the crowd's behavior? It starts out the same: Mr. Crazy leads off just as before, and his sidekick and the guy with a threshold of two join in like clockwork. But then it hits a snag, because nobody has a threshold of three. The next most susceptible individuals are the pair who both have thresholds of four; yet we have only three rioters. So the potential riot stops before it even gets started.

Now imagine, finally, what observers in these two neighboring towns would see. In town A, they would witness an all-out riot, complete with smashed shop windows and overturned cars. In town B, they would see a few loutish individuals jostling an otherwise orderly crowd. If these observers were to compare notes later, they would try to figure out what it was about the *people* or their *circumstances* that must have been different. Perhaps the students in town A were angrier or more desperate than those in town B. Perhaps the shops were less well protected, or perhaps the police were more aggressive, or perhaps the crowd in town A had a particularly inflammatory speaker. These are the kinds of explanations that common sense would suggest. Obviously something must have been different, or else how can we explain such dramatically divergent outcomes? But in fact we know that apart from the threshold of a single individual, *nothing* about the people or their circumstances was different at all. This last point is critical because the only way a representative agent model could account for the different outcomes observed in town A and town B would be if there were some critical difference between the average properties of the two populations, and the averages are for all intents and purposes the same.

The problem sounds similar to the one my students encountered when trying to explain the difference between organ-donor rates in Austria and Germany, but it's actually quite different. In the organ-donor case, remember, the problem was that my students tried to understand the difference in terms of rational incentives, when in reality it was dominated by the default setting. In other words, they had the wrong model of individual behavior. But in the organ-donor case at least, once you understand how important the default bias is, it becomes clear why the donor rates are so wildly different. In Granovetter's riot model, by contrast, it doesn't matter *what* model of individual behavior you have—because in any reasonable sense the two populations are indistinguishable. To understand how the different outcomes emerge, you must take into account the interactions *between* individuals, which in turn requires that you follow the full sequence of individual decisions, each unfolding on top of the others. This is the micro-macro problem arriving in full force. And the minute you try to skip over it, say by substituting a representative agent for the behavior of the collective, you will have missed the whole essence of what is happening, no matter what you assume about the agent.

CUMULATIVE ADVANTAGE

Granovetter's "riot model" makes a profound statement about the limits of what can be understood about collective behavior by thinking only about individual behavior. That said, the model is extremely—almost comically—simple, and is likely to be wrong in all sorts of ways. In most real-world choices, for example, we are choosing between potentially many options, not just the two—riot or don't riot—in Granovetter's model. Nor does it seem likely that the manner in which we influence one another in the real world is anything as simple as the threshold rule that Granovetter proposed. In many routine situations, when choosing, say, a new artist to listen to, a new book to read, or a new restaurant to visit, it often makes sense to ask other people for advice, or simply to pay attention to the choices they have made, on the grounds that if they like something you're more likely to like it too. In addition, your friends may influence which music you choose to listen to or which books you choose to read not only because you assume that they have already done some work filtering out the various options but also because you will enjoy talking about them and sharing the same cultural references.[13]

Social influence of this general kind is likely ubiquitous. But unlike the simple threshold of Granovetter's thought experiment, the resulting decision rule is neither binary nor deterministic. Rather, when people tend to like something that other people like, differences in popularity are subject to what is called cumulative advantage, meaning that once, say, a song or a book becomes more popular than another, it will tend to become more popular still. Over the years, researchers have studied a number of different types of cumulative advantage models, but they all have the flavor that even tiny random fluctuations tend to get bigger over time, generating potentially enormous differences in the long run, a phenomenon that is similar to the famous "butterfly effect" from chaos theory, which says that a butterfly fluttering its wings in China can lead to a hurricane months later and oceans away.[14]

As with Granovetter's model, cumulative advantage models have disruptive implications for the kinds of explanations that we give of success and failure in cultural markets. Commonsense explanations, remember, focus on the thing itself—the song, the book, or the company—and account for its success solely in terms of its intrinsic attributes. If we were to imagine history being somehow "rerun" many times, therefore, explanations in which intrinsic attributes were the only things that mattered would predict that the same outcome would pertain every time. By contrast, cumulative advantage would predict that even identical universes, starting out with the same set of people and objects and tastes, would nevertheless generate different cultural or marketplace winners. The *Mona Lisa* would be popular in this world, but in some other version of history it would be just one of many masterpieces, while another painting that most of us have never heard of would be in its place. Likewise, the success of *Harry Potter,* Facebook, and *The Hangover* would turn out to be a product of chance and timing as much as of intrinsic quality.

In real life, however, we have only one world—the one that we are living in—thus it's impossible to make the sort of "between world" comparisons that the models say we should. It may not surprise you, therefore, that when someone uses the output of a simulation model to argue that *Harry Potter* may not be as special as everyone thinks it is, *Harry Potter* fans tend not to be persuaded. Common sense tells us that

Harry Potter must be special—even if the half dozen or so children's book publishers who passed on the original manuscript didn't know it at the time—because more than 350 million people bought it. And because any model necessarily makes all manner of simplifying assumptions, whenever we have to choose between questioning common sense and questioning a model, our tendency is to do the latter.

For exactly this reason, several years ago my collaborators Matthew Salganik and Peter Dodds and I decided to try a different approach. Instead of using computer models, we would run a controlled, laboratory-style experiment in which real people made more or less the same kinds of choices that they make in the real world—in this case, between a selection of songs. By randomly assigning different people to different experimental conditions, we would effectively create the "many worlds" situation imagined in the computer models. In some conditions, people would be exposed to information about what other people were doing, but it would be up to them to decide whether or not to be influenced by the information and how. In other conditions, meanwhile, participants would be faced with exactly the same set of choices, but without any information about other participants' decisions; thus they would be forced to behave independently. By comparing the outcomes in the "social influence" conditions with those in the "independent" condition, we would be able to observe the effects of social influence on collective outcomes directly. In particular, by running many such worlds in parallel, we would be able to measure how much of a song's success depended on its intrinsic attributes, and how much on cumulative advantage.

Unfortunately, running such experiments is easier said than done. In psychology experiments of the kind I discussed in the previous chapter, each "run" of the experiment involves at most a few individuals; thus conducting the entire experiment requires at most a few hundred subjects, typically undergraduate students who participate in exchange for money or course credit. The kind of experiment we had in mind, however, required us to observe how all these individual-level "nudges" added up to create differences at the collective level. In effect, we wanted to study the micro-macro problem in a lab. But to observe effects like these we would need to recruit hundreds of people for each run of the experiment, and we would need to conduct the experiment through many independent runs. Even for a single experiment, therefore, we would need thousands of subjects, and if we wanted to run multiple experiments under different conditions, we'd need tens of thousands.

In 1969, the sociologist Morris Zelditch described exactly this problem in a paper with the provocative title "Can You Really Study an Army in a Laboratory?" At the time, his conclusion was that you couldn't—at least not literally. Therefore he advocated that sociologists should instead study how small groups worked, and rely on theory to generalize their findings to large groups. Macrosociology, in other words, like macroeconomics, couldn't ever be an experimental discipline, simply because it would be impossible to run the relevant experiments. Coincidentally, however, the year 1969 also marked the genesis of the Internet, and in the years since, the world had changed in ways that would have been hard for Zelditch to imagine. With the social and economic activity of hundreds of millions of people migrating online, we wondered if it might be time to revisit Zelditch's question. Perhaps, we thought, one *could* study an army in the laboratory—only this lab would be a virtual one.[15]

EXPERIMENTAL SOCIOLOGY

So that's what we did. With the help of our resident computer programmer, a young Hungarian named Peter Hausel, and some friends at Bolt media, an early social networking site for teenagers, we set up a Web-based experiment designed to emulate a "market" for music. Bolt agreed to advertise our experiment, called Music Lab, on their site, and over the course of several weeks about fourteen thousand of its members clicked through on the banner ads and agreed to participate. Once they got to our site they were asked to listen to, rate, and if they chose to, download songs by unknown bands. Some of the participants saw only the names of the songs while others also saw how many times the songs had been downloaded by previous participants. People in the latter "social influence" category were further split into eight parallel "worlds" such that they could only see the prior downloads of people in their own world. Thus if a new arrival were to be allocated (randomly) to World #1, she might see the song "She Said" by the band Parker Theory in first place. But if she were allocated instead to World #4, Parker Theory might be in tenth place and "Lockdown" by 52 Metro might be first instead.[16]

We didn't manipulate any of the rankings—all the worlds started out identically, with zero downloads. But because the different worlds were carefully kept separate, they could subsequently evolve independently of one another. This setup therefore enabled us to test the effects of social influence directly. If people know what they like regardless of what other people think, there ought not to be any difference between the social influence and independent conditions. In all cases, the same songs should win by roughly the same amount. But if people do not make decisions independently, and if cumulative advantage applies, the different worlds within the social influence condition should look very different from one another, and they should all look different from the independent condition.

What we found was that when people had information about what other people downloaded, they were indeed influenced by it in the way that cumulative advantage theory would predict. In all the "social influence" worlds, that is, popular songs were more popular (and unpopular songs were less popular) than in the independent condition. At the same time, however, which particular songs turned out to be the most popular—the "hits"—were different in different worlds. Introducing social influence into human decision making, in other words, increased not just inequality but unpredictability as well. Nor could this unpredictability be eliminated by accumulating more information about the songs any more than studying the surfaces of a pair of dice could help you predict the outcome of a roll. Rather, unpredictability was *inherent* to the dynamics of the market itself.

Social influence, it should be noted, didn't eliminate quality altogether: It was still the case that, on average, "good" songs (as measured by their popularity in the independent condition) did better than "bad" ones. It was also true that the very best songs never did terribly, while the very worst songs never actually won. That said, even the best songs could fail to win sometimes, while the worst songs could do pretty well. And for everything in the middle—the majority of songs that were neither the best nor the worst—virtually any outcome was possible. The song "Lockdown" by 52 Metro, for example, ranked twenty-sixth out of forty-eight in quality; yet it was the no. 1 song in one social-influence world, and fortieth in another. The "average" performance of a particular song, in other words, is only meaningful if the variability that it exhibits from world to world is small. But it was precisely this random variability that turned out to be large. For example, by changing the format of the website from a randomly arranged grid of songs to a ranked list we found we could increase the effective strength of the social signal, thereby increasing both the inequality and unpredictability. In this "strong influence" experiment, the random fluctuations played a bigger role in determining a song's ranking than even the largest differences in quality. Overall, a song in the Top 5 in terms of quality had only a 50 percent chance of finishing in the Top 5 of success.

Many observers interpreted our findings as a commentary on the arbitrariness of teenage music tastes or the vacuousness of contemporary pop music. But in principle the experiment could have been about any choice that people make in a social setting: whom we vote for, what we think about gay marriage, which phone we buy or social networking service we join, what clothes we wear to work, or how we deal with our credit card debt. In many cases designing these experiments is easier said than done, and that's why we chose to study music. People like to listen to music and they're used to downloading it from the Web, so by setting up what looked like a site for music downloads we could conduct an experiment that was not only cheap to run (we didn't have to pay our subjects) but was also reasonably close to a "natural" environment. But in the end all that really mattered was that our subjects were making choices among competing options, and that their choices were being influenced by what they thought other people had chosen. Teenagers also were an expedient choice, because that's mostly who was hanging around on social networking sites in 2004. But once again, there was nothing special about teenagers—as we showed in a subsequent version of the experiment for which we recruited mostly adult professionals. As you might expect, this population had different preferences than the teenagers, and so the average performance of the songs changed slightly. Nevertheless, they were just as influenced by one another's behavior as the teenagers were, and so generated the same kind of inequality and unpredictability.[17]

What the Music Lab experiment really showed, therefore, was remarkably similar to the basic insight from Granovetter's riot model—that when individuals are influenced by what other people are doing, similar groups of people can end up behaving in very different ways. This may not sound like a big deal, but it fundamentally undermines the kind of commonsense explanations that we offer for why some things succeed and others fail, why social norms dictate that we do some things and not others, or even why we believe what we believe. Commonsense explanations sidestep the whole problem of how individual choices aggregate to collective behavior simply by replacing the collective with a representative individual. And because we think we know why individual people do what they do, as soon as we know what happened, we can always claim that it was what this fictitious individual—"the people," "the market," whatever—wanted.

By pulling apart the micro-macro problem, experiments like Music Lab expose the fallacy that arises from this form of circular reasoning. Just as you can know everything about the behavior of individual neurons and still be mystified by the emergence of consciousness in the human brain, so too you could know everything about individuals in a given population—their likes, dislikes, experiences, attitudes, beliefs, hopes, and dreams—and still not be able to predict much about their collective behavior. To explain the outcome of some social process in terms of the preferences of some fictitious representative individual therefore greatly exaggerates our ability to isolate cause and effect.

For example, if you'd asked the 500 million people who currently belong to Facebook back in 2004 whether or not they wanted to post profiles of themselves online and share updates with hundreds of friends and acquaintances about their everyday goings-on, many of them would have likely said no, and they probably would have meant it. The world, in other words, wasn't sitting around waiting for someone to invent Facebook so that we could all join it. Rather, a few people joined it for whatever reasons and began to play around with it. Only then, because of what those people experienced through using the service as it existed back then—and even more so because of the experiences they created for one another in the course of using it—did other people begin to join. And then other people joined because those people joined, and so on, until here we are today. Yet now that Facebook *is* tremendously popular, it just seems obvious that it must have been what people wanted—otherwise, why would they be using it?

This is not to say that Facebook, the company, hasn't made a lot of smart moves over the years, or doesn't deserve to be as successful as it is. Rather, the point is just that the explanations we give for its success are less relevant than they seem. Facebook, that is, has a particular set of features, just as *Harry Potter* and the *Mona Lisa* have their own particular sets of features, and all of them have experienced their own particular outcomes. But it does not follow that those features *caused* the outcomes in any meaningful way. Ultimately, in fact, it may simply not be possible to say *why* the *Mona Lisa* is the most famous painting in the world or *why* the *Harry Potter* books sold more than 350 million copies within ten years, or *why* Facebook has attracted more than 500 million users. In the end, the only honest explanation may be the one given by the publisher of Lynne Truss's surprise bestseller, *Eats, Shoots and Leaves,* who, when asked to explain its success, replied that "it sold well because lots of people bought it."

It may not surprise you to learn that many people do not particularly like this conclusion. Most of us would be prepared to admit that our decisions are influenced by what other people think—sometimes, anyway. But it's one thing to acknowledge that once in a while our behavior gets nudged this way or that by what other people are doing, and it's quite another to concede that as a consequence, true explanations for the success of an author or a company, unexpected changes in social norms, or the sudden collapse of a seemingly impregnable political regime may simply lie beyond our reach. When faced with the prospect that some outcome of interest cannot be explained in terms of special attributes or conditions, therefore, a common fallback is to assume that it was instead determined by a small number of important or influential people. So it is to this topic that we turn next.

CHAPTER 4

Special People

It may seem hard to believe in a time when "social networking" has become so commonplace an idea that it shows up in everything from feature films to Foster's beer commercials, but it wasn't that long ago—as recently as the mid-1990s—that the study of social networks was relatively obscure, pursued mostly by a small cadre of mathematically inclined sociologists interested in mapping the social interactions among individuals.[1] The field has exploded in recent years, in large part because fast computers, along with communication technologies like e-mail, cell phones, and social networking sites such as Facebook have made it possible to record and analyze these interactions with great precision, even for hundreds of millions of people at a time. Nowadays, thousands of computer scientists, physicists, mathematicians, and even biologists count themselves as "network scientists," and new discoveries about the structure and dynamics of networked systems arrive daily.[2]

SIX DEGREES OF SEPARATION

Back in 1995, however, when I was a graduate student at Cornell studying the synchronization of chirping crickets, all this was in the future. Back then, in fact, the idea that everyone in the world is connected through a giant social network through which information, ideas, and influence might flow, was still sufficiently novel that when my father asked me during one of our regular phone conversations if I'd ever heard of the notion that "everyone in the world is only six handshakes away from the president of the United States," I assumed it was folklore. And in some sense it was. People have been fascinated with what sociologists call the small-world problem for nearly a century, since the Hungarian poet Frigyes Karinthy published a short story called "Chains" in which his protagonist boasts that he can connect himself to any other person in the world, whether a Nobel Prize winner or a worker in a Ford Motor factory, through a chain of no more than five acquaintances. Four decades later, in her polemic on urban planning *The Death and Life of Great American Cities*, the journalist Jane Jacobs described a similar game, called messages, that she used to play with her sister when they first moved to New York:

> The idea was to pick two wildly dissimilar individuals— say a headhunter in the Solomon Islands and a cobbler in Rock Island, Illinois—and assume that one had to get a message to the other by word of mouth; then we would each silently figure out a plausible, or at least possible, chain of persons through whom the message could go. The one who could make the shortest plausible chain of messages won.

But how long are these chains in reality? One way to answer the question would be to map out all the links in the social network of the whole world and then simply count by brute force how many people you can reach in one "degree of separation," how many at "two degrees," and so on, until you have reached everyone. In Jacobs's day that was impossible, but in 2008 two computer scientists at Microsoft Research got somewhat close when they computed the length of paths connecting pairs of individuals in Microsoft's 240-million-strong instant messenger network, where being "friends" in this case meant being on each other's buddy lists.[3] On average they found that people were separated by about seven steps—remarkably close to the six handshakes that my father had mentioned. Yet this can't be the real answer to the question. The characters in Jacobs's fictional game didn't have access to this network, so they couldn't have computed the paths the way the Microsoft researchers did even if they had the computing power to do so. Clearly they must have used some other method to direct their messages. And indeed, according to Jacobs, they did:

> The headhunter would speak to the headman of his village, who would speak to the trader who came to buy copra, who would speak to the Australian patrol officer when he came through, who would tell the man who was next slated to go to Melbourne on leave, etc. Down at the other end, the cobbler would hear from his priest, who got it from the mayor, who got it from the state senator, who got it from the governor, etc. We soon had these close-to-home messengers down to a routine for almost everybody we could conjure up, but we would get tangled up in long chains at the middle until we began employing Mrs. Roosevelt. Mrs. Roosevelt made it suddenly possible to skip whole chains of intermediate connections. She knew the most unlikely people. The world shrank remarkably.[4]

Jacobs's solution, in other words, assumes that social networks are organized in a hierarchy: Messages flow up the hierarchy from the periphery and then back down again, with high-status figures like Mrs. Roosevelt occupying the critical center. We are so used to a world of hierarchies—whether inside formal organizations, across the economy, or in society—that it is natural to assume that social networks should be hierarchical as well. Karinthy, in fact, used a similar line of reasoning to Jacobs's, where in place of Mrs. Roosevelt he invoked Mr. Ford, writing that "to find a chain of contacts linking myself with an anonymous riveter at the Ford Motor Company...The worker knows his foreman, who knows Mr. Ford himself, who in turn is on good terms with the director general of the Hearst publishing empire. It would take but one word from my friend to send a cable to the general director of Hearst asking him to contact Ford who could in turn contact the foreman, who could then contact the riveter, who could then assemble a new automobile for me, should I need one."

As plausible as this method sounds, however, it is *not* how messages actually propagate through social networks, as we know now from a series of "small-world experiments" that began not long after Jacobs was writing. The first of these experiments was conducted by none other than Stanley Milgram, the social psychologist whose subway experiment I discussed in Chapter 1. Milgram recruited three hundred people, two hundred from Omaha, Nebraska, and the other hundred from around Boston, to play a version of the messages game with a Boston stockbroker who was a friend of Milgram's and who had volunteered to serve as the "target" of the exercise. Much as in Jacobs's imaginary version, participants in Milgram's experiment knew whom they were trying to reach, but could only send the message to someone whom they knew on a first-name basis; thus each of the three hundred "starters" would send it to a friend, who would send it to a friend, and so on, until someone either refused to participate or else the message chain reached the target. As luck would have it, sixty-four of the initial chains made it all the way to their destination, and the average length of those that did was indeed about six; hence the famous phrase "six degrees of separation."[5]

But although Milgram's subjects were able to find paths as short as those hypothesized by Karinthy and Jacobs, it wasn't because they employed Mrs. Roosevelt or anyone like her. Instead, ordinary people passed messages to other ordinary people, tracking along the same social stratum rather than going up and down the hierarchy as both Karinthy and Jacobs imagined. Nor did the chains get tangled up in the middle as Jacobs worried they might. Instead they experienced their greatest difficulties after they had already gotten close to their targets. Social networking, it seems, is less like a pyramid than it is like a game of golf—where, the old adage goes, you "drive for show, putt for dough." When you are far away from the target, that is, it's relatively easy to jump large distances simply by sending the message to someone in the right country, and from there to someone in the right city, and then to someone in the right profession. But once you get close to the target, big jumps don't help you anymore and messages have a tendency to bounce around until they find someone who knows the target.

Nevertheless, Milgram still found that not all message handlers are created equal. In fact, of the sixty-four messages that got through, nearly half of them were delivered to the target by one of three people, and half of those—sixteen chains—were delivered by a single person, "Mr. Jacobs," a clothing merchant who was a neighbor of the target. Struck by this concentration of messages into the hands of a few individuals, Milgram speculated that what he called sociometric stars might be important to understanding how the small-world phenomenon worked.[6] Milgram himself didn't conclude much more than that, but three decades later, in an essay called "Six Degrees of Lois Weisberg," *New Yorker* writer Malcolm Gladwell used Milgram's finding about Mr. Jacobs to make the argument that "a very small number of people [like Mrs. Weisberg] are linked to everyone else in a few steps, and the rest of us are linked to the world through those few."[7] In other words, even though Mr. Jacobs and Ms. Weisberg are not "important" in the same way that Mrs. Roosevelt or Mr. Ford were important, from a network perspective they end up serving the same kind of function—like hubs in an airline network that we necessarily pass through in order to get from one part of the world to another.

Like Jacobs's hierarchy, the airline network metaphor is an appealing one, but it says more about how we would organize the world if given the opportunity to do so than it says about how the world is actually organized. If you think about it for minute, in fact, the metaphor is actually quite implausible. Some people clearly have more friends than others. But people are not like airports—they can't just tack on an extra wing when they need to handle more traffic. As a result, the number of friends that people have doesn't vary by nearly as much as the traffic in airports. An average person, for example, has a few hundred friends, while the most gregarious top out around a couple of thousand—roughly ten times as many. That is a big difference, but not remotely comparable to a true hub like O'Hare, which handles thousands of times as many passengers as a small airport. So how is it that connectors in social networks can nevertheless act like hubs in airline networks?[8]

In fact, they do not, as my collaborators Roby Muhamad and Peter Dodds and I found several years ago when we replicated Milgram's original experiment—only this time we used e-mail in place of physical packets, allowing us to work on a much larger scale. Whereas Milgram had three hundred initial senders in two cities attempting to reach a single target in Boston, we had more than twenty thousand chains in search of one of eighteen targets in thirteen different countries around the world. By the time the experiment had ended, the chains had passed through over 60,000 people in 166 countries. Using some more up-to-date statistical analysis than Milgram had available to him, we were also able to estimate not only the length of the chains that made it to their targets, but also how long the chains that failed would have been had they continued. Our main finding was remarkably close to Milgram's—roughly half of all chains should be expected to reach their targets in seven steps or fewer. Given the differences between the two experiments, which were conducted on very different scales using different technologies and nearly forty years apart, it is actually sort of amazing that the results accorded so closely, and provides strong support for the claim that many people—although certainly not all people—can connect to one another through short chains.[9]

Unlike Milgram's findings, however, we discovered no "hubs" in the delivery process. Rather, messages reached their targets through almost as many recipients as there were chains. We also asked people why they chose the next person in the chain, and here, too, we discovered little evidence of hubs or stars. Subjects in small-world experiments, it turns out, do not typically pass messages to their highest-status or most-connected friends. Instead, they pass them to people they think have something in common with the target, like geographic proximity or a similar occupation, or they simply pass them to people they think will be likely to continue passing it along. Ordinary individuals, in other words, are just as

capable of spanning critical divides between social and professional circles, between different nations, or between different neighborhoods, as exceptional people. When you want to
get a message to a graduate student in Novosibirsk, Russia,
for example, you don't think about whom you know who has
a lot of friends, or goes to lots of parties, or has connections
to the White House. You think about whether you know any
Russians. And if you don't know any Russians, then maybe
you know someone from Eastern Europe, or someone who
has traveled to Eastern Europe, or has studied Russian, or
who lives in a part of your city that is known for its Eastern
European immigrants. Mrs. Roosevelt, or Lois Weisberg for
that matter, may indeed connect many people. But those same
people have many other ways of connecting as well. And it is
these other, less obvious ways that they tend to actually use,
if only because there are so many more of them.

The overall message here is that real social networks are
connected in more complex and more egalitarian ways than
Jacobs or even Milgram imagined—a result that has now been
confirmed with many experiments, empirical studies, and theoretical models.[10] In spite of all this evidence, however, when
we think about how social networks work, we continue to
be drawn to the idea that certain "special people," whether
famous wives of presidents or gregarious local businessmen,
are disproportionately responsible for connecting the rest of
us. Evidence, in fact, seems to have very little to do with why
we think this way. After all, Jacobs was writing years before Milgram's experiments and long before anyone had the
kind of data that might have supported her claim about Mrs.
Roosevelt. So wherever she got the idea from, it obviously
wasn't based on any actual evidence. Rather, it seems that Jacobs was drawn to the idea that a few special people connect
everyone else simply because without invoking such people

it's hard to come up with any explanation at all. The result is that no matter how many times the evidence rules out one kind of special person, we simply insert another. If it's not Mrs. Roosevelt, then it must be Lois Weisberg, and if it's not Lois Weisberg, then it must be Mr. Jacobs the clothing merchant. And if it's not him, then it must be our friend Ed who seems to know everyone. "It's got to be someone special." We feel compelled to conclude: "How else could it work?"

Nor is the intuitive appeal of special-people explanations restricted to problems to do with networks. The "great man" view of history explains important historical events in terms of the actions of a few critical leaders. Conspiracy theorists imbue shadowy government agents or secret cabals with near infinite capabilities to meddle with society. Media analysts credit high-profile celebrities with setting fashion trends or selling products. Corporate boards pay exorbitant amounts for a CEO whose decisions will shape the fate of the entire company. Epidemiologists worry that a few "superspreaders" can trigger an epidemic. And marketers extol the power of "influencers" to make or break a brand, change social norms, or otherwise shift public opinion.[11] In his book *The Tipping Point,* for example, Gladwell explains the origins of what he calls social epidemics, meaning everything from fads and fashions to shifts in cultural norms and sudden drops in crime rates, in terms of what he calls the law of the few. Just as superspreaders drive real epidemics and great men drive history, so too the law of the few claims that social epidemics are "driven by the efforts of a handful of exceptional people." For example, in discussing the mysterious resurgence of Hush Puppies in the mid-1990s, Gladwell explains that

the great mystery is how those shoes went from something worn by a few fashion-forward downtown Manhattan hipsters to being sold in malls across the country. What was the connection between the East Village and Middle America? The Law of the Few says the answer is that one of these exceptional people found out about the trend, and through social connections and energy and enthusiasm and personality spread the word about Hush Puppies just as people like Gaeten Dugas and Nushawn Williams were able to spread HIV.[12]

Gladwell's law of the few is catnip to marketers and businessmen and community organizers and just about anyone else in the business of shaping or manipulating people. And it's easy to see why. If you can just find these special people and influence *them*, their connections and energy and enthusiasm and personality would be put to work for you. It's a plausible-sounding story, and yet as with so many appealing ideas about human behavior, the law of the few turns out to be more a matter of perception than reality.

THE INFLUENCERS

The culprit again is common sense. As marketing consultants Ed Keller and Jon Berry argue, "Some people are better connected, better read, and better informed. You probably know this from your own experience. You don't turn to just anyone when you're deciding what neighborhood to live in, how to invest for retirement, or what kind of car or computer to buy."[13] As a description of our perceptions, this statement is probably accurate—when we think about what we're doing when we seek out information, access, or advice, it does indeed seem that we focus on some people over others. But as I've already discussed, our perceptions of how we behave are far from a perfect reflection of reality. A number of studies, for example, have suggested that social influence is mostly subconscious, arising out of subtle cues that we receive from our friends and neighbors, not necessarily by "turning to them" at all.[14] Nor is it clear that when we are influenced in these other, less conscious ways, we recognize that we have been influenced. Employees, for example, may well influence their bosses as much as their bosses influence them, but they are not equally likely to name each other as sources of influence—simply because bosses are supposed to be influential, whereas employees are not. In other words, our perceptions of who influences us may say more about social and hierarchical relations than influence per se.

One of the most confusing aspects of the influencer debate, in fact, is that no one can really agree on who the influencers are in the first place. Originally the term referred to "ordinary" people who just happened to exert extraordinary influence over their friends and neighbors. But in practice all sorts of people are referred to as influencers: media giants like Oprah Winfrey; gatekeepers like Anna Wintour, the editor of *Vogue;* celebrity actors and socialites; popular bloggers; and so on. All of these people may or may not be influential in their own way, but the kind of influence they exert varies tremendously. Oprah Winfrey's advocacy of an unknown book, for example, may dramatically improve its chances of appearing on the bestseller lists, but that is mostly because her individual influence is magnified enormously by the media empire that she runs. Likewise, a fashion designer might be well advised to have a famous actress arrive at the Oscars wearing his dress, but that is again because her arrival is being recorded, broadcast, and commented upon by the mass media. And when a popular blogger expresses his enthusiasm for a particular product, potentially thousands of people read his opinion. But is his or her influence analogous to that of an Oprah endorsement, a personal recommendation from a friend, or something else?

Even if we narrow down the problem to direct, interpersonal influence of the kind that excludes the media, celebrities, and bloggers of the world, measuring influence is a lot more difficult than simply measuring the length of message chains. For example, to demonstrate just one incident of influence between two friends, Anna and Bill, you need to demonstrate that whenever Anna adopts a certain idea or product, Bill is more likely to adopt the same idea or product as well.[15] Even keeping track of just one such relationship would not be easy. And as researchers quickly discovered, doing it for many people simultaneously is prohibitively difficult. In place of observing influence directly, therefore, researchers have proposed numerous proxies for influence, such as how many friends an individual has, or how many opinions they voice, or how expert or passionate they are about a topic, or how highly they score on some personality test—things that are easier to measure than influence itself. Unfortunately, while all these measures are plausible substitutes for influence, they all derive from assumptions about how people are influenced, and no one has ever tested these assumptions. In practice, therefore, nobody really knows who is an influencer and who isn't.[16]

This ambiguity is confusing, but it's still not the real source of the problem. If we could invent a perfect instrument for measuring influence, presumably we would find that some people are indeed more influential than others. Yet some people are also taller than others and that is not necessarily something about which marketers should care. So why are they so excited about influencers? Consider, for example, that many studies count someone as an influencer if at least three acquaintances named them as someone to whom they would turn for advice. Now, in a world where the average person influences just one other person, influencing three others makes you 300 percent as influential as average—a big difference. But on its own it doesn't solve the kinds of problems that marketers care about, like generating a hit product, driving public health awareness, or influencing a political candidate's election chances. All these problems require influencing millions of individuals. So even if each one of your influencers can influence three other ordinary people, you will still need to find and influence a million of them, which is rather different from what the law of the few promises. As it turns out, there's a solution to this problem as well, but it requires that we incorporate another related but distinct idea from network theory—that of social contagion.

THE ACCIDENTAL INFLUENTIALS

Contagion—the idea that information, and potentially influence, can spread along network ties like an infectious disease—is one of the most intriguing ideas in network science. As we saw in the last chapter, when everyone is being influenced by what other people are doing, surprising things can happen. But contagion also has important implications for influencers—because once you include the effects of contagion, the ultimate importance of an influencer is not just the individuals he or she influences directly but also all those influenced indirectly, via his neighbors, his neighbors' neighbors, and so on. It is through contagion, in fact, that the law of the few gets its real power. Because if just the right influencers can trigger a social epidemic, then influencing four million people may in fact require only a few of them. That's not a good deal—that's a *great* deal. And because finding and influencing just a few people is quite different from finding and influencing a million, it qualitatively changes the nature of influence.[17]

What it means, though, is that the law of the few is not one, but two hypotheses that have been mashed together: first that some people are more influential than others; and second, that the influence of these people is greatly magnified by some contagion process that generates social epidemics.[18] It was therefore this combination of claims that Peter Dodds and I set out to test a few years ago in a series of computer simulations. Because these simulations required us to write down explicit mathematical models of how influence spreads, we had to specify all the assumptions that are typically left unstated in anecdotal descriptions of influencers. How should an influencer be defined? Who influences whom? What kinds of choices are individuals making? And how are these choices influenced by others? As I've discussed, no one really knows the answers to any of these questions; thus it's necessary, as in any modeling exercise, to make a number of assumptions, which could of course be wrong. Nevertheless, to cover our bases as much as possible, we considered two very different classes of models, each of which has been studied for decades by social and marketing scientists.[19]

The first was a version of Granovetter's riot model from the previous chapter. Unlike Granovetter's model, however, where everyone in the crowd observed everyone else, the interactions among individuals were specified by a network in which each individual got to observe only some relatively small circle of friends or acquaintances. The second model was a version of the "Bass model," named for Frank Bass, the marketing scientist who first proposed it as a model of product adoption, but closely related to an even older model used by mathematical epidemiologists to study the spread of biological diseases. In other words, whereas Granovetter's model assumes that individuals adopt something when a certain fraction of their neighbors do, the Bass model assumes that adoption works like an infection process, with "susceptible" and "infected" individuals interacting along network ties.[20] The two models sound similar, but they're actually very different—which was important, because we didn't want our conclusions about the effect of influencers to depend too much on the assumptions of any one model.

What we found was that under most conditions, highly influential individuals were indeed more effective than the average person in triggering social epidemics. But their relative importance was much less than what the law of the few would suggest. To illustrate, consider an "influencer" who directly influences three times as many of his peers as the average person. Intuitively, one would expect that, all other things being equal, the influencer would also influence three times as many people indirectly as well. In other words, the influencer would exhibit a "multiplier effect" of three. The law of the few, it bears noting, claims that the effect would be much greater—that the disproportionality should be "extreme"—but what we found was the opposite.[21] Typically the multiplier effect for an influencer like this was less than three, and in many cases, they were not any more effective at all. Influencers may exist, in other words, but not the kind of influencers posited by the law of the few.

The reason is simply that when influence is spread via some contagious process, the outcome depends far more on the overall structure of the network than on the properties of the individuals who trigger it. Just as forest fires require a conspiracy of wind, temperature, low humidity, and combustible fuel to rage out of control over large tracts of land, social epidemics require just the right conditions to be satisfied by the network of influence. And as it turned out, the most important condition had nothing to do with a few highly influential individuals at all. Rather, it depended on the existence of a critical mass of *easily influenced* people who influence other easy-to-influence people. When this critical mass existed, even an average individual was capable of triggering a large cascade—just as any spark will suffice to trigger a large forest fire when the conditions are primed for it. Conversely, when the critical mass did not exist, not even the most influential individual could trigger any more than a small cascade. The result is that unless one can see where particular individuals fit into the entire network, one cannot say much about how influential they will be—no matter what you can measure about them.

When we hear about a large forest fire, of course, we don't think that there must have been anything special about the spark that started it. Indeed, such an idea would be laughable. Yet when we see something special happen in the social world, we are instantly drawn to the idea that whoever started it must have been special also. And of course, whenever a large cascade did take place in our simulations, it was necessarily the case that someone had to have started it. However unexceptional that person might have seemed in advance, in retrospect they would seem to fit exactly the description of the law of the few: the "tiny percentage of people who do the majority of the work." What we knew from our simulations, however, was that there really *was* nothing special about these individuals—because we had created them that way. The majority of the work was being done not by a tiny percentage of people who acted as the triggers, but rather by the much larger critical mass of easily influenced people. What we concluded, therefore, is that the kind of influential person whose energy and connections can turn your book into a bestseller or your product into a hit is most likely an accident of timing and circumstances. An "accidental influential" as it were.[22]

"ORDINARY INFLUENCERS" ON TWITTER

As many people immediately pointed out, this conclusion was based entirely on computer simulations. And as I've already mentioned, these simulations were highly simplified versions of reality, and made a large number of assumptions, any of which could have been wrong. Computer simulations are useful tools that can generate great insight. But in the end they are more like thought experiments than real experiments, and as such are better suited to provoking new questions than to answering them. So if we really want to know whether particular individuals are capable of stimulating the diffusion of ideas, information, and influence—and if these influencers exist, which attributes distinguish them from ordinary people—then we need to run experiments in the real world. But studying the relationship between individual influence and large-scale impact in the real world is easier said than done.

The main problem is that you need an enormous amount of data, and most of it is very hard to collect. Just demonstrating that one person has influenced another is difficult enough. And if you wanted to make the connection to how they influence larger populations, you need to gather similar information for whole chains of influence, in which one person influences another who in turn influences another, and so on. Pretty soon, you're talking about thousands or even millions of relationships, just to track how a single piece of information was spread. And ideally you would want to study many such cases. It's an overwhelming amount of data to test what seems to be a relatively straightforward claim—that some people matter more than others—but there's no getting around it. It also helps explain why diffusion research, as it is known, has remained such a myth-laden business for so long: when it's impossible to prove anything, everyone is free to propose whatever plausible story they like. There's no way to decide who is right.

As with experiments like Music Lab, however, the Internet is starting to change this picture in important ways. A handful of recent studies have begun to explore diffusion in social networks on a scale that would have been unimaginable just a decade ago. Blog postings diffuse among networks of bloggers. Fan pages diffuse among networks of friends on Facebook. Special capabilities called "gestures" diffuse among players on the online game Second Life. And premium voice services have been shown to diffuse among networks of IM buddies.[23] Inspired by these studies, my Yahoo! colleagues Jake Hofman and Winter Mason and I, along with Eytan Bakshy, a talented graduate student at the University of Michigan, decided to look for the diffusion of information in the largest communication network we could get our hands on: Twitter. In the process, we would look for influencers.[24]

In many respects, Twitter is ideally suited to this objective. Unlike Facebook, say, where people connect to one another for a multitude of reasons, the whole point of Twitter is to broadcast information to other people—your "followers"— who have explicitly indicated that they want to hear from you. Getting people to pay attention to you—influencing them, in other words—is what Twitter is all about. Second, Twitter is remarkably diverse. Many users are regular people whose followers are mostly friends interested in hearing from them. But many of the most followed users on Twitter are public figures, including bloggers, journalists, celebrities (Ashton Kutcher, Shaquille O'Neal, Oprah), media organizations such as CNN, and even government agencies and nonprofits (the Obama administration, No. 10 Downing Street, the World Economic Forum). This diversity is helpful because it allowed us to compare the influence of all manner of would-be influencers—ordinary people all the way up to Oprah and Ashton—in a consistent way.

Finally, although many tweets are mundane updates ("Having coffee at Starbucks on Broadway! It's a beautiful day!!"), many of them refer either to other online content, like breaking news stories and funny videos, or to other things in the world, like books, movies, and so on, about which Twitter users wish to express their opinions. And because the format of Twitter forces users to keep every message to no more than 140 characters, users often make use of "URL shorteners," such as bit.ly, to replace the long, messy URL of the original website with something like http://bit .ly/beRKJo. The nice thing about these shortened URLs is that they effectively assign a unique code to every piece of content broadcast on Twitter. Thus when a user wishes to "retweet" something, it's possible to see whom it came from originally, and thereby trace chains of diffusion across the follower graph.

In total, we tracked more than 74 million of these diffusion chains initiated by more than 1.6 million users, over a two-month interval in late 2009. For each event, we counted how many times the URL in question was retweeted—first by the original "seed" user's immediate followers, then by their followers, and their followers' followers, and so on—thereby tracing out the full "cascade" of retweets triggered by each original tweet. As the figure on page 102 shows, some of these cascades were broad and shallow, while others were narrow and deep. Others still were very large, with complex structure, starting out small and trickling along before gaining momentum somewhere else in the network. Most of all, however, we found that the vast majority of attempted cascades—roughly 98 percent of the total—didn't actually spread at all.

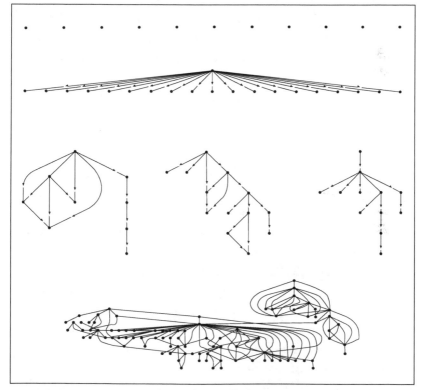

Cascades on Twitter

This result is important because, as I'll discuss in more detail in the next chapter, if you want to understand why some things "go viral"—those occasional YouTube videos that attract millions of downloads, or funny messages that circulate wildly through e-mail or on Facebook—it's a mistake to consider only the rare few that actually succeed. In most settings, unfortunately, it is only possible to study the "successes" for the simple reason that nobody bothers to keep track of all the failures, which have a tendency to get swept under the rug. On Twitter, however, we can keep track of every single event, no matter how small, thereby enabling us to learn who is influential, how much more influential than average they really are, and whether or not it is possible to tell the differences between individuals in a way that could potentially be exploited.

The way we went about this exercise was to imitate what a hypothetical marketer might try to do—that is, using everything known about the attributes and past performance of a million or so individuals, to predict how influential each of them will be in the future. Based on these predictions, the marketer could then "sponsor" some group of individuals to tweet whatever information it is trying to disseminate, thereby generating a series of cascades. The better the marketer can predict how large a cascade any particular individual can trigger, the more efficiently it can allocate its budget for sponsored tweets. Actually running such an experiment is still extremely difficult in practice, so we instead did our best to approximate it using the data we had already collected. Specifically, we divided our data in two, artificially setting the first month of our time period as our "history" and the second half as the "future." We then fed all our "historical" data into a statistical model, including how many followers each user had, how many others they were following, how frequently they tweeted, when they had joined, and how successful they had been at triggering cascades during this period. Finally, we used the model to "predict" how influential each user would be in our "future" data and checked the model's performance against what actually transpired.

In a nutshell, what we found was that individual-level predictions are extremely noisy. Even though it was the case that on average, individuals with many followers who had been successful at triggering cascades of retweets in the past were more likely to be successful in the future, individual cases fluctuated wildly at random. Just as with the *Mona Lisa,* for every individual who exhibited the attributes of a successful influencer, there were many other users with indistinguishable attributes who were not successful. Nor did this uncertainty arise simply because we weren't able to measure the right attributes—in reality we had more data than any marketer would normally have—or to measure them accurately. Rather, the problem was that, like the simulations above, much of what drives successful diffusion depends on factors outside the control of the individual seeds. What this result suggests, in other words, is that marketing strategies that focus on targeting a few "special" individuals are bound to be unreliable. Like responsible financial managers, therefore, marketers should adopt a "portfolio" approach, targeting a large number of potential influencers and harnessing their average effect, thereby effectively reducing the individual-level randomness.[24]

Although promising in theory, a portfolio approach also raises a new issue, of cost effectiveness. To illustrate the point, consider a recent story in the *New York Times* that claimed that Kim Kardashian, the reality TV actress, was getting paid $10,000 per tweet by various sponsors who wanted her to mention their products. Kardashian at the time had well over a million followers, so it seems plausible that paying someone like her would generate more attention than paying some ordinary person with only a few hundred followers. But how did they come up with that particular figure? Ordinary people, that is, might be prepared to tweet about their products for much less than $10,000. Assuming, therefore, that more visible individuals "cost" more than less visible ones, should marketers be targeting a relatively small number of more influential, more expensive, individuals or a larger number of less influential, less expensive individuals? Better yet, how should one strike the optimal balance?[25]

Ultimately, the answer to this question will depend on the specifics of how much different Twitter users would charge prospective marketers to sponsor their tweets—if indeed, they would agree to such an arrangement at all. Nevertheless, as a speculative exercise, we tested a range of plausible assumptions, each corresponding to a different hypothetical "influencer-based" marketing campaign, and measured their return on investment using the same statistical model as before. What we found was surprising even to us: Even though the Kim Kardashians of the world were indeed more influential than average, they were so much more expensive that they did not provide the best value for the money. Rather, it was what we called ordinary influencers, meaning individuals who exhibit average or even less-than-average influence, who often proved to be the most cost-effective means to disseminate information.

CIRCULAR REASONING AGAIN

Before you rush out to short stock in Kim Kardashian, I should emphasize that we didn't actually run the experiment that we imagined. Even though we were studying data from the real world, not a computer simulation, our statistical models still made a lot of assumptions. Assuming, for example, that our hypothetical marketer could persuade a few thousand ordinary influencers to tweet about their product, it is not at all obvious that their followers would respond as favorably as they do to normal tweets. As anyone whose friend has tried to sell them on Amway products would know, there is something a little icky about a sales message embedded in a personal communication. People who follow Kim Kardashian, however, might have no such concerns; thus she may be far more effective in real life than our study could determine. Or perhaps our measure of influence—the number of retweets—was the wrong measure. We measured retweets because that's what we could measure, and that was definitely better than nothing. But presumably what you really care about is how many people click through to a story, or donate money to a charitable cause, or buy your product. Possibly Kardashian followers act on her tweets even when they don't retweet them to their friends—in which case, once again, we would have underestimated her influence.

Then again, we may not have. In the end, we simply don't know who is influential or what influencers, however defined, can accomplish. Until it is possible to measure influence with respect to some outcome that we actually care about, and until someone runs the real-world experiments that can measure the influence of different individuals, every result—including ours—ought to be taken with a grain of salt. Nevertheless, the findings I have discussed—from the small-world experiment, from the simulation studies of influence spreading on networks, and from the Twitter study—ought to raise some serious doubts about claims like the law of the few that explain social epidemics as the work of a tiny minority of special people.

It's not even clear, in fact, that social epidemics are the right way to think about social change to begin with. Although our Twitter study found that epidemic-like events do occur, we also found that they are incredibly rare. Of 74 million events in our data, only a few dozen generated even a thousand retweets, and only one or two got to ten thousand. In a network of tens of millions of users, ten thousand retweets doesn't seem like that big a number, but what our data showed is that even that is almost impossible to achieve. For practical purposes, therefore, it may be better to forget about the large cascades altogether and instead try to generate lots of small ones. And for that purpose, ordinary influencers may work just fine. They don't accomplish anything dramatic, so you may need a lot of them, but in harnessing many such individuals, you can also average out much of the randomness, generating a consistently positive effect.

Finally, and quite apart from any specific findings, these studies help us to see a major shortcoming of commonsense thinking. It is ironic in a way that the law of the few is portrayed as a counterintuitive idea because in fact we're so used to thinking in terms of special people that the claim that a few special people do the bulk of the work is actually extremely natural. We think that by acknowledging the importance of interpersonal influence and social networks, we have somehow moved beyond the circular claim from the previous chapter that "X happened because that's what people wanted." But when we try to imagine how a complex network of millions of people is connected—or worse still, how influence propagates through it—our intuition is immediately defeated. By effectively concentrating *all* the agency into the hands of a few individuals, "special people" arguments like the law of the few reduce the problem of understanding how network structure affects outcomes to the much simpler problem of understanding what it is that motivates the special people. As with all commonsense explanations, it sounds reasonable and it might be right. But in claiming that "X happened because a few special people made it happen," we have effectively replaced one piece of circular reasoning with another.

CHAPTER 5

History, the Fickle Teacher

The message of the previous three chapters is that commonsense explanations are often characterized by circular reasoning. Teachers cheated on their students' tests because that's what their incentives led them to do. The *Mona Lisa* is the most famous painting in the world because it has all the attributes of the *Mona Lisa*. People have stopped buying gas-guzzling SUVs because social norms now dictate that people shouldn't buy gas-guzzling SUVs. And a few special people revived the fortunes of the Hush Puppies shoe brand because a few people started buying Hush Puppies before everyone else did. All of these statements may be true, but all they are really telling us is that what we know happened, happened, and not something else. Because they can only be constructed after we know the outcome itself, we can never be sure how much these explanations really explain, versus simply describe.

What's curious about this problem, however, is that even once you see the inherent circularity of commonsense explanations, it's still not obvious what's wrong with them. After all, in science we don't necessarily know why things happen either, but we can often figure it out by doing experiments in a lab or by observing systematic regularities in the world. Why can't we learn from history the same way? That is, think of history as a series of experiments in which certain general "laws" of cause and effect determine the outcomes that we observe. By systematically piecing together the regularities in our observations, can we not infer these laws just as we do in science? For example, imagine that the contest for attention between great works of art is an experiment designed to identify the attributes of great art. Even if it's true that prior to the twentieth century, it might not have been obvious that the *Mona Lisa* was going to become the most famous painting in the world, we have now run the experiment, and we have the answer. We may still not be able to say what it is about the *Mona Lisa* that makes it uniquely great, but we do at least have some data. Even if our commonsense explanations have a tendency to conflate what happened with why it happened, are we not simply doing our best to act like good experimentalists?[1]

In a sense, the answer is yes. We probably are doing our best, and under the right circumstances learning from observation and experience can work pretty well. But there's a catch: In order to be able to infer that "A causes B," we need to be able to run the experiment many times. Let's say, for example, that A is a new drug to reduce "bad" cholesterol and B is a patient's chance of developing heart disease in the next ten years. If the manufacturer can show that a patient who receives drug A is significantly less likely to develop heart disease than one who doesn't, they're allowed to claim that the drug can help prevent heart disease; otherwise they can't. But because any one person can only either receive the drug or not receive it, the only way to show that the drug is causing anything is to run the "experiment" many times, where each person's experience counts as a single run. A drug trial therefore requires many participants, each of whom is randomly assigned either to receive the treatment or not. The effect of the drug is then measured as the difference in outcomes between the "treatment" and the "control" groups, where the smaller the effect, the larger the trial needs to be in order to rule out random chance as the explanation.

In certain everyday problem-solving situations, where we encounter more or less similar circumstances over and over again, we can get pretty close to imitating the conditions of the drug trial. Driving home from work every day, for example, we can experiment with different routes or with different departure times. By repeating these variations many times, and assuming that traffic on any given day is more or less like traffic on any other day, we can effectively bypass all the complex cause-and-effect relationships simply by observing which route results in the shortest commute time, on average. Likewise, the kind of experience-based expertise that derives from professional training, whether in medicine, engineering, or the military, works in the same way—by repeatedly exposing trainees to situations that are as similar as possible to those they will be expected to deal with in their eventual careers.[2]

HISTORY IS ONLY RUN ONCE

Given how well this quasi-experimental approach to learning works in everyday situations and professional training, it's perhaps not surprising that our commonsense explanations implicitly apply the same reasoning to explain economic, political, and cultural events as well. By now, however, you probably suspect where this is heading. For problems of economics, politics, and culture—problems that involve many people interacting over time—the combination of the frame problem and the micro-macro problem means that *every* situation is in some important respect different from the situations we have seen before. Thus, we never really get to run the same experiment more than once. At some level, we understand this problem. Nobody really thinks that the war in

Iraq is directly comparable to the Vietnam War or even the war in Afghanistan, and one must therefore be cautious in applying the lessons from one to another. Likewise, nobody thinks that by studying the success of the *Mona Lisa* we can realistically expect to understand much about the success and failure of contemporary artists. Nevertheless, we do still expect to learn some lessons from history, and it is all too easy to persuade ourselves that we have learned more than we really have.

For example, did the so-called surge in Iraq in the fall of 2007 cause the subsequent drop in violence in the summer of 2008? Intuitively the answer seems to be yes—not only did the drop in violence take place reasonably soon after the surge was implemented, but the surge was specifically intended to have that effect. The combination of intentionality and timing strongly suggests causality, as did the often-repeated claims of an administration looking for something good to take credit for. But many other things happened between the fall of 2007 and the summer of 2008 as well. Sunni resistance fighters, seeing an even greater menace from hard-core terrorist organizations like Al Qaeda than from American soldiers, began to cooperate with their erstwhile occupiers. The Shiite militia—most importantly Moktada Sadr's Mahdi Army—also began to experience a backlash from their grassroots, possibly leading them to moderate their behavior. And the Iraqi Army and police forces, finally displaying sufficient competence to take on the militias, began to assert themselves, as did the Iraqi government. Any one of these other factors might have been at least as responsible for the drop in violence as the surge. Or perhaps it was some combination. Or perhaps it was something else entirely. How are we to know?

One way to be sure would be to "rerun" history many

times, much as we did in the Music Lab experiment, and see what would have happened both in the presence and also the absence of the surge. If across all of these alternate versions of history, violence drops whenever there is a surge and doesn't drop whenever there isn't, then we can say with some confidence that the surge is causing the drop. And if instead we find that most of the time we have a surge, nothing happens to the level of violence, or alternatively we find that violence drops whether we have a surge or not, then whatever it is that is causing the drop, clearly it isn't the surge. In reality, of course, this experiment got run only once, and so we never got to see all the other versions of it that may or may not have turned out differently. As a result, we can't ever really be sure what caused the drop in violence. But rather than producing doubt, the absence of "counterfactual" versions of history tends to have the opposite effect—namely that we tend to perceive what actually happened as having been inevitable.

This tendency, which psychologists call creeping determinism, is related to the better-known phenomenon of hindsight bias, the after-the-fact tendency to think that we "knew it all along." In a variety of lab experiments, psychologists have asked participants to make predictions about future events and then reinterviewed them after the events in question had taken place. When recalling their previous predictions, subjects consistently report being more certain of their correct predictions, and less certain of their incorrect predictions, than they had reported at the time they made them. Creeping determinism, however, is subtly different from hindsight bias and even more deceptive. Hindsight bias, it turns out, can be counteracted by reminding people of what they said before they knew the answer or by forcing them to keep records of their predictions. But even when we recall perfectly accurately how uncertain we were about the way events would transpire—even when we concede to have been caught completely by surprise—we still have a tendency to treat the realized outcome as inevitable. Ahead of time, for example, it might have seemed that the surge was just as likely to have had no effect as to lead to a drop in violence. But once we know that the drop in violence is what actually happened, it doesn't matter whether or not we knew all along that it was going to happen (hindsight bias). We still believe that it *was* going to happen, because it did.[3]

SAMPLING BIAS

Creeping determinism means that we pay less attention than we should to the things that don't happen. But we also pay too little attention to most of what does happen. We notice when we just miss the train, but not all the times when it arrives shortly after we do. We notice when we unexpectedly run into an acquaintance at the airport, but not all the times when we do not. We notice when a mutual fund manager beats the S&P 500 ten years in a row or when a basketball player has a "hot hand" or when a baseball player has a long hitting streak, but not all the times when fund managers and sportsmen alike do not display streaks of any kind. And we notice when a new trend appears or a small company becomes phenomenally successful, but not all the times when potential trends or new companies disappear before even registering on the public consciousness.

Just as with our tendency to emphasize the things that happened over those that didn't, our bias toward "interesting" things is completely understandable. Why would we be interested in uninteresting things? Nevertheless, it exacerbates our tendency to construct explanations that account for only some of the data. If we want to know why some people are rich, for example, or why some companies are successful, it may seem sensible to look for rich people or successful companies and identify which attributes they share. But what this exercise can't reveal is that if we instead looked at people who aren't rich or companies that aren't successful, we might have found that they exhibit many of the same attributes. The only way to identify attributes that differentiate successful from unsuccessful entities is to consider both kinds, and to look for systematic differences. Yet because what we care about is success, it seems pointless—or simply uninteresting—to worry about the absence of success. Thus we infer that certain attributes are related to success when in fact they may be equally related to failure.

This problem of "sampling bias" is especially acute when the things we pay attention to—the interesting events— happen only rarely. For example, when Western Airlines Flight 2605 crashed into a truck that had been left on an unused runway at Mexico City on October 31, 1979, investigators quickly identified five contributing factors. First, both the pilot and the navigator were fatigued, each having had only a few hours' sleep in the past twenty-four hours. Second, there was a communication mix-up between the crew and the air traffic controller, who had instructed the plane to come in on the radar beam that was oriented on the unused runway, and then shift to the active runway for the landing. Third, this mix-up was compounded by a malfunctioning radio, which failed for a critical part of the approach, during which time the confusion might have been clarified. Fourth, the airport was shrouded in heavy fog, obscuring both the truck and the active runway from the pilot's view. And fifth, the ground controller got confused during the final approach, probably due to the stressful situation, and thought that it was the inactive runway that had been lit.

As the psychologist Robyn Dawes explains in his account of the accident, the investigation concluded that although no one of these factors—fatigue, communication mix-up, radio failure, weather, and stress—had caused the accident on its own, the combination of all five together had proven fatal. It seems like a pretty reasonable conclusion, and it's consistent with the explanations we're familiar with for plane crashes in general. But as Dawes also points out, these same five factors arise all the time, including many, many instances where the planes did not crash. So if instead of starting with the crash and working backward to identify its causes, we worked forward, counting all the times when we observed some combination of fatigue, communication mix-up, radio failure, weather, and stress, chances are that most of those events would not result in crashes either.[4]

The difference between these two ways of looking at the world is illustrated in the figure below. In the left-hand panel, we see the five risk factors identified by the Flight 2605 investigation and all the corresponding outcomes. One of those outcomes is indeed the crash, but there are many other noncrash outcomes as well. These factors, in other words, are "necessary but not sufficient" conditions: Without them, it's extremely unlikely that we'd have a crash; but just because they're present doesn't mean that a crash will happen, or is even all that likely. Once we do see a crash, however, our view of the world shifts to the right-hand panel. Now all the "noncrashes" have disappeared, because we're no longer trying to explain them—we're only trying to account for the crash—and all the arrows from the factors to the noncrashes have disappeared as well. The result is that the very same set of factors that in the left-hand panel appeared do a poor job of predicting the crash now seems to do an excellent job.

By identifying necessary conditions, the investigations that follow plane crashes help to keep them rare—which is obviously a good thing—but the resulting temptation to treat them as sufficient conditions nevertheless plays havoc with our intuition for why crashes happen when they do. And much the same is true of other rare events, like school shootings, terrorist attacks, and stock market crashes. Most school shooters, for example, are teenage boys who have distant or

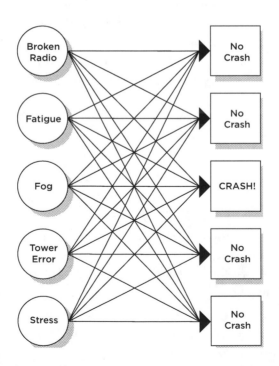

strained relationships with their parents, have been exposed to violent TV and video games, are alienated from their peers, and have fantasized about taking revenge. But these same attributes describe literally thousands of teenage boys, almost all of whom do not go on to hurt anyone, ever.[5] Likewise, the so-called systemic failure that almost allowed Umar Farouk Abdulmutallab, a twenty-three-year-old Nigerian, to bring down a Northwest Airlines flight landing in Detroit on Christmas Day 2009 comprised the sorts of errors and oversights that likely happen in the intelligence and homeland security agencies thousands of times every year—almost always with no adverse consequences. And for every day in

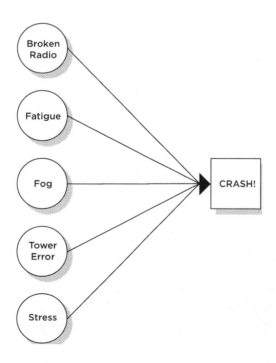

which the stock market experiences a wild plunge, there are thousands of days in which roughly the same sorts of circumstances produce nothing remarkable at all.

IMAGINED CAUSES

Together, creeping determinism and sampling bias lead commonsense explanations to suffer from what is called the post-hoc fallacy. The fallacy is related to a fundamental requirement of cause and effect—that in order for A to be said to cause B, A must precede B in time. If a billiard ball starts to move before it is struck by another billiard ball, something else must have caused it to move. Conversely, if we feel the wind blow and only then see the branches of a nearby tree begin to sway, we feel safe concluding that it was the wind that caused the movement. All of this is fine. But just because B follows A doesn't mean that A has *caused* B. If you hear a bird sing or see a cat walk along a wall, and then see the branches start to wave, you probably don't conclude that either the bird or the cat is causing the branches to move. It's an obvious point, and in the physical world we have good enough theories about how things work that we can usually sort plausible from implausible. But when it comes to social phenomena, common sense is extremely good at making all sorts of potential causes seem plausible. The result is that we are tempted to infer a cause-and-effect relationship when all we have witnessed is a sequence of events. This is the post-hoc fallacy.

Malcolm Gladwell's "law of the few," discussed in the last chapter, is a poster child for the post-hoc fallacy. Any time something interesting happens, whether it is a surprise best seller, a breakout artist, or a hit product, it will invariably be the case that someone was buying it or doing it before everyone else, and that person is going to seem influential.

The Tipping Point, in fact, is replete with stories about interesting people who seem to have played critical roles in important events: Paul Revere and his famous midnight ride from Boston to Lexington that energized the local militias and triggered the American Revolution. Gaëtan Dugas, the sexually voracious Canadian flight attendant who became known as Patient Zero of the American HIV epidemic. Lois Weisberg, the title character of Gladwell's earlier *New Yorker* article, who seems to know everyone, and has a gift for connecting people. And the group of East Village hipsters whose ironic embrace of Hush Puppies shoes preceded a dramatic revival in the brand's fortunes.

These are all great stories, and it's hard to read them and not agree with Gladwell that when something happens that is as surprising and dramatic as the Minutemen's unexpectedly fierce defense of Lexington on April 19, 1775, someone special—someone like Paul Revere—must have helped it along. Gladwell's explanation is especially convincing because he also relates the story of William Dawes, another rider that night who also tried to alert the local militia, but who rode a different route than Revere. Whereas the locals along Revere's route turned out in force the next day, the townsfolk in places like Waltham, Massachusetts, which Dawes visited, seemed not to have found out about the British movements until it was too late. Because Revere rode one route and Dawes rode the other, it seems clear that the difference in outcomes can be attributed to differences between the two men. Revere was a connector, and Dawes wasn't.[6]

What Gladwell doesn't consider, however, is that many other factors were also different about the two rides: different routes, different towns, and different people who made different choices about whom to alert once they had heard the news themselves. Paul Revere may well have been as remarkable and charismatic as Gladwell claims, while William Dawes may not have been. But in reality there was so much else going on that night that it's no more possible to attribute the outcomes the next day to the intrinsic attributes of the two men than it is to attribute the success of the *Mona Lisa* to its particular features, or the drop in violence in the Sunni Triangle of Iraq in 2008 to the surge. Rather, people like Revere, who after the fact seem to have been influential in causing some dramatic outcome, may instead be more like the "accidental influentials" that Peter Dodds and I found in our simulations—individuals whose apparent role actually depended on a confluence of other factors.

To illustrate how easily the post-hoc fallacy can generate accidental influentials, consider the following example from a real epidemic: the SARS epidemic that exploded in Hong Kong in early 2003. One of the most striking findings of the subsequent investigation was that a single patient, a young man who had traveled to Hong Kong by train from mainland China, and had been admitted to the Prince of Wales Hospital, had directly infected fifty others, leading eventually to 156 cases in the hospital alone. Subsequently the Prince of Wales outbreak led to a second major outbreak in Hong Kong, which in turn led to the epidemic's spread to Canada and other countries. Based on examples like the SARS epidemic, a growing number of epidemiologists have become convinced that the ultimate seriousness of the epidemic depends disproportionately on the activities of superspreaders—individuals like Gaëtan Dugas and the Prince of Wales patient who single-handedly infect many others.[7]

But how special are these people really? A closer look at the SARS case reveals that the real source of the problem was a misdiagnosis of pneumonia when the patient checked into the hospital. Instead of being isolated—the standard procedure for a patient infected with an unknown respiratory virus—the misdiagnosed SARS victim was placed in an open ward with poor air circulation. Even worse, because the diagnosis was pneumonia, a bronchial ventilator was placed into his lungs, which then proceeded to spew vast numbers of viral particles into the air around him. The conditions in the crowded ward resulted in a number of medical workers as well as other patients becoming infected. The event was important in spreading the disease—at least locally. But what was important about it was not the patient himself so much as the particular details of how he was treated. Prior to that, nothing you could have known about the patient would have led you to suspect that there was anything special about him, because there *was* nothing special about him.

Even after the Prince of Wales outbreak, it would have been a mistake to focus on superspreading individuals rather than the circumstances that led to the virus being spread. The next major SARS outbreak, for example, took place shortly afterward in a Hong Kong apartment building, the Amoy Gardens. This time the responsible person, who had become infected at the hospital while being treated for renal failure, also had a bad case of diarrhea. Unfortunately, the building's plumbing system was also poorly maintained, and the infection spread to three hundred other individuals in the building via a leaking drain, where none of these victims were even in the same room. Whatever lessons one might have inferred about superspreaders by studying the particular characteristics of the patient in the Prince of Wales Hospital, therefore, would have been next to useless in the Amoy Gardens. In both cases, the so-called superspreaders were simply accidental by-products of other, more complicated circumstances.

We'll never know what would have happened at Lexington on July 17, 1775, had Paul Revere instead ridden William

Dawes's midnight ride and Dawes ridden Revere's. But it's entirely possible that it would have worked out the same way, with the exception that it would have been William Dawes's name that was passed down in history, not Paul Revere's. Just as the outbreaks at the Prince of Wales Hospital and the Amoy Gardens happened for a complex combination of reasons, so too the victory at Lexington depended on the decisions and interactions of thousands of people, not to mention other accidents of fate. In other words, although it is tempting to attribute the outcome to a single special person, we should remember that the temptation arises simply because this is how we'd *like* the world to work, not because that is how it actually works. In this example, as in many others, common sense and history conspire to generate the illusion of cause and effect where none exists. On the one hand, common sense excels in generating plausible causes, whether special people, or special attributes, or special circumstances. And on the other hand, history obligingly discards most of the evidence, leaving only a single thread of events to explain. Commonsense explanations therefore seem to tell us *why* something happened when in fact all they're doing is describing *what* happened.

HISTORY CANNOT BE TOLD WHILE IT'S HAPPENING

The inability to differentiate the "why" from the "what" of historical events presents a serious problem to anyone hoping to learn from the past. But surely we can at least be confident that we know what happened, even if we can't be sure why. If anything seems like a matter of common sense, it is that history is a literal description of past events. And yet as the Russian-British philosopher Isaiah Berlin argued, the kinds of descriptions that historians give of historical events wouldn't have made much sense to the people who actually participated in them. Berlin illustrated this problem with a scene from Tolstoy's *War and Peace,* in which "Pierre Bezukhov wanders about, 'lost' on the battlefield of Borodino, looking for something which he imagines as a kind of set-piece; a battle as depicted by the historians or the painters. But he finds only the ordinary confusion of individual human beings haphazardly attending to this or that human want...a succession of 'accidents' whose origins and consequences are, by and large, untraceable and unpredictable; only loosely strung groups of events forming an ever-varying pattern, following no discernable order."[8]

Faced with such an objection, a historian might reasonably respond that Bezukhov simply lacked the ability to observe all the various parts of the battlefield puzzle, or else the wherewithal to put all the pieces together in his mind in real time. Perhaps, in other words, the only difference between the historian's view of the battle and Bezukhov's is that the historian has had the time and leisure to gather and synthesize information from many different participants, none of who was in a position to witness the whole picture. Viewed from this perspective, it may indeed be difficult or even impossible to understand what is happening at the time it is happening. But the difficulty derives solely from a practical problem about the speed with which one can realistically assemble the relevant facts. If true, this response implies that it ought to be possible for someone like Bezukhov to have known what was going on at the battle of Borodino *in principle,* even if not in practice.[9]

But let's imagine for a moment that we could solve this practical problem. Imagine that we could summon up a truly panoptical being, able to observe in real time every single person, object, action, thought, and intention in Tolstoy's battle, or any other event. In fact, the philosopher Arthur Danto proposed precisely such a hypothetical being, which he called the Ideal Chronicler, or IC. Replacing Pierre Bezukhov with Danto's Ideal Chronicler, one could then ask the question, What would the IC observe? To begin with, the Ideal Chronicler would have a lot of advantages over poor Bezukhov. Not only could it observe every action of every combatant at Borodino, but it could also observe everything else going on in the world as well. Having been around forever, moreover, the Ideal Chronicler would also know everything that had happened right up to that point, and would have the power to synthesize all that information, and even make inferences about where it might be leading. The IC, in other words, would have far more information, and infinitely greater ability to process it, than any mortal historian.

Amazingly, in spite of all that, the Ideal Chronicler would still have essentially the same problem as Bezukhov; it could not give the kind of descriptions of *what was happening* that historians provide. The reason is that when historians describe the past, they invariably rely on what Danto calls narrative sentences, meaning sentences that purport to be describing something that happened at a particular point in time but do so in a way that invokes knowledge of a later point. For example, consider the following sentence: "One afternoon about a year ago, Bob was out in his garden planting roses." This is what Danto calls a normal sentence, in that it does nothing more than describe what was happening at the time. But consider now the same sentence, slightly modified: "One afternoon about a year ago, Bob was out in his garden planting his prize-winning roses." This is a narrative sentence, because it implicitly refers to an event—Bob's roses winning a prize—that hadn't happened at the time of the planting.

The difference between the two sentences seems negligible. But what Danto points out is that only the first kind of sentence—the normal one—would have made sense to the participants at the time. That is, Bob might have said at the time "I am planting roses" or even "I am planting roses and they are going to be prizewinners." But it would be very strange for him to have said "I am planting my prize-winning roses" before they'd actually won any prizes. The reason is that while the first two statements make predictions about the future—that the roots Bob is putting in the ground will one day bloom into a rosebush, or that he intends to submit them to a contest and thinks he will win—the third is something different: It assumes foreknowledge of a very specific event that will only color the events of the present after it has actually happened. It's the kind of thing that Bob could say only if he were a prophet—a character who sees the future with sufficient clarity that he can speak about the present as though looking back on it.

Danto's point is that the all-knowing, hypothetical Ideal Chronicler can't use narrative sentences either. It knows everything that is happening now, as well as everything that has led up to now. It can even make inferences about how all the events it knows about might fit together. But what it can't do is foresee the future; it cannot refer to what is happening now in light of future events. So when English and French ships began to skirmish in the English Channel in 1337, the Ideal Chronicler might have noted that a war of some kind seemed likely, but it could not have recorded the observation "The Hundred Years War began today." Not only was the extent of the conflict between the two countries unknown at the time, but the term "Hundred Years War" was only invented long after it ended as shorthand to describe what was in actuality a series of intermittent conflicts from 1337 to 1453. Likewise, when Isaac Newton published his masterpiece, *Principia,* the Ideal Chronicler might have been able to say it was a major contribution to celestial mechanics, and even predicted that it would revolutionize science. But to claim that Newton was laying the foundation for what became modern science, or was playing a key role in the Enlightenment, would be beyond the IC. These are narrative sentences that could only be uttered after the future events had taken place.[10]

This may sound like a trivial argument over semantics. Surely even if the Ideal Chronicler can't use exactly the *words* that historians use, it can still perceive the essence of what is happening as well as they do. But in fact Danto's point is precisely that historical descriptions of "what is happening" are *impossible* without narrative sentences—that narrative sentences are the very essence of historical explanations. This is a critical distinction, because historical accounts do often claim to be describing "only" what happened in detached, dispassionate detail. Yet as Berlin and Danto both argue, literal descriptions of what happened are impossible. Perhaps even more important, they would also not serve the purpose of historical explanation, which is not to reproduce the events of the past so much as to explain why they mattered. And the only way to know what mattered, and why, is to have been able to see what happened as a result—information that, by definition, not even the impossibly talented Ideal Chronicler possesses. History cannot be told while it is happening, therefore, not only because the people involved are too busy or too confused to puzzle it out, but because what is happening can't be made sense of until its implications have been resolved. And when will that be? As it turns out, even this innocent question can pose problems for commonsense explanations.

IT'S NOT OVER TILL IT'S OVER

In the classic movie *Butch Cassidy and the Sundance Kid*, Butch, Sundance, and Etta decide to escape their troubles in the United States by fleeing to Bolivia, where, according to Butch, the gold is practically digging itself out of the ground. But when they finally arrive, after a long and glamorous journey aboard a steamer from New York, they are greeted by a dusty yard filled with pigs and chickens and a couple of run-down stone huts. The Sundance Kid is furious and even Etta looks depressed. "You get much more for your money in Bolivia," claims Butch optimistically. "What could they possibly have that you could possibly want to buy?" replies the Kid in disgust. Of course we know that things will soon be looking up for our pair of charming bank robbers. And sure enough, after some amusing misadventures with the language, they are. But we also know that it is eventually going to end in tears, with Butch and Sundance frozen in that timeless sepia image, bursting out of their hiding place, pistols drawn, into a barrage of gunfire.

So was the decision to go to Bolivia a good decision or a bad one? Intuitively, it seems like the latter because it led inexorably to Butch and the Kid's ultimate demise. But now we know that that way of thinking suffers from creeping determinism—the assumption that because we know things ended badly, they had to have ended badly. To avoid this error, therefore, we need to imagine "running" history many times, and comparing the different potential outcomes that Butch and the Kid might have experienced had they made different decisions. But at what point in these various histories should we make our comparison? At first, leaving the United States seemed like a great idea—they were escaping what seemed like certain death at the hands of the lawman Joe Lefors and his posse, and the journey was all fun and games. Later in the story, the decision seemed like a terrible idea—of all the many places they might have escaped to, why this godforsaken wasteland? Then it seemed like a good decision again—they were making loads of easy money robbing small-town banks. And then, finally, it seemed like a bad idea again as their exploits caught up to them. Even if you granted them the benefit of foresight, in other words—something we already know is impossible—they may still have reached very different conclusions about their choice, depending on which point in the future they chose to evaluate it. Which one is right?

Within the narrow confines of a movie narrative, it seems obvious that the right time to evaluate everything should be at the end. But in real life, the situation is far more ambiguous. Just as the characters in a story don't know when the ending is, we can't know when the movie of our own life will reach its final scene. And even if we did, we could hardly go around evaluating all choices, however trivial, in light of our final state on our deathbed. In fact, even then we couldn't be sure of the meaning of what we had accomplished. At least when Achilles decided to go to Troy, he knew what the bargain was: his life, in return for everlasting fame. But for the rest of us, the choices we make are far less certain. Today's embarrassment may become tomorrow's valuable lesson. Or yesterday's "mission accomplished" may become today's painful irony. Perhaps that painting we picked up at the market will turn out to be an old master. Perhaps our leadership of the family firm will be sullied by the unearthing of some ethical scandal, about which we may not have known. Perhaps our children will go on to achieve great things and attribute their success to the many small lessons we taught them. Or perhaps we will have unwittingly pushed them into the wrong career and undermined their chances of real happiness. Choices that seem insignificant at the time we make them may one day turn out to be of immense import. And choices that seem incredibly important to us now may later seem to have been of little consequence. We just won't know until we know. And even then we still may not know, because it may not be entirely up to us to decide.

In much of life, in other words, the very notion of a well-defined "outcome," at which point we can evaluate, once and for all, the consequences of an action is a convenient fiction. In reality, the events that we label as outcomes are never really endpoints. Instead, they are artificially imposed milestones, just as the ending of a movie is really an artificial end to what in reality would be an ongoing story. And depending on where we choose to impose an "end" to a process, we may infer very different lessons from the outcome. Let's say, for example, that we observe that a company is hugely successful and we want to emulate that success with our own company. How should we go about doing that? Common sense (along with a number of bestselling business books) suggests that we should study the successful company, identify the key drivers of its success, and then replicate those practices and attributes in our own organization. But what if I told you that a year later this same company has lost 80 percent of its market value, and the same business press that is raving about it now will be howling for blood? Common sense would suggest that perhaps you should look somewhere else for a model of success. But how will you know that? And how will you know what will happen the year after, or the year after that?

Problems like this actually arise in the business world all the time. In the late 1990s, for example, Cisco Systems—a manufacturer of Internet routers and telecommunications switching equipment—was a star of Silicon Valley and the darling of Wall Street. It rose from humble beginnings at the dawn of the Internet era to become, in March 2000, the most valuable company in the world, with a market capitalization of over $500 billion. As you might expect, the business press went wild. *Fortune* called Cisco "computing's new superpower" and hailed John Chambers, the CEO, as the best CEO of the information age. In 2001, however, Cisco's stock plummeted, and in April of 2001, it bottomed out at $14, down from its high of $80 just over a year earlier. The same business press that had fallen over itself to praise the firm now lambasted its strategy, its execution, and its leadership. Was it all a sham? It seemed so at the time, and many articles were written explaining how a company that had seemed so successful could have been so flawed. But not so fast: by late 2007, the stock had more than doubled to over $33, and the company, still guided by the same CEO, was handsomely profitable.[11]

So was Cisco the great company that it was supposed to have been in the late 1990s after all? Or was it still the house of cards that it appeared to be in 2001? Or was it both, or neither? Following the stock price since 2007, you couldn't tell. At first, Cisco dropped again to $14 in early 2009 in the depths of the financial crisis. But by 2010, it had recovered yet again to $24. No one knows where Cisco's stock price will be a year from now, or ten years from now. But chances are that the business press at the time will have a story that "explains" all the ups and downs it has experienced to that point in a way that leads neatly to whatever the current valuation is. Unfortunately, these explanations will suffer from exactly the same problem as all the explanations that went before them—that at no point in time is the story ever really "over." Something always happens afterward, and what happens afterward is liable to change our perception of the current outcome, as well as our perception of the outcomes that we have already explained. It's actually quite remarkable in a way that we are able to completely rewrite our previous explanations without experiencing any discomfort about the one we are currently articulating, each time acting as if *now* is the right time to evaluate the outcome. Yet as we can see from the example of Cisco, not to mention countless other examples from business, politics, and planning, there is no reason to think that now is any better time to stop and evaluate than any other.

WHOEVER TELLS THE BEST STORY WINS

Historical explanations, in other words, are neither causal explanations nor even really descriptions—at least not in the sense that we imagine them to be. Rather, they are stories. As the historian John Lewis Gaddis points out, they are stories that are constrained by certain historical facts and other observable evidence.[12] Nevertheless, like a good story, historical explanations concentrate on what's interesting, downplaying multiple causes and omitting all the things that might have happened but didn't. As with a good story, they enhance drama by focusing the action around a few events and actors, thereby imbuing them with special significance or meaning. And like good stories, good historical explanations are also coherent, which means they tend to emphasize simple, linear determinism over complexity, randomness, and ambiguity. Most of all, they have a beginning, a middle, and an end, at which point everything—including the characters identified, the order in which the events are presented, and the manner in which both characters and events are described—all has to make sense.

So powerful is the appeal of a good story that even when we are trying to evaluate an explanation scientifically—that is, on the basis of how well it accounts for the data—we can't help judging it in terms of its narrative attributes. In a range of experiments, for example, psychologists have found that simpler explanations are judged more likely to be true than complex explanations, not because simpler explanations actually explain more, but rather *just because* they are simpler. In one study, for example, when faced with a choice of explanations for a fictitious set of medical symptoms, a majority of respondents chose an explanation involving only one disease over an alternative explanation involving two diseases, even when the combination of the two diseases was statistically twice as likely as the single-disease explanation.[13] Somewhat paradoxically, explanations are also judged to be more likely to be true when they have informative details added, even when the extra details are irrelevant or actually make the explanation less likely. In one famous experiment, for example, students shown descriptions of two fictitious individuals, "Bill" and "Linda" consistently preferred more detailed backstories— that Bill was both an accountant and a jazz player rather than simply a jazz player, or that Linda was a feminist bank teller rather than just a bank teller—even though the less detailed descriptions were logically more likely.[14] In addition to their content, moreover, explanations that are skillfully delivered are judged more plausible than poorly delivered ones, even when the explanations themselves are identical. And explanations that are intuitively plausible are judged more likely than those that are counterintuitive—even though, as we know from all those Agatha Christie novels, the most plausible explanation can be badly wrong. Finally, people are observed to be more confident about their judgments when they have an explanation at hand, even when they have no idea how likely the explanation is to be correct.[15]

It's true, of course, that scientific explanations often start out as stories as well, and so have some of the same attributes.[16] The key difference between science and storytelling, however, is that in science we perform experiments that explicitly test our "stories." And when they don't work, we modify them until they do. Even in branches of science like astronomy, where true experiments are impossible, we do something analogous—building theories based on past observations and testing them on future ones. Because history is only run once, however, our inability to do experiments effectively excludes precisely the kind of evidence that would be necessary to infer a genuine cause-and-effect relation. In the absence of experiments, therefore, our storytelling abilities are allowed to run unchecked, in the process burying most of the evidence that is left, either because it's not interesting or doesn't fit with the story we want to tell. Expecting history to obey the standards of scientific explanation is therefore not just unrealistic, but fundamentally confused—it is, as Berlin concluded, "to ask it to contradict its essence."[17]

For much the same reason, professional historians are often at pains to emphasize the difficulty of generalizing from any one particular context to any other. Nevertheless, because accounts of the past, once constructed, bear such a strong resemblance to the sorts of theories that we construct in science, it is tempting to treat them as if they have the same power of generalization—even for the most careful historians.[18] When we try to understand *why* a particular book became a bestseller, in other words, we are implicitly asking a question about how books in general become bestsellers, and therefore how that experience can be repeated by other authors or publishers. When we investigate the *causes* of the recent housing bubble or of the terrorist attacks of September 11, we are inevitably also seeking insight that we hope we'll be able to apply in the future—to improve our national security or the stability of our financial markets. And when we conclude from the surge in Iraq that it *caused* the subsequent drop in violence, we are invariably tempted to apply the same strategy again, as indeed the current administration has done in Afghanistan. No matter what we say we are doing, in other words, whenever we seek to learn *about* the past, we are invariably seeking to learn *from* it as well—an association that is implicit in the words of the philosopher George Santayana: "Those who cannot remember the past are condemned to repeat it."[19]

This confusion between stories and theories gets to the heart of the problem with using common sense as a way of understanding the world. In one breath, we speak as if all we're trying to do is to make sense of something that has already happened. But in the next breath we're applying the "lesson" that we think we have learned to whatever plan or policy we're intending to implement in the future. We make this switch between storytelling and theory building so easily and instinctively that most of the time we're not even aware that we're doing it. But the switch overlooks that the two are fundamentally different exercises with different objectives and standards of evidence. It should not be surprising then that explanations that were chosen on the basis of their qualities as stories do a poor job of predicting future patterns or trends. Yet that is nonetheless what we use them for. Understanding the limits of what we can explain about the past ought therefore to shed light on what it is that we can predict about the future. And because prediction is so central to planning, policy, strategy, management, marketing, and all the other problems that we will discuss later, it is to prediction that we now turn.

CHAPTER 6

The Dream of Prediction

Humans love to make predictions—whether about the movements of the stars, the gyrations of the stock market, or the upcoming season's hot color. Pick up the newspaper on any given day and you'll immediately encounter a mass of predictions—so many, in fact, that you probably don't even notice them. To illustrate the point, let's consider a single news story chosen more or less at random from the front page of the *New York Times*. The story, which was published in the summer of 2009, was about trends in retail sales and contained no fewer than ten predictions about the upcoming back-to-school season. For example, according to one source cited in the article—an industry group called the National Retail Federation—the average family with school-age children was predicted to spend "nearly 8 percent less this year than last," while according to the research firm ShopperTrak, customer traffic in stores was predicted to be down 10 percent. Finally, an expert who was identified as president of Customer Growth Partners, a retailing consultant firm, was quoted as claiming that the season was "going to be the worst back-to-school season in many, many years."[1]

All three predictions were made by authoritative-sounding sources and were explicit enough to have been scored for accuracy. But how accurate were they? To be honest, I have no idea. The *New York Times* doesn't publish statistics on the accuracy of the predictions made in its pages, nor do most of the research companies that provide them. One of the strange things about predictions, in fact, is that our eagerness to make pronouncements about the future is matched only by our reluctance to be held accountable for the predictions we make. In the mid-1980s, the psychologist Philip Tetlock noticed exactly this pattern among political experts of the day. Determined to make them put their proverbial money where their mouths were, Tetlock designed a remarkable test that was to unfold over twenty years. To begin with, he convinced 284 political experts to make nearly a hundred predictions each about a variety of possible future events, ranging from the outcomes of specific elections to the likelihood that two nations would engage in armed conflict with each other. For each of these predictions, Tetlock insisted that the experts specify which of two outcomes they expected and also assign a probability to their prediction. He did so in a way that confident predictions scored more points when correct, but also lost more points when mistaken. With those predictions in hand, he then sat back and waited for the events themselves to play out. Twenty years later, he published his results, and what he found was striking: Although the experts performed slightly better than random guessing, they did not perform as well as even a minimally sophisticated statistical model. Even more surprisingly, the experts did slightly better when operating *outside* their area of expertise than within it.[2]

Tetlock's results are often interpreted as demonstrating the fatuousness of so-called experts, and no doubt there's some truth to that. But although experts are probably no better than the rest of us at making predictions, they are also probably no worse. When I was young, for example, many people believed that the future would be filled with flying cars, orbiting space cities, and endless free time. Instead, we drive internal combustion cars on crumbling, congested freeways; endure endless cuts in airplane service, and work more hours than ever. Meanwhile, Web search, mobile phones, and online shopping—the technologies that have, in fact, affected our lives—came more or less out of nowhere. Around the same time that Tetlock was beginning his experiment, in fact, a management scientist named Steven Schnaars tried to quantify the accuracy of technology-trend predictions by combing through a large collection of books, magazines, and industry reports, and recording hundreds of predictions that had been made during the 1970s. He concluded that roughly 80 percent of all predictions were wrong, whether they were made by experts or not.[3]

Nor is it just forecasters of long-term social and technology trends that have lousy records. Publishers, producers, and marketers—experienced and motivated professionals in business with plenty of skin in the game—have just as much difficulty predicting which books, movies, and products will become the next big hit as political experts have in predicting the next revolution. In fact, the history of cultural markets is crowded with examples of future blockbusters—Elvis, *Star Wars, Seinfeld, Harry Potter, American Idol*—that publishers and movie studios left for dead while simultaneously betting big on total failures.[4] And whether we consider the most spectacular business meltdowns of recent times—Long-Term Capital Management in 1998, Enron in 2001, WorldCom in 2002, the near-collapse of the entire financial system in 2008—or spectacular success stories like the rise of Google and Facebook, what is perhaps most striking about them is that virtually *nobody* seems to have had any idea what was about to happen. In September 2008, for example, even as Lehman Brothers' collapse was imminent, Treasury and Federal Reserve officials—who arguably had the best information available to anyone in the world—failed to anticipate the devastating freeze in global credit markets that followed. Conversely, in the late 1990s the founders of Google, Sergey Brin and Larry Page, tried to sell their company for $1.6M. Fortunately for them, nobody was interested, because Google went on to attain a market value of over $160 billion, or about 100,000 times what they and everybody else apparently thought it was worth only a few years earlier.[5]

Results like these seem to show that humans are simply bad at making predictions, but in fact that's not quite right either. In reality there are all sorts of predictions that we could make very well if we chose to. I would bet, for example, that I could do a pretty good job of forecasting the weather in Santa Fe, New Mexico—in fact, I bet I would be correct more than 80 percent of the time. As impressive as that sounds compared to the lousy record of Tetlock's experts, however, my ability to predict the weather in Santa Fe is not going to land me a job at the Weather Bureau. The problem is that in Santa Fe it is sunny roughly 300 days a year, so one can be right 300 days out of 365 simply by making the mindless prediction that "tomorrow it will be sunny." Likewise, predictions that the United States will not go to war with Canada in the next decade or that the sun will continue to rise in the east are also likely to be accurate, but impress no one. The real problem of prediction, in other words, is not that we are universally good or bad at it, but rather that we are bad at distinguishing predictions that we can make reliably from those that we can't.

LAPLACE'S DEMON

In a way this problem goes all the way back to Newton. Starting from his three laws of motion, along with his universal law of gravitation, Newton was able to derive not only Kepler's laws of planetary motion but also the timing of the tides, the trajectories of projectiles, and a truly astonishing array of other natural phenomena. It was a singular scientific accomplishment, but it also set an expectation for what could be accomplished by mathematical laws that would prove difficult to match. The movements of the planets, the timing of the tides—these are amazing things to be able to predict. But aside from maybe the vibrations of electrons or the time required for light to travel a certain distance, they are also about the most predictable phenomena in all of nature. And yet, because predicting these movements was among the first problems that scientists and mathematicians set their sights on, and because they met with such stunning success, it was tempting to conclude that everything worked that way. As Newton himself wrote:

If only we could derive the other phenomena of nature from mechanical principles by the same kind of reasoning! For many things lead me to have a suspicion that all phenomena may depend on certain forces by which particles of bodies, by causes not yet known, either are impelled toward one another and cohere in regular figures, or are repelled from one another and recede.[6]

A century later, the French mathematician and astronomer Pierre-Simon Laplace pushed Newton's vision to its logical extreme, claiming in effect that Newtonian mechanics had reduced the prediction of the future—even the future of the universe—to a matter of mere computation. Laplace envisioned an "intellect" that knew all the forces that "set nature in motion, and all positions of all items of which nature is composed." Laplace went on, "for such an intellect nothing would be uncertain and the future just like the past would be present before its eyes."[7]

The "intellect" of Laplace's imagination eventually received a name—"Laplace's demon"—and it has been lurking around the edges of mankind's view of the future ever since. For philosophers, the demon was controversial because in reducing the prediction of the future to a mechanical exercise, it seemed to rob humanity of free will. As it turned out, though, they needn't have worried too much. Starting with the second law of thermodynamics, and continuing through quantum mechanics and finally chaos theory, Laplace's idea of a clockwork universe—and with it the concerns about free will—has been receding for more than a century now. But that doesn't mean the demon has gone away. In spite of the controversy over free will, there was something incredibly appealing about the notion that the laws of nature, applied to the appropriate data, could be used to predict the future. People of course had been making predictions about the future since the beginnings of civilization, but what was different about Laplace's boast was that it wasn't based on any claim to magical powers, or even special insight, that he possessed himself. Rather it depended only on the existence of scientific laws that in principle anyone could master. Thus prediction, once the realm of oracles and mystics, was brought within the objective, rational sphere of modern science.

In doing so, however, the demon obscured a critical difference between two different sorts of processes, which for the sake of argument I'll call simple and complex.[8] Simple systems are those for which a model can capture all or most of the variation in what we observe. The oscillations of pendulums and the orbits of satellites are therefore "simple" in this sense, even though it's not necessarily a simple matter to be able to model and predict them. Somewhat paradoxically, in fact, the most complicated models in science—models that predict the trajectories of interplanetary space probes, or pinpoint the location of GPS devices—often describe relatively simple processes. The basic equations of motion governing the orbit of a communications satellite or the lift on an aircraft wing can be taught to a high-school physics student. But because the difference in performance between a good model and a slightly better one can be critical, the actual models used by engineers to build satellite GPS systems and 747s need to account for all sorts of tiny corrections, and so end up being far more complicated. When the NASA Mars Climate Orbiter burned up and disintegrated in the Martian atmosphere in 1999, for example, the mishap was traced to a simple programming error (imperial units were used instead of metric) that put the probe into an orbit of about 60km instead of 140km from Mars's surface. When you consider that in order to get to Mars, the orbiter first had to traverse more than 50 million kilometers, the magnitude of the error seems trivial. Yet it was the difference between a triumphant success for NASA and an embarrassing failure.

Complex systems are another animal entirely. Nobody really agrees on what makes a complex system "complex" but it's generally accepted that complexity arises out of many interdependent components interacting in nonlinear ways. The U.S. economy, for example, is the product of the individual actions of millions of people, as well as hundreds of thousands of firms, thousands of government agencies, and countless other external and internal factors, ranging from the weather in Texas to interest rates in China. Modeling the trajectory of the economy is therefore not like modeling the trajectory of a rocket. In complex systems, tiny disturbances in one part of the system can get amplified to produce large effects somewhere else—the "butterfly effect" from chaos theory that came up in the earlier discussion of cumulative advantage and unpredictability. When every tiny factor in a complex system can get potentially amplified in unpredictable ways, there is only so much that a model can predict. As a result, models of complex systems tend to be rather simple—not because simple models perform well, but because incremental improvements make little difference in the face of the massive errors that remain. Economists, for example, can only dream of modeling the economy with the same kind of accuracy that led to the destruction of the Mars Climate Orbiter. The problem, however, is not so much that their models are bad as that all models of complex systems are bad.[9]

The fatal flaw in Laplace's vision, therefore, is that his demon works only for simple systems. Yet pretty much everything in the social world—from the effect of a marketing campaign to the consequences of some economic policy or the outcome of a corporate plan—falls into the category of complex systems. Whenever people get together—in social gatherings, sports crowds, business firms, volunteer organizations, markets, political parties, or even entire societies—they affect one another's thinking and behavior. As I discussed in Chapter 3, it is these interactions that make social systems "social" in the first place—because they cause a collection of people to be something other than just a collection of people. But in the process they also produce tremendous complexity.

THE FUTURE IS NOT LIKE THE PAST

The ubiquity of complex systems in the social world is important because it severely restricts the kinds of predictions we can make. In simple systems, that is, it is possible to predict with high probability what will *actually* happen—for example when Halley's Comet will next return or what orbit a particular satellite will enter. For complex systems, by contrast, the best that we can hope for is to correctly predict the *probability* that something will happen.[10] At first glance, these two exercises sound similar, but they're fundamentally different. To see how, imagine that you're calling the toss of a coin. Because it's a random event, the best you can do is predict that it will come up heads, on average, half the time. A rule that says "over the long run, 50 percent of coin tosses will be heads, and 50 percent will be tails" is, in fact, perfectly accurate in the sense that heads and tails do, on average, show up exactly half the time. But even knowing this rule, we still can't correctly predict the *outcome* of a single coin toss any more than 50 percent of the time, no matter what strategy we adopt.[11] Complex systems are not really random in the same way that a coin toss is random, but in practice it's extremely difficult to tell the difference. As the Music Lab experiment demonstrated earlier, you could know everything about every person in the market—you could ask them a thousand survey questions, follow them around to see what they do, and put them in brain scanners while they're doing it—and still the best you could do would be to predict the probability that a particular song will be the winner in any particular virtual world. Some songs were more likely to win on average than others, but in any given world the interactions between individuals magnified tiny random fluctuations to produce unpredictable outcomes.

To understand why this kind of unpredictability is problematic, consider another example of a complex system about which we like to make predictions—namely, the weather. At least in the very near future—which generally means the next forty-eight hours—weather predictions are actually pretty accurate, or as forecasters call it, "reliable." That is, of the days when the weather service says there is a 60 percent chance of rain, it does, in fact, rain on about 60 percent of them.[12] So why is it that people complain about the accuracy of weather forecasts? The reason is not that they aren't reliable—although possibly they could be more reliable than they are—but rather that reliability isn't the kind of accuracy that we want. We don't want to know what is going to happen 60 percent of the time on days like tomorrow. Rather, we want to know what is actually going to happen tomorrow—and tomorrow, it will either rain or it will not. So when we hear "60 percent chance of rain tomorrow," it's natural to interpret the information as the weather service telling us that it's probably going to rain tomorrow. And when it fails to rain almost half the times we listen to them and take an umbrella to work, we conclude that they don't know what they're talking about.

Thinking of future events in terms of probabilities is difficult enough for even coin tossing or weather forecasting, where more or less the same kind of thing is happening over and over again. But for events that happen only once in a lifetime, like the outbreak of a war, the election of a president, or even which college you get accepted to, the distinction becomes almost impossible to grasp. What does it mean, for example, to have said the day before Barack Obama's victory in the 2008 presidential election that he had a 90 percent chance of winning? That he would have won nine out of ten attempts? Clearly not, as there will only ever be one election, and any attempt to repeat it—say in the next election—will not be comparable in the way that consecutive coin tosses are. So does it instead translate to the odds one ought to take in a gamble? That is, to win $10 if he is elected, I will have to bet $9, whereas if he loses, you can win $10 by betting only $1? But how are we to determine what the "correct" odds are, seeing as this gamble will only ever be resolved once? If the answer isn't clear to you, you're not alone—even mathematicians argue about what it means to assign a probability to a single event.[13] So if even they have trouble wrapping their heads around the meaning of the statement that "the probability of rain tomorrow is 60 percent," then it's no surprise that the rest of us do as well.

The difficulty that we experience in trying to think about the future in terms of probabilities is the mirror image of our preference for explanations that account for known outcomes at the expense of alternative possibilities. As discussed in the previous chapter, when we look back in time, all we see is a sequence of events that happened. Yesterday it rained, two years ago Barack Obama was elected president of the United States, and so on. At some level, we understand that these events could have played out differently. But no matter how much we might remind ourselves that things might be other than they are, it remains the case that what actually happened, happened. Not 40 percent of the time or 60 percent of the time, but 100 percent of the time. It follows naturally, therefore, that when we think about the future, we care mostly about what will *actually happen*. To arrive at our prediction, we might contemplate a range of possible alternative futures, and maybe we even go as far as to determine that some of them are more likely than others. But at the end of the day, we know that only one such possible future will actually come to be, and we want to know which one that is.

The relationship between our view of the past and our view

of the future is illustrated in the figure on the facing page, which shows the stock price of a fictitious company over time. Looking back in time from the present, one sees the history of the stock (the solid line), which naturally traces out a unique path. Looking forward, however, all we can say about the stock price is its probability of falling within a particular range. My Yahoo! colleagues David Pennock and Dan Reeves have actually built an application that generates pictures like this one by mining data on the prices of stock options. Because the value of an option depends on the price of the underlying stock, the prices at which various options are being traded now can be interpreted as predictions about the price of the stock on the date when the option is scheduled to mature. More precisely, one can use the option prices to infer various "probability envelopes" like those shown in the figure. For example, the inner envelope shows the range of prices within which the stock is likely to fall with a 20 percent probability, while the outer envelope shows the 60 percent probability range.

We also know, however, that at some later time, the stock price will have been revealed—as indicated by the dotted "future" trajectory. At that time, we know the hazy cloud of probabilities defined by the envelope will have been replaced by a single, certain price at each time, just like prices that we can currently see in the past. And knowing this, it's tempting to take the next step of assuming that this future trajectory has in some cosmic sense already been determined, even if it has not yet been revealed to us. But this last step would be a mistake. Until it is actually realized, all we can say about the future stock price is that it has a certain probability of being within a certain range—not because it actually lies somewhere in this range and we're just not sure where it is, but in the stronger sense that it only exists *at all* as a range of probabilities. Put another way, there is a difference between being uncertain about the future and the future itself being uncertain. The former is really just a lack of information—something we don't know—whereas the latter implies that the information is, in principle, unknowable. The former is the orderly universe of Laplace's demon, where if we just try hard enough, if we're just smart enough, we can predict the future. The latter is an essentially random world, where the best we can ever hope for is to express our predictions of various outcomes as probabilities.

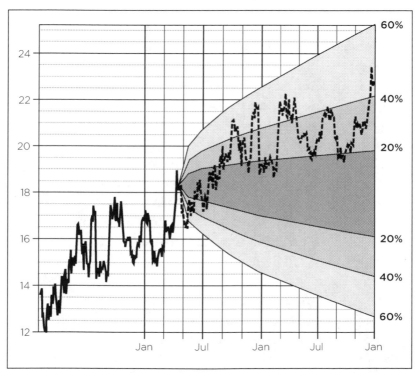

Past Versus Future Stock Price

PREDICTING WHAT TO PREDICT

The distinction between predicting outcomes and predicting probabilities of outcomes is a fundamental one that should change our view about what *kinds* of predictions we can make. But there is another problem that also arises from the way we learn from the past, which is if anything even more counterintuitive—namely that we can't know *which* outcomes we ought to be making predictions about in the first place. Truth be told, there is an infinitude of predictions that we could make at any given time, just as there is an infinitude of "things that happened" in the past. And just as we don't care at all about almost all of these past events, we don't care about almost all such potential predictions. Rather, what we care about is the very small number of predictions that, had we been able to make them correctly, might have changed things in a way that actually mattered. Had U.S. aviation officials predicted that terrorists armed with box cutters would hijack planes with the intention of flying them into the World Trade Center and the Pentagon, they could have taken preventative measures, such as strengthening cockpit doors and clamping down on airport screening, that would have averted such a threat. Likewise, had an investor known in the late 1990s that a small startup company called Google would one day grow into an Internet behemoth, she could have made a fortune investing in it.

Looking back in history, it seems we ought to have been able to predict events like these. But what we don't appreciate is that hindsight tells us more than the outcomes of the predictions that we could have made in the past. It also reveals what predictions we should have been making. In November of 1963, how would one have known that it was important to worry about snipers, and not food poisoning, during JFK's visit to Dallas? How was one to know before 9/11 that the strength of cockpit doors, not the absence of bomb-sniffing dogs, was the key to preventing airplane hijackings? Or that hijacked aircraft, and not dirty bombs or nerve gas in the subway, were the main terrorist threat to the United States? How was one to know that search engines would make money from advertising and not some other business model? Or that one should even be interested in the monetization of search engines rather than content sites or e-commerce sites, or something else entirely?

In effect, this problem is the flip side of Danto's argument about history in the previous chapter—that what is *relevant* cannot be known until later. The kinds of predictions we most want to make, that is, require us to first determine which of all the things that might happen in the future will turn out to be relevant, in order that we can start paying attention to them now. It seems we ought to be able to do this, in the same way that it seems Danto's Ideal Chronicler ought to be able to say what is going on. But if we tried to state our predictions for everything that might conceivably happen, we would immediately drown in the possibilities. Should we worry about what time the garbage truck will show up tonight? Probably not. On the other hand, if our dog gets off the leash and runs out on the street at exactly that time, we will have wished we'd known before we went for a walk. Should we attempt to predict whether our flight will be canceled? Again, probably not. But if we get bumped onto another flight that subsequently crashes, or we sit next to the person we will one day marry, that event will seem tremendously significant.

This relevance problem is fundamental, and can't be eliminated simply by having more information or a smarter algorithm. For example, in his book about prediction the political scientist and "predictioneer" Bruce Bueno de Mesquita extols the power of game theory to predict the outcomes of complex political negotiations.[14] Given the intrinsic unpredictability of complex systems, it seems unlikely that his computer models can in fact predict what he says they can. But leaving that aside for the moment, let's look at the larger question of what they could predict even if they worked perfectly. Take for example his claim to have successfully predicted the outcome of the 1993 Oslo Accords between Israel and the then Palestine Liberation Organization. At the time, that would have seemed like an impressive feat. But what the algorithm didn't predict was that the Oslo Accords were, in effect, a mirage, a temporary flicker of hope that was quickly extinguished by subsequent events. From what we now know about what happened afterward, in other words, it is clear that the outcome of the Oslo negotiations wasn't the most important outcome to have predicted in the first place.

Of course, Bueno de Mesquita might reasonably point out that his models aren't designed to make that sort of prediction. But that's precisely the point: *Making the right prediction is just as important as getting the prediction right.* When we look back at the past, we do not wish that we had predicted what the search market share for Google would be in 1999, or how many days it would take for US soldiers to reach Baghdad during the second Gulf war. Those are certainly valid predictions that we might have thought to make. But at some point we would have realized that it didn't really matter whether they were right or wrong—because they just weren't that important. Instead we would end up wishing we'd been able to predict on the day of Google's IPO that within a few years its stock price would peak above $500, because then we could have invested in it and become rich. We wish we'd been able to foresee the carnage that would follow the toppling of Saddam Hussein and the dismantling of his security forces, because then we could have adopted a different strategy or even avoided the whole mess in the first place.

Even when we are dealing with more mundane types of predictions—like how consumers will respond to such and such a color or design, or whether doctors would spend more time on preventative care if they were compensated on the basis of patients' health outcomes rather than the number and expense of their prescribed procedures—we have the same problem. These sorts of predictions seem less problematic than predictions about the next great company or the next war. But as soon as we think about why we care about these predictions, we are forced immediately to make other predictions—about the effects of the predictions we're making now. For example, we are concerned about how customers will react to the color not because we care about the reaction per se, but because we want the product to be a success, and we think the color will matter. Likewise, we care about the reaction of doctors to incentives because we wish to control healthcare costs and ultimately design a system that provides affordable healthcare to everyone without bankrupting the country. If our prediction does not somehow help to bring about larger results, then it is of little interest or value to us. Once again, we care about things that matter, yet it is precisely these larger, more significant predictions about the future that pose the greatest difficulties.

BLACK SWANS AND OTHER "EVENTS"

Nowhere is this problem of predicting the things that matter more acute than for what former derivatives trader and gadfly of the financial industry Nassim Taleb calls black swans, meaning events that—like the invention of the printing press, the storming of the Bastille, and the attacks on the World

Trade Center—happen rarely but carry great import when they do.[15] But what makes an event a black swan? This is where matters get confusing. We tend to speak about events as if they are separate and distinct, and can be assigned a level of importance in the way that we describe natural events such as earthquakes, avalanches, and storms by their magnitude or size. As it turns out, many of these natural events are characterized not by "normal" distributions, but instead by heavily skewed distributions that range over many orders of magnitude. Heights of people, for example, are roughly normally distributed: the typical U.S. male is 5 feet 9 inches, and we essentially never see adults who are 2 feet tall or 12 feet tall. Earthquakes, by contrast, along with avalanches, storms, and forest fires, display "heavy-tailed" distributions, meaning that most are relatively small and draw little attention, whereas a small number can be extremely large.

It's tempting to think that historical events also follow a heavy-tailed distribution, where Taleb's black swans lie far out in the tail of the distribution. But as the sociologist William Sewell explains, historical events are not merely "bigger" than others in the sense that some hurricanes are bigger than others. Rather, "events" in the historical sense acquire their significance via the transformations they trigger in wider social arrangements. To illustrate, Sewell revisits the storming of the Bastille on July 14, 1789, an event that certainly seems to satisfy Taleb's definition of a black swan. Yet as Sewell points out, the event was not just the series of actions that happened in Paris on July 14, but rather encompassed the whole period between July 14 and July 23, during which Louis XVI struggled to control the insurrection in Paris, while the National Assembly at Versailles debated whether to condemn the violence or to embrace it as an expression of the people's will. It was only after the king withdrew his troops from the outskirts of the city and traveled to Paris in contrition that the Assembly managed to assert itself, and the Bastille became an "event" in the historical sense. It's hard to stop even there, in fact, because of course the only reason we care about the Bastille at all is because of what came next—the French Revolution, and its transformation of the notion of sovereignty from the divine right of a king, handed down by birth, to a power inherent in the people themselves. And *that* event included not only the days up until July 23, but also the subsequent repercussions, like the bizarre mass panic, often called the Great Fear, that gripped the provinces over the next week, and the famous legislative session that lasted the entire night of August 4, during which the entire social and political order of the old regime was dismantled.[16]

The more you want to explain about a black swan event like the storming of the Bastille, in other words, the broader you have to draw the boundaries around what you consider to be the event itself. This is true not only for political events but also for "technological black swans," like the computer, the Internet, and the laser. For example, it might be true that the Internet was a black swan, but what does that mean? Does it mean that the invention of packet-switched networks was a black swan? Or was the black swan the growth of this original network into something much larger, eventually forming what would at first be called the ARPANET and then this thing called the Internet? Was it solely the development of the physical infrastructure on which other technological innovations, such as the Web and voice-over IP, were built? Or was it that these technologies, in turn, led to new business models and modes of social interaction? Or that these developments ultimately changed the way that we discover information, share opinions, and express our identities? Presumably it is all these developments together that give the

Internet its black swan status. But then the Internet isn't really a thing at all. Rather, it's shorthand for an entire period of history, and all the interlocking technological, economic, and social changes that happened therein.

Much the same is true even of natural events that acquire black swan status. Hurricane Katrina, for example, was a huge storm, but it wasn't the biggest storm we've ever witnessed, or even the biggest that summer. What made it a black swan, therefore, had less to do with the storm itself than it did with what happened subsequently: the failure of the levees; the flooding of large portions of the city; the slow and ineffective emergency response; the thousands of residents who were subjected to unnecessary suffering and humiliation; the more than 1,800 people who died; the hundreds of thousands more who were evacuated; the decision of many of these evacuees not to return; the economic effect on the city of New Orleans of losing a large chunk of its population; and the impression left in the public mind of a monstrous debacle, shot through with latent racial and class discrimination, administrative incompetence, and the indifference of the powerful and privileged to the weak and vulnerable. When we talk about Hurricane Katrina as a black swan, in other words, we are not speaking primarily about the storm itself, but rather about the whole complex of events that unfolded around it, along with an equally complicated series of social, cultural, and political consequences—consequences that are still playing out.

Predicting black swans is therefore fundamentally different than predicting events like plane crashes or changes in the rate of unemployment. The latter kind of event may be impossible to predict with certainty—and hence we may have to make do with predicting probabilities of outcomes rather than the outcomes themselves—but it is at least possible to say in advance what it is that we are trying to predict. Black swans, by contrast, can only be identified in retrospect because only then can we synthesize all the various elements of history under a neat label. Predicting black swans, in other words, requires us not only to see the future outcome about which we're making a prediction but also to see the future *beyond* that outcome, because only then will its importance be known. As with Danto's example from the previous chapter about Bob describing his prizewinning roses before they've actually won any prizes, this kind of prediction is not really prediction at all, but prophecy—the ability to foresee not only what will happen, but also what its meaning will be.[17]

Nevertheless, once we know about black swans, we can't help wishing that we had been able to predict them. And just as commonsense explanations of the past confuse stories with theories—the topic of the last chapter—so too does commonsense intuition about the future tend to conflate predictions with prophecies. When we look to the past, we see only the things that happened—not all the things that might have happened but didn't—and as a result, our commonsense explanations often mistake for cause and effect what is really just a sequence of events. Correspondingly, when we think about the future, we imagine it to be a unique thread of events that simply hasn't been revealed to us yet. In reality no such thread exists—rather, the future is more like a bundle of possible threads, each of which is assigned some probability of being drawn, where the best we can manage is to estimate the probabilities of the different threads. But because we know that at some point in the future, all these probabilities will have collapsed onto a single thread, we naturally want to focus on the one thread that will actually matter.

Likewise, when we look to the past, we do not feel any confusion about what we mean by the "events" that happened, nor does it seem difficult to say which of these events were important. And just as the uniqueness of the past causes us to think of the future as unique as well, so too does the apparent obviousness of past events tempt us into thinking that we ought to be able to anticipate which events will be important in the future. Yet what these commonsense notions overlook is that this view of the past is a product of a collective story-telling effort—not only by professional historians but also by journalists, experts, political leaders, and other shapers of public opinion—the goal of which is to make sense of "what happened." Only once this story has been completed and agreed upon can we say what the relevant events were, or which were the most important. Thus it follows that predicting the importance of events requires predicting not just the events themselves but also the outcome of the social process that makes sense of them.

FROM COMMON SENSE TO UNCOMMON SENSE

For the purpose of going about our everyday business, none of this confusion may cause us serious problems. As I argued earlier, common sense is extraordinarily good at navigating particular circumstances. And because everyday decisions and circumstances are effectively broken up into many small chunks, each of which we get to deal with separately, it does not matter much that the sprawling hodgepodge of rules, facts, perceptions, beliefs, and instincts on which common sense relies forms a coherent whole. For the same reason, it may not matter much that commonsense reasoning leads us to think that we have understood the cause of something when in fact we have only described it, or to believe that we can make predictions that in fact we cannot make. By the time the future has arrived we have already forgotten most of the predictions we might have made about it, and so are untroubled by the possibility that most of them might have been wrong, or simply irrelevant. And by the time we get around to making sense of what did happen, history has already buried most of the inconvenient facts, freeing us to tell stories about whatever is left. In this way, we can skip from day to day and observation to observation, perpetually replacing the chaos of reality with the soothing fiction of our explanations. And for everyday purposes, that's good enough, because the mistakes that we inevitably make don't generally have any important consequences.

Where these mistakes do start to have important consequences is when we rely on our common sense to make the kinds of plans that underpin government policy or corporate strategy or marketing campaigns. By their very nature, foreign policy or economic development plans affect large numbers of people over extended periods of time, and so do need to work consistently across many different specific contexts. By their very nature, effective marketing or public health plans do depend on being able to reliably associate cause and effect, and so do need to differentiate scientific explanation from mere storytelling. By their very nature, strategic plans, whether for corporations or political parties, do necessarily make predictions about the future, and so do need to differentiate predictions that can be made reliably from those that cannot. And finally, all these sorts of plans do often have consequences of sufficient magnitude—whether financial, or political, or social—that it is worth asking whether or not there is a better, *uncommonsense* way to go about making them. It is therefore to the virtues of uncommon sense, and its implications for prediction, planning, social justice, and even social science, that we now turn.

PART TWO

UNCOMMON SENSE

CHAPTER 7

The Best-Laid Plans

The message of the previous chapter is that the kinds of predictions that common sense tells us we ought to be able to make are in fact impossible—for two reasons. First, common sense tells us that only one future will actually play out, and so it is natural to want to make specific predictions about it. In complex systems, however, which comprise most of our social and economic life, the best we can hope for is to reliably estimate the probabilities with which certain kinds of events will occur. Second, common sense also demands that we ignore the many uninteresting, unimportant predictions that we could be making all the time, and focus on those outcomes that actually matter. In reality, however, there is no way to anticipate, even in principle, which events will be important in the future. Even worse, the black swan events that we most wish we could have predicted are not really events at all, but rather shorthand descriptions—"the French Revolution," "the Internet," "Hurricane Katrina," "the global financial crisis"—of what are in reality whole swaths of history. Predicting black swans is therefore doubly hopeless, because until history has played out it's impossible even to know what the relevant terms are.

It's a sobering message. But just because we can't make the kinds of predictions we'd like to make doesn't mean that we can't predict anything *at all*. As any good poker player can tell you, counting cards won't tell you exactly which card is going to show up next, but by knowing the odds better than your opponents you can still make a lot of money over time by placing more informed bets, and winning more often than you lose.[1] And even for outcomes that truly can't be predicted with any reliability whatsoever, just knowing the limits of what's possible can still be helpful—because it forces us to change the way we plan. So what kinds of predictions can we make, and how can we make them as accurately as possible? And how should we change the way we think about planning—in politics, business, policy, marketing, and management—to accommodate the understanding that some predictions cannot be made at all? These questions may seem distant from the kinds of issues and puzzles that we grapple with on an everyday basis, but one way or another—through their influence on the firms we work for, or the economy at large, or the issues that we read about every day in the newspaper—they affect us all.

WHAT CAN WE PREDICT?

To oversimplify somewhat, there are two kinds of events that arise in complex social systems—events that conform to some stable historical pattern, and events that do not—and it is only the first kind about which we can make reliable predictions. As I discussed in the previous chapter, even for these events we can't predict any particular outcome any more than we can predict the outcome of any particular die roll. But as long as we can gather enough data on their past behavior, we can do a reasonable job of predicting probabilities, and that can be enough for many purposes.

Every year, for example, each of us may or may not be unlucky enough to catch the flu. The best anyone can predict is that in any given season we would have some probability of getting sick. Because there are so many of us, however, and because seasonal influenza trends are relatively consistent from year to year, drug companies can do a reasonable job of anticipating how many flu shots they will need to ship to a given part of the world in a given month. Likewise, consumers with identical financial backgrounds may vary widely in their likelihood of defaulting on a credit card, depending on what is going on in their lives. But credit card companies can do a surprisingly good job of predicting aggregate default rates by paying attention to a range of socioeconomic, demographic, and behavioral variables. And Internet companies are increasingly taking advantage of the mountains of Web-browsing data generated by their users to predict the probability that a given user will click on a given search result, respond favorably to particular news story, or be swayed by a particular recommendation. As the political scientist Ian Ayres writes in his book *Super Crunchers,* predictions of this kind are being made increasingly in highly data-intensive industries like finance, healthcare, and e-commerce, where the often modest gains associated with data-driven predictions can add up over millions or even billions of tiny decisions—in some cases every day—to produce very substantial gains to the bottom line.[2]

So far, so good. But there are also many areas of business—as well as of government and policy—that rely on predictions that do not quite fit into this supercrunching mold. For example, whenever a book publisher decides how much of an advance to offer a potential author, it is effectively making a prediction about the future sales of the proposed book. The more copies the book sells, the more royalties the author is entitled to, and so the more of an advance the publisher should offer to prevent the author from signing with a different publisher. But if in making this calculation, the publisher overestimates how well the book will sell, it will end up over-paying the author—good for the author but bad for the publisher's bottom line. Likewise when a movie studio decides to green-light a project, it is effectively making a prediction about the future revenues of the movie, and thus how much it can afford to spend making and marketing it. Or when a drug company decides to proceed with the clinical testing stage of a new drug, it must justify the enormous expense in terms of some prediction about the likely success of the trial and the eventual market size for the drug.

All these lines of business therefore depend on predictions, but they are considerably more complicated predictions than predictions about the number of flu cases expected in North America this winter, or the probability that a given user will click on a given ad online. When a publisher offers an advance for a book, the book itself is typically at least a year or two away from publication; so the publisher has to make a prediction not only about how the book itself will turn out but also what the market will be like for that kind of book when it is eventually published, how it will be reviewed, and any number of other related factors. Likewise predictions about movies, new drugs, and other kinds of business or development projects are, in effect, predictions about complex, multifaceted processes that play out over months or years. Even worse, because decision makers are constrained to making only a handful of such decisions every year, they do not have the luxury of averaging out their uncertainty over huge numbers of predictions.

Nevertheless, even in these cases, decision makers often have at least some historical data on which to draw. Publishers can keep track of how many copies they have sold of similar books in the past, while movie studios can do the same for box office revenues, DVD sales, and merchandising profits. Likewise, drug companies can assess the rates with which similar drugs have succeeded in reaching the market, marketers can track the historical success of comparable products, and magazine publishers can track the newsstand sales of previous cover stories. Decision makers often also have a lot of other data on which to draw—including market research, internal evaluations of the project in question, and their knowledge of the industry in general. So as long as nothing dramatic changes in the world between when they commit to a project and when it launches, then they are still in the realm of predictions that are at least possible to make reliably. How should they go about making them?

MARKETS, CROWDS, AND MODELS

One increasingly popular method is to use what is called a prediction market—meaning a market in which buyers and sellers can trade specially designed securities whose prices correspond to the predicted probability that a specific outcome will take place. For example, the day before the 2008 US presidential election, an investor could have paid $0.92 for a contract in the Iowa Electronic Markets—one of the longest-running and best-known prediction markets—that would have yielded him or her $1 if Barack Obama had won. Participants in prediction markets therefore behave much like participants in financial markets, buying and selling contracts for whatever price is on offer. But in the case of prediction markets, the prices are explicitly interpreted as making a prediction about the outcome in question—for example, the probability of an Obama victory on the eve of Election Day was predicted by the Iowa Electronic Markets to be 92 percent.

In generating predictions like this one, prediction markets exploit a phenomenon that *New Yorker* writer James Surowiecki dubbed the "wisdom of crowds"—the notion that although individual people tend to make highly error-prone predictions, when lots of these estimates are averaged together, the errors have a tendency to cancel out; hence the market is in some sense "smarter" than its constitutents. Many such markets also require participants to bet real money, thus people who know something about a particular topic are more likely to participate than people who don't. What's so powerful about this feature of prediction markets is that it doesn't matter *who* has the relevant market information—a single expert or a large number of nonexperts, or any combination in between. In theory, the market should incorporate all their opinions in proportion to how much each is willing to bet. In theory, in fact, no one should be able to consistently outperform a properly designed prediction market. The reason is that if someone *could* outperform the market, they would have an incentive to make money in it. But the very act of making money in the market would immediately shift the prices to incorporate the new information.[3]

The potential of prediction markets to tap into collective wisdom has generated a tremendous amount of excitement among professional economists and policy makers alike. Imagine, for example, that a market had been set up to predict the possibility of a catastrophic failure in deep-water oil drilling in the Gulf prior to the BP disaster in April 2010. Possibly insiders like BP engineers could have participated in the market, effectively making public what they knew about the risks their firms were taking. Possibly then regulators would have had a more accurate assessment of those risks and been more inclined to crack down on the oil industry before a disaster took place. Possibly the disaster could have been averted. These are the sorts of claims that the proponents of prediction markets tend to make, and it's easy to see why they've generated so much interest. In recent years, in fact, prediction markets have been set up to make predictions as varied as the likely success of new products, the box office revenues of upcoming movies, and the outcomes of sporting events.

In practice, however, prediction markets are more complicated than the theory suggests. In the 2008 presidential election, for example, one of the most popular prediction markets, Intrade, experienced a series of strange fluctuations when an unknown trader started placing very large bets on John McCain, generating large spikes in the market's prediction for a McCain victory. Nobody figured out who was behind these bets, but the suspicion was that it was a McCain supporter or even a member of the campaign. By manipulating the market prices, he or she was trying to create the impression that a respected source of election forecasts was calling the election for McCain, presumably with the hope of creating a self-fulfilling prophecy. It didn't work. The spikes were quickly reversed by other traders, and the mystery bettor ended up losing money; thus the market functioned essentially as it was supposed to. Nevertheless, it exposed a potential vulnerability of the theory, which assumes that rational traders will not deliberately lose money. The problem is that if the goal of a participant is instead to manipulate perceptions of people *outside* the market (like the media) and if the amounts involved are relatively small (tens of thousands of dollars, say, compared with the tens of millions of dollars spent on TV advertising), then they may not care about losing money, in which case it's no longer clear what signal the market is sending.[4]

Problems like this one have led some skeptics to claim that prediction markets are not necessarily superior to other less sophisticated methods, such as opinion polls, that are harder to manipulate in practice. However, little attention has been paid to evaluating the relative performance of different methods, so nobody really knows for sure.[5] To try to settle the matter, my colleagues at Yahoo! Research and I conducted a systematic comparison of several different prediction methods, where the predictions in question were the outcomes of NFL football games. To begin with, for each of the fourteen to sixteen games taking place each weekend over the course of the 2008 season, we conducted a poll in which we asked respondents to state the probability that the home team would win as well as their confidence in their prediction. We also collected similar data from the website Probability Sports, an online contest where participants can win cash prizes by predicting the outcomes of sporting events. Next, we compared the performance of these two polls with the Vegas sports betting market—one of the oldest and most popular betting markets in the world—as well as with another prediction market, TradeSports. And finally, we compared the prediction of both the markets and the polls against two simple statistical models. The first model relied only on the historical probability that home teams win—which they do 58 percent of the time—while the second model also factored in the recent win-loss records of the two teams in question. In this way, we set up a six-way comparison between different prediction methods—two statistical models, two markets, and two polls.[6]

Given how different these methods were, what we found was surprising: All of them performed about the same. To be fair, the two prediction markets performed a little better than the other methods, which is consistent with the theoretical argument above. But the very best performing method—the Las Vegas Market—was only about 3 percentage points more accurate than the worst-performing method, which was the model that always predicted the home team would win with

58 percent probability. All the other methods were somewhere in between. In fact, the model that also included recent win-loss records was so close to the Vegas market that if you used both methods to predict the actual point differences between the teams, the average error in their predictions would differ by less than a tenth of a point. Now, if you're betting on the outcomes of hundreds or thousands of games, these tiny differences may still be the difference between making and losing money. At the same time, however, it's surprising that the aggregated wisdom of thousands of market participants, who collectively devote countless hours to analyzing upcoming games for any shred of useful information, is only incrementally better than a simple statistical model that relies only on historical averages.

When we first told some prediction market researchers about this result, their reaction was that it must reflect some special feature of football. The NFL, they argued, has lots of rules like salary caps and draft picks that help to keep teams as equal as possible. And football, of course, is a game where the result can be decided by tiny random acts, like the wide receiver dragging in the quarterback's desperate pass with his fingertips as he runs full tilt across the goal line to win the game in its closing seconds. Football games, in other words, have a lot of randomness built into them—arguably, in fact, that's what makes them exciting. Perhaps it's not so surprising after all, then, that all the information and analysis that is generated by the small army of football pundits who bombard fans with predictions every week is not superhelpful (although it might be surprising to the pundits). In order to be persuaded, our colleagues insisted, we would have to find the same result in some other domain for which the signal-to-noise ratio might be considerably higher than it is in the specific case of football.

OK, what about baseball? Baseball fans pride themselves on their near-fanatical attention to every measurable detail of the game, from batting averages to pitching rotations. Indeed, an entire field of research called sabermetrics has developed specifically for the purpose of analyzing baseball statistics, even spawning its own journal, the *Baseball Research Journal*. One might think, therefore, that prediction markets, with their far greater capacity to factor in different sorts of information, would outperform simplistic statistical models by a much wider margin for baseball than they do for football. But that turns out not to be true either. We compared the predictions of the Las Vegas sports betting markets over nearly twenty thousand Major League baseball games played from 1999 to 2006 with a simple statistical model based again on home-team advantage and the recent win-loss records of the two teams. This time, the difference between the two was even smaller—in fact, the performance of the market and the model were indistinguishable. In spite of all the statistics and analysis, in other words, and in spite of the absence of meaningful salary caps in baseball and the resulting concentration of superstar players on teams like the New York Yankees and Boston Red Sox, the outcomes of baseball games are even closer to random events than football games.

Since then, we have either found or learned about the same kind of result for other kinds of events that prediction markets have been used to predict, from the opening weekend box office revenues for feature films to the outcomes of presidential elections. Unlike sports, these events occur without any of the rules or conditions that are designed to make sports competitive. There is also a lot of relevant information that prediction markets could conceivably exploit to boost their performance well beyond that of a simple model or a poll of relatively uninformed individuals. Yet when we compared the Hollywood Stock Exchange (HSX)—one of the most popular prediction markets, which has a reputation for accurate prediction—with a simple statistical model, the HSX did only slightly better.[7] And in a separate study of the outcomes of five US presidential elections from 1988 to 2004, political scientists Robert Erikson and Christopher Wlezien found that a simple statistical correction of ordinary opinion polls outperformed even the vaunted Iowa Electronic Markets.[8]

TRUST NO ONE, ESPECIALLY YOURSELF

So what's going on here? We are not really sure, but our suspicion is that the strikingly similar performance of different methods is an unexpected side effect of the prediction puzzle from the previous chapter. On the one hand, when it comes to complex systems—whether they involve sporting matches, elections, or movie audiences—there are strict limits to how accurately we can predict what will happen. But on the other hand, it seems that one can get pretty close to the limit of what *is* possible with relatively simple methods. By analogy, if you're handed a weighted die, you might be able to figure out which sides will come up more frequently in a few dozen rolls, after which you would do well to bet on those outcomes. But beyond that, more elaborate methods like studying the die under a microscope to map out all the tiny fissures and irregularities on its surface, or building a complex computer simulation, aren't going to help you much in improving your prediction.

In the same way, we found that with football games a single piece of information—that the home team wins slightly more than half the time—is enough to boost one's performance in predicting the outcome above random guessing. In addition, a second simple insight, that the team with the better win-loss record should have a slight advantage, gives you another significant boost. Beyond that, however, all the additional information you might consider gathering—the recent performance of the quarterback, the injuries on the team, the girlfriend troubles of the star running back—will only improve your predictions incrementally at best. Predictions about complex systems, in other words, are highly subject to the law of diminishing returns: The first pieces of information help a lot, but very quickly you exhaust whatever potential for improvement exists.

Of course, there are circumstances in which we may care about very small improvements in prediction accuracy. In online advertising or high-frequency stock trading, for example, one might be making millions or even billions of predictions every day, and large sums of money may be at stake. Under these circumstances, it's probably worth the effort and expense to invest in sophisticated methods that can exploit the subtlest patterns. But in just about any other business, from making movies or publishing books to developing new technologies, where you get to make only dozens or at most hundreds of predictions a year, and where the predictions you are making are usually just one aspect of your overall decision-making process, you can probably predict about as well as possible with the help of a relatively simple method.

The one method you don't want to use when making predictions is to rely on a single person's opinion—especially not your own. The reason is that although humans are generally good at perceiving which factors are potentially relevant to a particular problem, they are generally bad at estimating how important one factor is relative to another. In predicting the opening weekend box office revenue for a movie, for example, you might think that variables such as the movie's production and marketing budgets, the number of screens on which it will open, and advance ratings by reviewers are all highly relevant—and you'd be correct. But how much should you weight a slightly worse-than-average review against an extra $10 million marketing budget? It isn't clear. Nor is it clear, when deciding how to allocate a marketing budget, how much people will be influenced by the ads they see online or in a magazine versus what they hear about the product from their friends—even though all these factors are likely to be relevant.

You might think that making these sorts of judgments accurately is what experts would be good at, but as Tetlock showed in his experiment, experts are just as bad at making quantitative predictions as nonexperts and maybe even worse.[9] The real problem with relying on experts, however, is not that they are appreciably worse than nonexperts, but rather that because they are experts we tend to consult only one at a time. Instead, what we should do is poll *many* individual opinions—whether experts or not—and take the average. Precisely how you do this, it turns out, may not matter so much. With all their fancy bells and whistles, prediction markets may produce slightly better predictions than a simple method like a poll, but the difference between the two is much less important than the gain from simply averaging lots of opinions *somehow*. Alternatively, one can estimate the relative importance of the various predictors directly from historical data, which is really all a statistical model accomplishes. And once again, although a fancy model may work slightly better than a simple model, the difference is small relative to using no model at all.[10] At the end of the day, both models and crowds accomplish the same objective. First, they rely on some version of human judgment to identify which factors are relevant to the prediction in question. And second, they estimate and weight the relative importance of each of these factors. As the psychologist Robyn Dawes once pointed out, "the whole trick is to know what variables to look at and then know how to add."[11]

By applying this trick consistently, one can also learn over time which predictions can be made with relatively low error, and which cannot be. All else being equal, for example, the further in advance you predict the outcome of an event, the larger your error will be. It is simply harder to predict the box office potential of a movie at green light stage than a week or two before its release, no matter what methods you use. In the same way, predictions about new product sales, say, are likely to be less accurate than predictions about the sales of existing products no matter when you make them. There's nothing you can do about that, but what you can do is start using any one of several different methods—or even use all of them together, as we did in our study of prediction markets—and keep track of their performance over time. As I mentioned at the beginning of the previous chapter, keeping track of our predictions is not something that comes naturally to us: We make lots of predictions, but rarely check back to see how often we got them right. But keeping track of performance is possibly the most important activity of all—because only then can you learn how accurately it is possible to predict, and therefore how much weight you should put on the predictions you make.[12]

FUTURE SHOCK

No matter how carefully you adhere to this advice, a serious limitation with all prediction methods is that they are only reliable to the extent that the same kind of events will happen in the future as happened in the past, and with the same average frequency.[13] In regular times, for example, credit card companies may be able to do a pretty good job of predicting default rates. Individual people may be complicated and unpredictable, but they tend to be complicated and unpredictable in much the same way this week as they were last week, and so on average the models work reasonably well. But as critics of predictive modeling have pointed out, many of the outcomes that we care about most—like the onset of the financial crisis, the emergence of a revolutionary new technology, the overthrow of an oppressive regime, or a precipitous drop in violent crime—are interesting to us precisely because they are *not* regular times. And in these situations some very serious problems arise from relying on historical data to predict future outcomes—as a number of credit card companies discovered when default rates soared in the aftermath of the recent financial crisis.

Even more important, the models that many banks were using to price mortgage-backed derivatives prior to 2008—like the infamous CDOs—now seem to have relied too much on data from the recent past, during which time housing prices had only gone up. As a result, ratings analysts and traders alike collectively placed too low a probability on a nationwide drop in real-estate values, and so badly underestimated the risk of mortgage defaults and foreclosure rates.[14] At first, it might seem that this would have been a perfect application for prediction markets, which might have done a better job of anticipating the crisis than all the "quants" working in the banks. But in fact it would have been precisely these people—along with the politicians, government regulators, and other financial market specialists who also failed to anticipate the crisis—who would have been participating in the prediction market, so it's unlikely that the wisdom of crowds would have been any help at all. Arguably, in fact, it was precisely the "wisdom" of the crowd that got us into the mess in the first place. So if models, markets, and crowds can't help predict black swan events like the financial crisis, then what are we supposed to do about them?

A second problem with methods that rely on historical data is that big, strategic decisions are not made frequently enough to benefit from a statistical approach. It may be the case, historically speaking, that most wars end poorly, or that most corporate mergers don't pay off. But it may also be true that some military interventions are justified and that some mergers succeed, and it may be impossible to tell the difference in advance. If you could make millions, or even hundreds, of such bets, it would make sense to go with the historical probabilities. But when facing a decision about whether or not to lead the country into war, or to make some strategic acquisition, you cannot count on getting more than one attempt. Even if you could measure the probabilities, therefore, the difference between a 60 percent and 40 percent probability of success may not be terribly meaningful.

Like anticipating black swans, making one-off strategic decisions is therefore ill suited to statistical models or crowd wisdom. Nevertheless, these sorts of decisions have to get made all the time, and they are potentially the most consequential decisions that anyone makes. Is there a way to improve our success here as well? Unfortunately, there's no clear answer to this question. A number of approaches have been tried over the years, but none of them has a consistently successful track record. In part that's because the techniques can be difficult to implement correctly, but mostly it's because of the problem raised in the previous chapter—that there is simply a level of uncertainty about the future that we're stuck with, and this uncertainty inevitably introduces errors into the best-laid plans.

THE STRATEGY PARADOX

Ironically, in fact, the organizations that embody what would seem to be the *best* practices in strategy planning—organizations, for example, that possess great clarity of vision and that act decisively—can also be the most vulnerable to planning errors. The problem is what strategy consultant and author Michael Raynor calls the strategy paradox. In his book of the same name, Raynor illustrates the paradox by revisiting the case of Sony's Betamax videocassette, which famously lost out to the cheaper, lower-quality VHS technology developed by Matsushita. According to conventional wisdom, Sony's blunder was twofold: First, they focused on image quality over running time, thereby conceding VHS the advantage of being able to tape full-length movies. And second, they designed Betamax to be a standalone format, whereas VHS was "open," meaning that multiple manufacturers could compete to make the devices, thereby driving down the price. As the video-rental market exploded, VHS gained a small but inevitable lead in market share, and this small lead then grew rapidly through a process of cumulative advantage. The more people bought VHS recorders, the more stores stocked VHS tapes, and vice versa. The result over time was near-total saturation of the market by the VHS format and a humiliating defeat for Sony.[15]

What the conventional wisdom overlooks, however, is that Sony's vision of the VCR wasn't as a device for watching rented movies at all. Rather, Sony expected people to use VCRs to tape TV shows, allowing them to watch their favorite shows at their leisure. Considering the exploding popularity of digital VCRs that are now used for precisely this purpose, Sony's view of the future wasn't implausible at all. And if it had come to pass, the superior picture quality of Betamax might well have made up for the extra cost, while the shorter taping time may have been irrelevant.[16] Nor was it the case that Matsushita had any better inkling than Sony how fast the video-rental market would take off—indeed, an earlier experiment in movie rentals by the Palo Alto–based firm CTI had failed dramatically. Regardless, by the time it had become clear that home movie viewing, not taping TV shows, would be the killer app of the VCR, it was too late. Sony did their best to correct course, and in fact very quickly produced a longer-playing BII version, eliminating the initial advantage held by Matsushita. But it was all to no avail. Once VHS got a sufficient market lead, the resulting network effects were impossible to overcome. Sony's failure, in other words, was not really the strategic blunder it is often made out to be, resulting instead from a shift in consumer demand that happened far more rapidly than *anyone* in the industry had anticipated.

Shortly after their debacle with Betamax, Sony made another big strategic bet on recording technology—this time with their MiniDisc players. Determined not to make the same mistake twice, Sony paid careful attention to where Betamax had gone wrong, and did their best to learn the appropriate lessons. In contrast with Betamax, Sony made sure that MiniDiscs had ample capacity to record whole albums. And mindful of the importance of content distribution to the outcome of the VCR wars, they acquired their own content repository in the form of Sony Music. At the time they were introduced in the early 1990s, MiniDiscs held clear technical advantages over the then-dominant CD format. In particular, the MiniDiscs could record as well as play, and because they were smaller and more resistant to jolts they were better suited to portable devices. Recordable CDs, by contrast, required entirely new machines, which at the time were extremely expensive.

By all reasonable measures the MiniDisc should have been an outrageous success. And yet it bombed. What happened? In a nutshell, the Internet happened. The cost of memory plummeted, allowing people to store entire libraries of music on their personal computers. High-speed Internet connections allowed for peer-to-peer file sharing. Flash drive memory allowed for easy downloading to portable devices. And new websites for finding and downloading music abounded. The explosive growth of the Internet was not driven by the music business in particular, nor was Sony the only company that failed to anticipate the profound effect that the Internet would have on production, distribution, and consumption of music. Nobody did. Sony, in other words, really was doing the best that anyone could have done to learn from the past and to anticipate the future—but they got rolled anyway, by forces beyond anyone's ability to predict or control.

Surprisingly, the company that "got it right" in the music industry was Apple, with their combination of the iPod player and their iTunes store. In retrospect, Apple's strategy looks visionary, and analysts and consumers alike fall over themselves to pay homage to Apple's dedication to design and quality. Yet the iPod was exactly the kind of strategic play that the lessons of Betamax, not to mention Apple's own experience in the PC market, should have taught them would fail. The iPod was large and expensive. It was based on closed architecture that Apple refused to license, ran on proprietary software, and was actively resisted by the major content providers. Nevertheless, it was a smashing success. So in what sense was Apple's strategy better than Sony's? Yes, Apple had made a great product, but so had Sony. Yes, they looked ahead and did their best to see which way the technological winds were blowing, but so did Sony. And yes, once they made their choices, they stuck to them and executed brilliantly; but that's exactly what Sony did as well. The only important difference, in Raynor's view, was that Sony's choices happened to be wrong while Apple's happened to be right.[17]

This is the strategy paradox. The main cause of strategic failure, Raynor argues, is not bad strategy, but great strategy that just happens to be wrong. Bad strategy is characterized by lack of vision, muddled leadership, and inept execution—not the stuff of success for sure, but more likely to lead to persistent mediocrity than colossal failure. Great strategy, by contrast, is marked by clarity of vision, bold leadership, and laser-focused execution. When applied to just the right set of commitments, great strategy can lead to resounding success—as it did for Apple with the iPod—but it can also lead to resounding failure. Whether great strategy succeeds or fails therefore depends entirely on whether the initial vision happens to be right or not. And that is not just difficult to know in advance, but impossible.

STRATEGIC FLEXIBILITY

The solution to the strategy paradox, Raynor argues, is to acknowledge openly that there are limits to what can be predicted, and to develop methods for planning that respect those limits. In particular, he recommends that planners look for ways to integrate what he calls strategic uncertainty—uncertainty about the future of the business you're in—into the planning process itself. Raynor's solution, in fact, is a variant of a much older planning technique called scenario planning, which was developed by Herman Kahn of the RAND Corporation in the 1950s as an aid for cold war military strategists. The basic idea of scenario planning is to create what strategy consultant Charles Perrottet calls "detailed, speculative, well thought out narratives of 'future history.'"

Critically, however, scenario planners attempt to sketch out a wide range of these hypothetical futures, where the main aim is not so much to decide which of these scenarios is most likely as to challenge possibly unstated assumptions that underpin existing strategies.[18]

In the early 1970s, for example, the economist and strategist Pierre Wack led a team at Royal Dutch/Shell that used scenario planning to test senior management's assumptions about the future success of oil exploration efforts, the political stability of the Middle East, and the emergence of alternative energy technologies. Although the main scenarios were constructed in the relatively placid years of energy production before the oil shocks of the 1970s and the subsequent rise of OPEC—events that definitely fall into the black swan category—Wack later claimed that the main trends had indeed been captured in one of his scenarios, and that the company was as a result better prepared both to exploit emerging opportunities and to hedge against potential pitfalls.[19]

Once these scenarios have been sketched out, Raynor argues that planners should formulate not one strategy, but rather a portfolio of strategies, each of which is optimized for a given scenario. In addition, one must differentiate *core* elements that are common to all these strategies from *contingent* elements that appear in only one or a few of them. Managing strategic uncertainty is then a matter of creating "strategic flexibility" by building strategies around the core elements and hedging the contingent elements through investments in various strategic options. In the Betamax case, for example, Sony expected the dominant use of VCRs would be to tape TV shows for the future, but it did have *some* evidence from the CTI experiment that the dominant use might instead turn out to be home movie viewing. Faced with these possibilities, Sony adopted a traditional planning approach, deciding first which of these outcomes they considered more likely, and then optimizing their strategy around that outcome. Optimizing for strategic flexibility, by contrast, would have led Sony to identify elements that would have worked no matter which version of the future played out, and then to hedge the residual uncertainty, perhaps by tasking different operating divisions to develop higher- and lower-quality models to be sold at different price points.

Raynor's approach to managing uncertainty through strategic flexibility is certainly intriguing. However, it is also a time-consuming process—constructing scenarios, deciding what is core and what is contingent, devising strategic hedges, and so on—that necessarily diverts attention from the equally important business of running a company. According to Raynor, the problem with most companies is that their senior management, meaning the board of directors and the top executives, spends too much time managing and optimizing their existing strategies—what he calls operational management—and not enough thinking through strategic uncertainty. Instead, he argues that they should devote *all* their time to managing strategic uncertainty, leaving the operational planning to division heads. As he puts it, "The board of directors and CEO of an organization should not be concerned primarily with the short-term performance of the organization, but instead occupy themselves with creating strategic options for the organization's operating divisions."[20]

Raynor's justification for this radical proposal is that the only way to deal adequately with strategic uncertainty is to manage it continuously—"Once an organization has gone through the process of building scenarios, developing optimal strategies, and identifying and acquiring the desired portfolio of strategic options, it is time to do it all over again." And if indeed strategic planning requires such a continuous loop, it does make a kind of sense that the best people to be doing it are senior management. Nevertheless, it is hard to imagine how senior managers can suddenly stop doing the sort of planning that got them promoted to senior management in the first place and start acting like an academic think tank. Nor does it seem likely that shareholders or even employees would tolerate a CEO who didn't consider it his or her business to execute strategy or to worry about short-term performance.[21] This isn't to say that Raynor isn't right—he may be—just that his proposals have not exactly been embraced by corporate America.

FROM PREDICTION TO REACTION

A more fundamental concern is that even if senior management did embrace Raynor's brand of strategic management as their primary task, it may still not work. Consider the example of a Houston-based oilfield drilling company that engaged in a scenario-planning exercise around 1980. As shown in the figure on page 184, the planners identified three different scenarios that they considered to represent the full range of possible futures, and they plotted out the corresponding predicted yields—exactly what they were supposed to do. Unfortunately, none of the scenarios considered the possibility that the boom in oil exploration that had begun in 1980 might be a historical aberration. In fact, that's exactly what it turned out to be, and as a result the actual future that unfolded wasn't anywhere within the ballpark of possibilities that the participants had envisaged. Scenario planning, therefore, left the company just as unprepared for the future as if they hadn't bothered to use the method at all. Arguably, in fact, the exercise had left them in an even worse position. Although it had accomplished its goal of challenging their initial assumptions, it had ultimately increased their confidence that they had considered the appropriate range of scenarios, which of course they hadn't, and therefore left them even more vulnerable to surprise than before.[22]

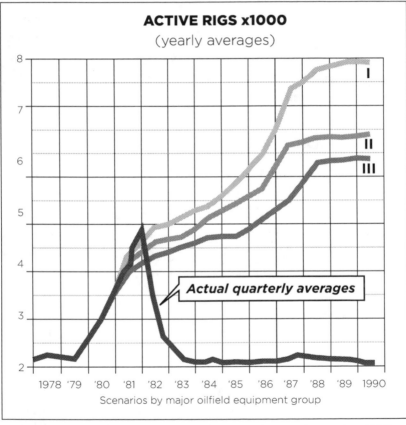

Scenario planning gone wrong (reprinted from Schoemaker 1991)

Possibly, this bad outcome was merely a consequence of poor execution of scenario planning, not a fundamental limitation of the method.[23] But how is a firm in the throes of a scenario analysis supposed to know that it isn't making the same mistake as the oil producer? Perhaps Sony could have taken the home video market more seriously, but what killed them was really the speed with which it exploded. It's hard to see how they could have anticipated that. Even worse, when developing the MiniDisc, it's unclear how Sony could possibly have anticipated the complicated combination of technological, economic, and cultural changes that arrived in short order with the explosive growth of the Internet. As Raynor puts it, "Not only did everything that could go wrong for Sony actually go wrong, everything that went wrong *had* to go wrong in order to sink what was in fact a brilliantly conceived and executed strategy."[24] So although more flexibility in their strategy might have helped, it's unclear how much flexibility they would have needed in order to adapt to such a radically shifting marketplace, or how they could have accomplished the requisite hedging without undermining their ability to execute any one strategy in particular.

Ultimately, the main problem with strategic flexibility as a planning approach is precisely the same problem that it is intended to solve—namely that in hindsight the trends that turned out to shape a given industry always appear obvious. And as a result, when we revisit history it is all too easy to persuade ourselves that had we been faced with a strategic decision "back then," we could have boiled down the list of possible futures to a small number of contenders—including, of course, the one future that did in fact transpire. But when we look to our own future, what we see instead is myriad potential trends, any one of which could be game changing and most of which will prove fleeting or irrelevant. How are we to know which is which? And without knowing what is relevant, how wide a range of possibilities should we consider? Techniques like scenario planning can help managers think through these questions in a systematic way. Likewise, an emphasis on strategic flexibility can help them manage the uncertainty that the scenarios expose. But no matter how you slice it, strategic planning involves prediction, and prediction runs into the fundamental "prophecy" problem I discussed in the previous chapter—that we just can't know what it is that we should be worrying about until after its importance has been revealed to us. An alternative approach, therefore— and the subject of the next chapter—is to rethink the whole philosophy of planning altogether, placing less emphasis on anticipating the future, or even multiple futures, and more on reacting to the present.

CHAPTER 8

The Measure of All Things

Of all the prognosticators, forecasters, and fortune-tellers, few are at once more confident and yet less accountable than those in the business of predicting fashion trends. Every year, the various industries in the business of designing, producing, selling, and commenting on shoes, clothing, and apparel are awash in predictions for what could be, might be, should be, and surely will be the next big thing. That these predictions are almost never checked for accuracy, that so many trends arrive unforeseen, and that the explanations given for them are only possible in hindsight, seems to have little effect on the breezy air of self-assurance that the arbiters of fashion so often exude. So it's encouraging that at least one successful fashion company pays no attention to any of it.

That company is Zara, the Spanish clothing retailer that has made business press headlines for over a decade with its novel approach to satisfying consumer demand. Rather than trying to anticipate what shoppers will buy next season, Zara effectively acknowledges that it has no idea. Instead, it adopts what we might call a measure-and-react strategy. First, it sends out agents to scour shopping malls, town centers, and other gathering places to observe what people are already wearing, thereby generating lots of ideas about what might work. Second, drawing on these and other sources of inspiration, it produces an extraordinarily large portfolio of styles, fabrics, and colors—where each combination is initially made in only a small batch—and sends them out to stores, where it can then measure directly what is selling and what isn't. And finally, it has a very flexible manufacturing and distribution operation that can react quickly to the information that is coming directly from stores, dropping those styles that aren't selling (with relatively little left-over inventory) and scaling up those that are. All this depends on Zara's ability to design, produce, ship, and sell a new garment anywhere in the world in just over two weeks—a stunning accomplishment to anyone who has waited in limbo for just about any designer good that isn't on the shelf.[1]

Ten years before Zara became a business-school case study, management theorist Henry Mintzberg anticipated their measure-and-react approach in a concept that he called "emergent strategy." Reflecting on the problem raised in the previous chapter—that traditional strategic planning invariably requires planners to make predictions about the future, leaving them vulnerable to inevitable errors—Mintzberg recommended that planners should rely less on making predictions about long-term strategic trends and more on reacting quickly to changes on the ground. Rather than attempting to anticipate correctly what will work in the future, that is, they should instead improve their ability to learn about what is working right now. Then, like Zara, they should react to it as rapidly as possible, dropping alternatives that are not working—no matter how promising they might have seemed in advance—and diverting resources to those that are succeeding, or even developing new alternatives on the fly.[2]

BUCKETS, MULLETS, AND CROWDS

Nowhere are the virtues of a measure-and-react strategy more apparent than in the online world, where the combination of low-cost development, large numbers of users, and rapid feedback cycles allows for many variants of virtually everything to be tested and selected on the basis of performance. Before Yahoo! rolled out its new home page in 2009, for example, the company spent months "bucket testing" every element of the design. Roughly 100 million people have Yahoo! as their home page, which in turn drives a great deal of traffic to other Yahoo! properties; so any changes have to be made with caution. Throughout the redesign process, therefore, whenever the home-page team came up with an idea for a new design element, a tiny percentage of users— the "bucket"—would be randomly chosen to see a version of the page containing the element. Then through a combination of user feedback and observational metrics like how long the users in the bucket stayed on the page, or what they clicked on, and comparing them to ordinary users, the home-page team could assess whether the element created a positive or negative effect. In this way, the company was able to learn what would work and what would not in real time and with real audience data.[3]

Bucket testing is now routine. Major Web companies like Google, Yahoo!, and Microsoft use it to optimize ad placement, content selection, search results, recommendations, pricing, even page layout.[4] A growing number of startup companies have also begun to offer advertisers automated services that winnow down a large suite of potential ads to those that perform the best, as measured by click-through rate.[5] But the measure-and-react philosophy of planning is not restricted to learning how consumers will respond to options they are presented with—it can also include the consumer as a producer of content. In the media world, this view is exemplified by what *Huffington Post* cofounder Jonah Peretti calls the Mullet Strategy, after the much-maligned hairstyle characterized by "business up front, party in the back."

The Mullet Strategy starts from the conventional view that user-generated content is a potential gold mine for media companies, in part because users can greatly amplify and extend the content of, say, a news story. But even more, it allows users to participate in conversations around the story that change the nature of the experience—from pure consumption to participation—thereby increasing their engagement and loyalty. Just as is true in real gold mines, however, a lot of user-generated content is closer to dirt than gold. As anyone who reads popular blogs or news sites can attest, many user comments are wildly inaccurate or simply dumb, and some of them are downright mean. Regardless, they do not constitute the kind of content that publishers want to promote or that advertisers want to be seen next to. Moderating online comments is the obvious solution to this problem, but it tends to alienate users, who resent the oversight and want to see their comments posted without filters. Editorial oversight also doesn't scale well, as the *Huffington Post* quickly discovered: A handful of editors simply can't read fast enough to keep up with potentially hundreds of blog posts every day. The solution is the Mullet Strategy: In the back pages where few people will see any particular story, let a thousand flowers bloom (or a million of them); then selectively promote material from the back to the front page, with all its premium advertising space, and keep that under strict editorial control.[6]

The Mullet Strategy is also an example of "crowdsourcing," a term coined in a 2006 *Wired* article by Jeff Howe to describe the outsourcing of small jobs to potentially very large numbers of individual workers. Online journalism, in fact, is increasingly moving toward a crowdsourced model—not just for generating community activity around a news story but also for creating the stories themselves, or even deciding what topics to cover in the first place. The *Huffington Post,* for example, relies on thousands of unpaid bloggers who contribute content either out of passion for the topic they write about or else to benefit from the visibility they receive from being published on a widely read news site. Other sites, like Examiner.com, meanwhile, retain armies of contributors to write about specific topics of interest to them, and pay them by the page view. And finally, sites like Yahoo!'s news blog "The Upshot" and Associated Content not only crowdsource the writing work but also track search queries and other indicators of current crowd interest to decide which topics to write about.[7]

The idea of measuring audience interest and reacting to it in close to real time has also started to gain traction beyond the revenue-challenged world of news media. For example, the cable channel Bravo regularly spins off new reality TV shows from its existing shows by tracking online buzz surrounding different characters. The shows can be launched quickly and at relatively low cost—and if they don't perform, the channel can quickly pull the plug. Following a similar principle, Cheezburger Network—a collection of nearly fifty websites featuring goofy user-contributed photos and videos, most with funny captions—is capable of launching a site within a week of noticing a new trend, and kills unsuccessful sites just as quickly. And BuzzFeed—a platform for launching "contagious media"—keeps track of hundreds of potential hits and only promotes those that are already generating enthusiastic responses from users.[8]

As creative as they are, these examples of crowdsourcing

work best for media sites that already attract millions of visitors, and so automatically generate real-time information about what people like or don't like. So if you're not Bravo or Cheezburger or BuzzFeed—if you're just some boring company that makes widgets or greeting cards or whatnot—how can you tap into the power of the crowd? Fortunately, crowdsourcing services like Amazon's Mechanical Turk (which Winter Mason and I used to run our experiments on pay and performance that I discussed in Chapter 2) can also be used to perform fast and inexpensive market research. Unsure what to call your next book? Rather than tossing around ideas with your editor, you can run a quick poll on Mechanical Turk and get a thousand opinions in a matter of hours, for about $10—or better yet, have the "turkers" come up with the suggestions as well as voting on them. Looking to get feedback on some design choices for a new product or advertising campaign? Throw the images up on Mechanical Turk and have users vote. Want an independent evaluation of your search engine results? Strip off the labels and throw your results up on Mechanical Turk next to your competitors', and let real Web users decide. Wondering if the media is biased against your candidate? Scrape several hundred news stories off the Web and have the turkers read them and rate them for positive or negative sentiment—all over a weekend.[9]

Clearly Mechanical Turk, along with other potential crowdsourcing solutions, comes with some limitations—most obviously the representativeness and reliability of the turkers. To many people it seems strange that anyone would work for pennies on mundane tasks, and therefore one might suspect either that the turkers are not representative of the general population or else that they do not take the work seriously. These are certainly valid concerns, but as the Mechanical Turk community matures, and as researchers learn more about it, the problems seem increasingly manageable. Turkers, for example, are far more diverse and representative than researchers initially suspected, and several recent studies have shown that they exhibit comparable reliability to "expert" workers. Finally, even where their reliability is poor—which sometimes it is—it can often be boosted through simple techniques, like soliciting independent ratings for every piece of content from several different turkers and taking the majority or the average score.[10]

PREDICTING THE PRESENT

At a higher level, the Web as a whole can also be viewed as a form of crowdsourcing. Hundreds of millions of people are increasingly turning to search engines for information and research, spending ever more time browsing news, entertainment, shopping, and travel sites, and increasingly sharing content and information with their friends via social networking sites like Facebook and Twitter. In principle, therefore, one might be able to aggregate all this activity to form a real-time picture of the world as viewed through the interests, concerns, and intentions of the global population of Internet users. By counting the number of searches for influenza-related terms like "flu," and "flu shots," for example, researchers at Google and Yahoo! have been able to estimate influenza caseloads remarkably close to those reported by the CDC.[11] Facebook, meanwhile, publishes a "gross national happiness" index based on users' status updates,[12] while Yahoo! compiles an annual list of most-searched-for items that serves as a rough guide to the cultural zeitgeist.[13] In the near future, no doubt, it will be possible to combine search and update data, along with tweets on Twitter, check-ins on Foursquare, and many other sources to develop more specific indices associated with real estate or auto sales or hotel vacancy rates—not just nationally, but down to the local level.[14]

Once properly developed and calibrated, Web-based indices such as these could enable businesses and governments alike to measure and react to the preferences and moods of their respective audiences—what Google's chief economist Hal Varian calls "predicting the present." In some cases, in fact, it may even be possible to use the crowd to make predictions about the near future. Consumers contemplating buying a new camera, for example, may search to compare models. Moviegoers may search to determine the opening date of an upcoming film or to locate cinemas showing it. And individuals planning a vacation may search for places of interest and look up airline costs or price hotel rooms. If so, it follows that by aggregating counts of search queries related to retail activity, moviegoing, or travel, one might be able to make near-term predictions about behavior of economic, cultural, or political interest.

Determining what kind of behavior can be predicted using searches, as well as the accuracy of such predictions and the timescale over which predictions can be usefully made are therefore all questions that researchers are beginning to address. For example, my colleagues at Yahoo! and I recently studied the usefulness of search-query volume to predict the opening weekend box office revenues of feature films, the first-month sales of newly released video games, and the Billboard "Hot 100" ranking of popular songs. All these predictions were made at most a few weeks in advance of the event itself, so we are not talking about long-term predictions here—as discussed in the previous chapter, those are much harder to make. Nevertheless, even having a slightly better idea a week in advance of audience interest might help a movie studio or a distributor decide how many screens to devote to which movies in different local regions.[15]

What we found is that the improvement one can get from search queries over other types of public data—like production budgets or distribution plans—is small but significant. As I discussed in the last chapter, simple models based on historical data are surprisingly hard to outperform, and the same rule applies to search-related data as well. But there are still plenty of ways in which search and other Web-based data could help with predictions. Sometimes, for example, you won't have access to reliable sources of historical data— say you're launching a new game that isn't like games you've launched in the past, or because you don't have access to a competitor's sales figures. And sometimes, as I've also discussed, the future is not like the past—such as when normally placid economic indicators suddenly increase in volatility or historically rising housing prices abruptly crash—and in these circumstances prediction methods based on historical data can be expected to perform poorly. Whenever historical data is unavailable or is simply uninformative, therefore, having access to the real-time state of collective consciousness—as revealed by what people are searching for—might give you a valuable edge.

In general, the power of the Web to facilitate measure-and-react strategies ought to be exciting news for business, scientists, and government alike. But it's important to keep in mind that the principle of measure and react is not restricted to Web-based technology, as indeed the very non-Web company Zara exemplifies. The real point is that our increasing ability to measure the state of the world ought to change the conventional mind-set toward planning. Rather than predicting how people will behave and attempting to design ways to make consumers respond in a particular way—whether to an advertisement, a product, or a policy—we can instead measure directly how they respond to a whole range of possibilities, and react accordingly. In other words, the shift from "predict and control" to "measure and react" is not just technological—although technology is needed—but psychological. Only once we concede that we cannot depend on our ability to predict the future are we open to a process that discovers it.[16]

DON'T JUST MEASURE: EXPERIMENT

In many circumstances, however, merely improving our ability to measure things does not, on its own, tell us what we need to know. For example, a colleague of mine recently related a conversation he'd had with the CFO of a major American corporation who confided that in the previous year his company had spent about $400 million on "brand advertising," meaning that it was not advertising particular products or services—just the brand. How effective was that money? According to my colleague, the CFO had lamented that he didn't know whether the correct number should have been $400 million or zero. Now let's think about that for a second. The CFO wasn't saying that the $400 million hadn't been effective—he was saying that he had *no idea* how effective it had been. As far as he could tell, it was entirely possible that if they had spent no money on brand advertising at all, their performance would have been no different. Alternatively, not spending the money might have been a disaster. He just didn't know.

Now, $400 million might seem like a lot of money not to know about, but in reality it's a drop in the ocean. Every year, US corporations collectively spend about $500 *billion* on marketing, and there's no reason to think that this CFO was any different from CFOs at other companies—more honest perhaps, but not any more or less certain. So really we should be asking the same question about the whole $500 billion. How much effect on consumer behavior does it really have? Does anybody have any idea? When pressed on this point, advertisers often quote the department-store magnate John Wanamaker, who is reputed to have said that "half the money I spend on advertising is wasted—I just don't know which half." It's entirely apropos and always seems to get a laugh. But what many people don't appreciate is that Wanamaker uttered it almost a century ago, around the time when Einstein published his theory of general relativity. How is it that in spite of the incredible scientific and technological boom since Wanamaker's time—penicillin, the atomic bomb, DNA, lasers, space flight, supercomputers, the Internet—his puzzlement remains as relevant today as it was then?

It's certainly *not* because advertisers haven't gotten better at measuring things. With their own electronic sales databases, third-party ratings agencies like Nielsen and comScore, and the recent tidal wave of clickstream data online, advertisers can measure many more variables, and at far greater resolution, than Wanamaker could. Arguably, in fact, the advertising world has more data than it knows what to do with. No, the real problem is that what advertisers want to know is whether their advertising is *causing* increased sales; yet almost always what they measure is the *correlation* between the two.

In theory, of course, everyone "knows" that correlation and causation are different, but it's so easy to get the two mixed up in practice that we do it all the time. If we go on a diet and then subsequently lose weight, it's all too tempting to conclude that the diet caused the weight loss. Yet often when people go on diets, they change other aspects of their lives as well—like exercising more or sleeping more or simply paying more attention to what they're eating. Any of these other changes, or more likely some combination of them, could be just as responsible for the weight loss as the particular choice of diet. But because it is the diet they are focused on, not these other changes, it is the diet to which they attribute the effect. Likewise, every ad campaign takes place in a world where lots of other factors are changing as well. Advertisers, for example, often set their budgets for the upcoming year as a function of their anticipated sales volume, or increase their spending during peak shopping periods like the holidays. Both these strategies will have the effect that sales and advertising will tend to be correlated whether or not the advertising is causing anything at all. But as with the diet, it is the advertising effort on which the business focuses its attention; thus if sales or some other metric of interest subsequently increases, it's tempting to conclude that it was the advertising, and not something else, that caused the increase.[17]

Differentiating correlation from causation can be extremely tricky in general. But one simple solution, at least in principle, is to run an experiment in which the "treatment"—whether the diet or the ad campaign—is applied in some cases and not in others. If the effect of interest (weight loss, increased sales, etc.) happens significantly more in the presence of the treatment than it does in the "control" group, we can conclude that it is in fact causing the effect. If it doesn't, we can't. In medical science, remember, a drug can be approved by the FDA only after it has been subjected to field studies in which some people are randomly assigned to receive the drug while others are randomly assigned to receive either nothing or a placebo. Only if people taking the drug get better more frequently than people who don't take the drug is the drug company allowed to claim that it works.

Precisely the same reasoning ought to apply in advertising. Without experiments, it's actually close to impossible to ascertain cause and effect, and therefore to measure the *real* return on investment of an advertising campaign. Let's say, for example, that a new product launch is accompanied by an advertising campaign, and the product sells like hotcakes. Clearly one could compute a return on investment based on how much was spent on the campaign and how much sales were generated, and that's generally what advertisers do. But what if the item was simply a great product that would have sold just as well anyway, even with no advertising campaign at all? Then clearly that money was wasted. Alternatively, what if a different campaign would have generated twice as many sales for the same cost? Once again, in a relative sense the campaign generated a poor return on investment, even though it "worked."[18]

Without experiments, moreover, it's extremely difficult to measure how much of the apparent effect of an ad was due simply to the predisposition of the person viewing it. It is often noted, for example, that search ads—the sponsored links you see on the right-hand side of a search results page—perform much better than display ads that appear on most other Web pages. But why is that? A big part of the reason is that which sponsored links you see depends very heavily on what you just searched for. People searching for "Visa card" are very likely to see ads for credit card vendors, while people searching for "Botox treatments" are likely to see ads for dermatologists. But these people are also more likely to be interested precisely in what those particular advertisers have to offer. As a result, the fact that someone who clicked on an ad for a Visa card subsequently signs up for one can only be partly attributed to the ad itself, for the simple reason that the same consumer might have signed up for the card anyway.

This seems like an obvious point, but it is widely misunderstood.[19] Advertisers, in fact, often pay a premium to reach customers they think are most likely to buy their products—because they have bought their products (e.g., Pampers) in the past; or because they have bought products in the same category (e.g., a competitor to Pampers); or because their attributes and circumstances make them likely to do so soon (e.g., a young couple expecting their first child). Targeted advertising of this kind is often held up as the quintessence of a scientific approach. But again, at least some of those consumers, and possibly many of them, would have bought the products anyway. As a result, the ads were just as wasted on them as they were on consumers who saw the ads and weren't interested. Viewed this way, the only ads that matter are those that sway the *marginal* consumer—the one who ends up buying the product, but who wouldn't have bought it had they not seen the ad. And the only way to determine the effect on marginal consumers is to conduct an experiment in which the decision about who sees the ad and who doesn't is made randomly.

FIELD EXPERIMENTS

A common objection to running these kinds of randomized experiments is that it can be difficult to do in practice. If you put up a billboard by the highway or place an ad in a magazine, it's generally impossible to know who sees it—even consumers themselves are often unaware of the ads they have seen. Moreover, the effects can be hard to measure. Consumers may make a purchase days or even weeks later, by which stage the connection between seeing the ad and acting on it has been lost. These are reasonable objections, but increasingly they can be dealt with, as three of my colleagues at Yahoo!—David Reiley, Taylor Schreiner, and Randall Lewis—demonstrated recently in a pioneering "field experiment" involving 1.6 million customers of a large retailer who were also active Yahoo! users.

To perform the experiment, Reiley and company randomly assigned 1.3 million users to the "treatment" group, meaning that when they arrived at Yahoo!-operated websites, they were shown ads for the retailer. The remaining 300,000, meanwhile, were assigned to the "control" group, meaning that they did not see these ads even if they visited exactly the same pages as the treatment group members. Because the assignment of individuals to treatment and control groups was random, the differences in behavior between the two groups had to be caused by the advertising itself. And because all the participants in the experiment were also in the retailer's database, the effect of the advertising could be measured in terms of their actual purchasing behavior—up to several weeks after the campaign itself concluded.[20]

Using this method, the researchers estimated that the additional revenue generated by the advertising was roughly four times the cost of the campaign in the short run, and possibly much higher over the long run. Overall, therefore, they concluded that the campaign had in fact been effective—a result that was clearly good news both for Yahoo! and the retailer. But what they also discovered was that almost all the effect was for older consumers—the ads were largely ineffective for people under forty. At first, this latter result seems like bad news. But the right way to think about it is that finding out that something doesn't work is also the first step toward learning what does work. For example, the advertiser could experiment with a variety of different approaches to appeal to younger people, including different formats, different styles, or even different sorts of incentives and offers. It's entirely possible that something would work, and it would be valuable to figure out what that is in a systematic way.

But let's say that none of these attempts is effective. Perhaps the brand in question is just not appealing to particular demographics, or perhaps those people don't respond to online advertising. Even in that event, however, the advertiser can at least stop wasting money advertising to them, freeing more resources to focus on the population that might actually be swayed. Regardless, the only way to improve one's marketing effectiveness over time is to first know what is working and what isn't. Advertising experiments, therefore, should not be viewed as a one-off exercise that either yields "the answer" or doesn't, but rather as part of an ongoing learning process that is built into all advertising.[21]

A small but growing community of researchers is now arguing that the same mentality should be applied not just to advertising but to all manner of business and policy planning, both online and off. In a recent article in *MIT Sloan Management Review,* for example, MIT professors Erik Brynjolfsson and Michael Schrage argue that new technologies for tracking inventory, sales, and other business parameters—whether the layout of links on a search page, the arrangement of products on a store shelf, or the details of a special direct mail offer— are bringing about a new era of controlled experiments in business. Brynjolfsson and Schrage even quote Gary Loveman, the chief executive of the casino company Harrah's, as saying, "There are two ways to get fired from Harrah's: stealing from the company, or failing to include a proper control group in your business experiment." You might find it disturbing that casino operators are ahead of the curve in terms of science-based business practice, but the mind-set of routinely including experimental controls is one from which other businesses could clearly benefit.[22]

Field experiments are even beginning to gain traction in the more tradition-bound worlds of economics and politics. Researchers associated with the MIT Poverty Action Lab, for example, have conducted more than a hundred field experiments to test the efficacy of various aid policies, mostly in the areas of public health, education, and savings and credit. Political scientists have tested the effect of advertising and phone solicitations on voter turnout, as well as the effect of newspapers on political opinions. And labor economists have conducted numerous field experiments to test the effectiveness of different compensation schemes, or how feedback affects performance. Typically the questions these researchers pose are quite specific. Should aid agencies give away mosquito nets or charge for them? How do workers respond to fixed wages versus performance-based pay? Does offering people a savings plan help them to save more? Yet answers to even these modest goals would be useful to managers and planners. And field experiments could be conducted on grander scales as well. For example, public policy analyst Randal O'Toole has advocated conducting field experiments for the National Park Service that would test different ways to manage and govern the national parks by applying them randomly to different parks (Yellowstone, Yosemite, Glacier, etc.) and measuring which ones work the best.[23]

THE IMPORTANCE OF LOCAL KNOWLEDGE

The potential of field experiments is exciting, and there is no doubt that they are used far less often than they could be. Nevertheless, it isn't always possible to conduct experiments.

The United States cannot go to war with half of Iraq and remain at peace with the other half just to see which strategy works better over the long haul. Nor can a company easily rebrand just a part of itself, or rebrand itself with respect to only some consumers and not others.[24] For decisions like these, it's unlikely that an experimental approach will be of much help; nevertheless, the decisions still have to get made. It's all well and good for academics and researchers to debate the finer points of cause and effect, but our politicians and business leaders must often act in the absence of certainty. In such a world, the first rule of order is not to let the perfect be the enemy of the good, or as my Navy instructors constantly reminded us, sometimes even a bad plan is better than no plan at all.

Fair enough. In many circumstances, it may well be true that realistically all one can do is pick the course of action that seems to have the greatest likelihood of success and commit to it. But the combination of power and necessity can also lead planners to have more faith in their instincts than they ought to, often with disastrous consequences. As I mentioned in Chapter 1, the late nineteenth and early twentieth centuries were characterized by pervasive optimism among engineers, architects, scientists, and government technocrats that the problems of society could be solved just like problems in science and engineering. Yet as the political scientist James Scott has written, this optimism was based on a misguided belief that the intuition of planners was as precise and reliable as mankind's accumulated scientific expertise.

According to Scott, the central flaw in this "high modernist" philosophy was that it underemphasized the importance of local, context-dependent knowledge in favor of rigid mental models of cause and effect. As Scott put it, applying generic rules to a complex world was "an invitation to practical failure, social disillusionment, or most likely both." The solution, Scott argued, is that plans should be designed to exploit "a wide array of practical skills and acquired intelligence in responding to a constantly changing natural and human environment." This kind of knowledge, moreover, is hard to reduce to generally applicable principles precisely because "the environments in which it is exercised are so complex and non-repeatable that formal procedures of rational decision making are impossible to apply." In other words, the knowledge on which a plan should be based is necessarily *local* to the concrete situation in which it is to be applied.[25]

Scott's argument in favor of local knowledge was in fact presaged many years earlier in a famous paper titled "The Use of Knowledge in Society" by the economist Friedrich Hayek, who argued that planning was fundamentally a matter of aggregating knowledge. Knowing what resources to allocate, and where, required knowing who needed how much of what relative to everyone else. Hayek also argued, however, that aggregating all this knowledge across a broad economy made up of hundreds of millions of people is impossible for any single central planner no matter how smart or well intentioned. Yet it is precisely the aggregation of all this information that markets achieve every day, without any oversight or direction. If, for example, someone, somewhere invents a new use for iron that allows him to make more profitable use of it than anyone else, that person will also be willing to pay more for the iron than anyone else will. And because aggregate demand has now gone up, then all else being equal, so will its price. The people who have less productive uses will therefore buy less iron, while the people who have more productive uses will buy more of it. Nobody needs to know why the price went up, or who it is that suddenly wants more iron—in fact, no one needs to know anything about the process at all. Rather, it is the "invisible hand" of the market that automatically allocates the limited amount of iron in the world to whomever can make the best use of it.

Hayek's paper is often held up by free market advocates as an argument that government-designed solutions are always worse than market-based ones, and no doubt there are cases where this conclusion is correct. For example, "cap and trade" policies to reduce carbon emissions explicitly invoke Hayek's reasoning. Rather than the government instructing businesses on how to reduce their carbon emissions—as would be the case with typical government regulation—it should simply place a cost on carbon by "capping" the total amount that can be emitted by the economy as a whole, and then leave it up to individual businesses to figure out how best to respond. Some businesses would find ways to reduce their energy consumption, while others would switch to alternative sources of energy, and others still would look for ways to clean up their existing emissions. Finally, some businesses would prefer to pay for the privilege of continuing to emit carbon by buying credits from those who prefer to cut back, where the price of the credits would depend on the overall supply and demand—just as in other markets.[26]

Market-based mechanisms like cap and trade do indeed seem to have more chance of working than centralized bureaucratic solutions. But market-based mechanisms are not the only way to exploit local knowledge, nor are they necessarily the best way. Critics of cap-and-trade policies, for example, point out that markets for carbon credits are likely to spawn all manner of complex derivatives—like the derivatives that brought the financial system to its knees in 2008—with consequences that may undermine the intent of the policy. A less easily gamed approach, they argue, would be to increase the cost of carbon simply by taxing it, thereby still offering incentives to businesses to reduce emissions and still giving them the flexibility to decide how best to reduce them, but without all the overhead and complexity of a market.

Another nonmarket approach to harnessing local knowledge that is increasingly popular among governments and foundations alike is the prize competition. Rather than allocating resources ahead of time to preselected recipients, prize competitions reverse the funding mechanism, allowing anyone to work on the problem, but only rewarding solutions that satisfy prespecified objectives. Prize competitions have attracted a lot of attention in recent years for the incredible amount of creativity they have managed to leverage out of relatively small prize pools. The funding agency DARPA, for example, was able to harness the collective creativity of dozens of university research labs to build self-driving robot vehicles by offering just a few million dollars in prize money—far less than it would have cost to fund the same amount of work with conventional research grants. Likewise, the $10 million Ansari X Prize elicited more than $100 million worth of research and development in pursuit of building a reusable spacecraft. And the video rental company Netflix got some of the world's most talented computer scientists to help it improve its movie recommendation algorithms for just a $1 million prize.

Inspired by these examples—along with "open innovation" companies like Innocentive, which conducts hundreds of prize competitions in engineering, computer science, math, chemistry, life sciences, physical sciences, and business— governments are wondering if the same approach can be used to solve otherwise intractable policy problems. In the past year, for example, the Obama administration has generated shock waves throughout the education establishment by announcing its "Race to the Top"—effectively a prize competition among US states for public education resources allocated on the basis of plans that the states must submit, which are scored on a variety of dimensions, including student performance measurement, teacher accountability, and labor contract reforms. Much of the controversy around the Race to the Top takes issue with its emphasis on teacher quality as the primary determinant of student performance and on standardized testing as a way to measure it. These legitimate critiques notwithstanding, however, the Race to the Top remains an interesting policy experiment for the simple reason that, like cap and trade, it specifies the "solution" only at the highest level, while leaving the specifics up to the states themselves.[27]

DON'T "SOLVE": BOOTSTRAP

Market-based solutions and prize competitions are both good ideas, but they're not the only way that centralized bureaucracies can take advantage of local knowledge. A different approach altogether begins with the observation that in any troubled system, there are often instances of individuals and groups—called bright spots by marketing scientists Chip and Dan Heath in their book *Switch*—who have figured out workable solutions to specific problems. The bright-spot approach was first developed by Tufts University nutrition professor Marian Zeitlin, who noticed that a number of studies of child nutrition in impoverished communities had found that within any given community, some children seemed to be better nourished than others. After understanding these naturally occurring success stories—how the children's mothers behaved differently, what they fed them and when—Zeitlin realized that he could help other mothers to take better care of their children simply by teaching them the homegrown solutions that already existed in their own communities. Subsequently, the bright-spot approach has been used successfully in developing nations, and even in the United States where certain hand-washing practices in a small number of hospitals are being replicated in order to help reduce bacterial infections—the leading cause of preventable hospital deaths—throughout the medical system.[28]

The bright-spot approach is also similar to what political scientist Charles Sabel calls bootstrapping, a philosophy that has begun to gain popularity in the world of economic development. Bootstrapping is modeled on the famous Toyota Production System, which has been embraced not only across the Japanese automotive firms but also more broadly across industries and cultures. The basic idea is that production systems should be engineered along "just in time" principles, which assure that if one part of the system fails, the whole system must stop until the problem is fixed. At first, this sounds like a bad idea (and it has led Toyota to the brink of disaster at least once), but its advantage is that it forces organizations to address problems quickly and aggressively. It also forces them to trace problems to their "root causes"—a process that frequently requires looking beyond the immediate cause of the failure to discover how flaws in one part of the system can result in failures somewhere else. And finally, it forces them to look either for existing solutions or else adapt solutions from related activities—a process known as benchmarking. Together these three practices—identifying failure points, tracing problems to root causes, and searching for solutions outside the confines of existing routines—can transform the organization itself from one that offers solutions to complex problems in a centralized managerial manner into one that searches for solutions among a broad network of collaborators.[29]

Like bright spots, bootstrapping focuses on concrete solutions to local problems, and seeks to extract solutions that are working from what is already happening on the ground. However, bootstrapping goes one step further, sniffing out not only what is working, but also what *could* work if certain impediments were removed, constraints lifted, or problems solved elsewhere in the system. A potential downside of bootstrapping is that it requires a motivated workforce with strong incentives to solve problems as they arise. So one might legitimately wonder whether the model can be translated from highly competitive industrial settings to the world of economic development or public policy. But as Sabel points out, there are now so many examples of local successes—footwear producers in the Sinos Valley of Brazil, wine growers in Mendoza, Argentina, or soccer ball manufacturers in Sialkot, Pakistan—that have flourished on the strength of the bootstrapping approach that it is hard to dismiss them as mere aberrations.[30]

PLANNING AND COMMON SENSE

Most important, what both bright spots and bootstrapping have in common is that they require a shift in mind-set on the part of planners. First, planners must recognize that no matter what the problem is—creating a more nutritious diet in impoverished villages, reducing infection rates in hospitals, or improving the competitiveness of local industries—chances are that somebody out there already has part of the solution and is willing to share it with others. And second, having realized that they do not need to figure out the solution to every problem on their own, planners can instead devote their resources to finding the existing solutions, wherever they occur, and spreading their practice more widely.[31]

In effect, this is also the lesson of thinkers like Scott and Hayek, whose proposed solutions also advocate that policy makers devise plans that revolve around the knowledge and motivation of local actors rather than relying on their own. Planners, in other words, need to learn to behave more like what the development economist William Easterly calls searchers. As Easterly puts it,

> A Planner thinks he already knows the answer; he thinks of poverty as a technical engineering problem that his answers will solve. A Searcher admits he doesn't know the answers in advance; he believes that poverty is a complicated tangle of political, social, historical, institutional, and technological factors...and hopes to find answers to individual problems by trial and error....A Planner believes outsiders know enough to impose solutions. A Searcher believes only insiders have enough knowledge to find solutions, and that most solutions must be homegrown.[32]

As different as they appear on the surface, in fact, all these approaches to planning—along with Mintzberg's emergent strategy, Peretti's mullet strategy, crowdsourcing, and field experiments—are really just variations on the same general theme of "measuring and reacting." Sometimes what is being measured is the detailed knowledge of local actors, and sometimes it is mouse clicks or search terms. Sometimes it is sufficient merely to gather data, and sometimes one must conduct a randomized experiment. Sometimes the appropriate reaction is to shift resources from one program or topic or ad campaign to another, while at other times it is to expand on someone else's homegrown solution. There are, in fact, as many ways to measure and react to different problems as there are problems to solve, and no one-size-fits-all approach exists. What they all have in common, however, is that they require planners—whether government planners trying to reduce global poverty or advertising planners trying to launch a new campaign for a client—to abandon the conceit that they can develop plans on the basis of intuition and experience alone. Plans fail, in other words, not because planners ignore common sense, but rather because they rely on their own common sense to reason about the behavior of people who are different from them.

This seems like an easy trap to avoid, but it isn't. Whenever we contemplate the question of why it is that things turned out the way they did, or why people do what they do, we are always able to come up with plausible answers. We may even be so convinced by our answers that whatever prediction or explanation we arrive at may seem obvious. We will always be tempted to think that we know how other people will react to a new product, or to a politician's campaign speech, or to a new tax law. "It'll never work," we will want to say, "because people just don't like that kind of thing," or "No one will be fooled by his obvious chicanery," or "Such a tax will reduce incentives to work hard and invest in the economy." None of this can be helped—we cannot suppress our commonsense intuition any more than we can will our heart to stop beating. What we can do, however, is remember that whenever it comes to questions of business strategy or government policy, or even marketing campaigns and website design, we must rely less on our common sense and more on what we can measure.

But measurement alone is not enough to prevent us from misleading ourselves. Commonsense reasoning can also mislead us with respect to more philosophical questions about society—like how we assign blame, or how we attribute success—where measurement may be impossible. In these circumstances too we will not be able to restrain our commonsense intuition from coming up with seemingly self-evident answers. But once again, we can suspect it, and instead look for ways to think about the world that benefit from understanding the limits of common sense.

CHAPTER 9

Fairness and Justice

August 4, 2001, was a Saturday, and Joseph Gray was having a fun day. Gray, a fifteen-year veteran of the New York City Police Department, had finished the late shift that morning, in the 72nd precinct in Brooklyn, and he and a bunch of his colleagues decided to stick around the station house to have a few beers. Shortly before noon, by which stage a few beers had turned into several beers, several of them decided to have lunch at the nearby Wild, Wild West topless bar. Officer Gray, apparently, was particularly pleased with the decision, as he stayed there all afternoon and into the evening, even after the rest of his friends had left. It was puzzling behavior, considering he had to report to work again later that night, but perhaps he was hoping to get there a few hours before his shift started and sleep it off. Regardless, by the time he poured himself into his burgundy Ford Windstar van, he had drunk somewhere between twelve and eighteen beers—enough to put his blood alcohol content at over twice the legal limit.

What happened next isn't completely clear, but the record indicates that as Officer Gray drove north on Third Avenue, under the Gowanus Expressway overpass, he ran a red light. Definitely not good, but also perhaps not a big deal. On any other Saturday evening he might have sailed right on through and gotten safely to Staten Island, where he planned to pick up one of his drinking partners from earlier in the day before returning to the station. But on this particular night, he was not to be so lucky. Nor were twenty-four-year-old Maria Herrera; her sixteen-year-old sister, Dilcia Peña; and Herrera's four-year old son, Andy, who were crossing the avenue at 46th Street at that moment. Officer Gray struck the three of them at full speed, killing them all and dragging the poor boy's body for nearly half a block under his front fender before coming to a halt. As he emerged from his vehicle, witnesses claimed his eyes were glassy, his voice was slurred, and he kept asking, "Why did they cross?" over and over again. But the nightmare didn't end there. Maria Herrera was also eight-and-a-half months pregnant. Her unborn baby, Ricardo, was delivered by cesarean section at Lutheran Medical Center, and the doctors there fought to save his life. But they failed. Twelve hours after his mother died, so did baby Ricardo, leaving his father, Victor Herrera, alone in the world.

Almost two years later, Joseph Gray was sentenced in State Supreme Court to the maximum penalty of five to fifteen years in prison on four counts of second-degree manslaughter. Gray pleaded with the judge for mercy, claiming that he'd never done "anything intentional in my entire life to hurt another human being," and more than one hundred supporters wrote letters to the court attesting to his decency. But Justice Anne Feldman was unsympathetic, pointing out that driving a half-ton van along city streets while intoxicated was "equivalent to waving a loaded gun around a crowded room." The four thousand members of the Herreras' community, who signed a petition demanding the maximum sentence, clearly concurred with the judge. Many felt that Gray had gotten off easy. Certainly Victor Herrera did. "Joseph Gray, fifteen years is not enough for you," he told the courtroom. "You will get out of prison one day. And when you do, you will still be able to see your family. I will have nothing. You killed everything I have."[1]

Even reading about these events years after they took place, it's impossible not to feel the grief and anger of the victims' family. As Victor Herrera expressed it to one reporter, God had blessed him with the family he'd dreamed of; then one drunk and reckless man had taken it all away from him in an instant. It's a horrible thought, and Herrera has every right to hate the man who destroyed his life. Nevertheless, as I read about the repercussions—the protests outside the police station, the condemnation of neighbors and politicians, the shock waves through the community, and of course the eventual sentence—I couldn't help but think about what would have happened had Joseph Gray come along an instant later. Naturally there would have been no accident, and Maria Herrera, her sister, and her son would have gone along their merry way. She would have given birth to Ricardo weeks later, hopefully lived a long and happy life, and would never have thought twice about the van speeding erratically along Third Avenue that summer evening. Joseph Gray would have picked up his fellow officer in Staten Island, who presumably would have insisted on driving back to Brooklyn. Gray might have gotten a reprimand from his supervisor, or he might have gotten away with it altogether. But regardless, he would have gone home to his wife and three children the next day and gotten on with his quiet, unremarkable existence.

ALL'S NOT WELL THAT ENDS WELL

OK, I know what you're thinking. Even if Gray's driving drunk did not make the accident inevitable, it did increase the likelihood that something bad would happen, and his punishment was justified in terms of his behavior. But if that's true, then versions of his crime play out all the time. Every day, police officers—not to mention public officials, parents, and others—get drunk and drive their cars. Some of them are as drunk as Joseph Gray was that night, and some of them drive just as irresponsibly. Most of them don't get caught, and even the few who do are rarely sent to jail. Few are subject to the punishment and public vilification that befell Joseph Gray, who was labeled a monster and a murderer. So what was it about Joseph Gray's actions that made him so much worse than all these others? No matter how reprehensible, even criminal, you think his actions that day were, they would have been exactly as bad had he walked out of the bar a minute later, or had the light been green, or had the Herreras been momentarily delayed while walking down the street, or had Gray been pulled over before reaching 46th Street. And conversely, even if you subscribe to Judge Feldman's logic that everyone who is driving a van drunk down a city street is a potential killer of mothers and children, it is hard to imagine charging every driver who has had a few too many drinks—or these days, anyone texting or talking on a cell phone—to fifteen years in prison, simply on the grounds that they *might* have killed someone.

That the nature of the outcome should matter is about as commonsense an observation as one can think of. If great harm is caused, great blame is called for—and conversely, if no harm is caused, we are correspondingly inclined to leniency. All's well that end's well, is it not? Well, maybe, but maybe not. To be clear, I'm not drawing any conclusion about whether Joseph Gray got a fair trial, or whether he deserved to spend the next fifteen years of his life in prison; nor am I insisting that all drunk drivers should be treated like murderers. What I am saying, however, is that in being swayed so heavily by the outcome, our commonsense notions of justice inevitably lead us to a *logical* conundrum. On the one hand, it seems an outrage not to punish a man who killed four innocent people with the full force of the law. And on the other hand, it seems grossly disproportionate to treat every otherwise decent, honest person who has ever had a few too many drinks and driven home as a criminal and a killer. Yet aside from the trembling hand of fate, there is no difference between these two instances.

Quite possibly this is an inconsistency that we simply have to live with. As sociologists who study institutions have long argued, the formal rules that officially govern behavior in organizations and even societies are rarely enforced in practice, and in fact are probably impossible to enforce both consistently and comprehensively. The real world of human interactions is simply too messy and ambiguous a place ever to be governed by any predefined set of rules and regulations; thus the business of getting on with life is something that is best left to individuals exercising their common sense about what is reasonable and acceptable in a given situation. Most of the time this works fine. Problems get resolved, and people learn from their mistakes, without regulators or courts of law getting involved. But occasionally an infraction is striking or serious enough that the rules have to be invoked, and the offender dealt with officially. Looked at on a case-by-case basis, the invocation of the rules can seem arbitrary and even unfair, for exactly the reasons I have just discussed, and the person who suffers the consequences can legitimately wonder "why me?" Yet the rules nevertheless serve a larger, social purpose of providing a rough global constraint on acceptable behavior. For society to function it isn't necessary that every case get dealt with consistently, as nice as that would be. It is enough simply to discourage certain kinds of antisocial behavior with the threat of punishment.[2]

Seen from this sociological perspective, it makes perfect sense that even if some irresponsible people are lucky enough to get away with their actions, society still has to make examples of violators occasionally—if only to keep the rest of us in check—and the threshold for action that has been chosen is that harm is done. But just because sociological sense and common sense happen to converge on the same solution in this particular case does not mean that they are saying the same thing, or that they will always agree. The sociological argument is not claiming that the commonsense emphasis on outcomes over processes is right—just that it's a tolerable error for the purpose of achieving certain social ends. It's the same kind of reasoning, in fact, that Oliver Wendell Holmes used to defend freedom of speech—not because he was fighting for the rights of individuals per se, but because he believed that allowing everyone to voice their opinion served the larger interest of creating a vibrant, innovative, and self-regulating society.[3] So even if we end up shrugging off the logical conundrum raised by cases like Joseph Gray's as an acceptable price to pay for a governable society, it doesn't follow that we should overlook the role of chance in determining outcomes. And yet we do tend to overlook it. Whether we are passing judgment on a crime, weighing up a person's career, assessing some work of art, analyzing a business strategy, or evaluating some public policy, our evaluation of the process is invariably and often heavily swayed by our knowledge of the outcome, even when that outcome may have been driven largely by chance.

THE HALO EFFECT

This problem is related to what management scientist Phil Rosenzweig calls the Halo Effect. In social psychology, the

Halo Effect refers to our tendency to extend our evaluation about one particular feature of another person—say that they're tall or good-looking—to judgments about other features, like their intelligence or character, that aren't necessarily related to the first feature at all. Just because someone is good-looking doesn't mean they're smart, for example, yet subjects in laboratory experiments consistently evaluate good-looking people as smarter than unattractive people, even when they have no reason to believe anything about either person's intelligence. Not for no reason, it seems, did John Adams once snipe that George Washington was considered a natural choice of leader by virtue of always being the tallest man in the room.[4]

Rosenzweig argues that the very same tendency also shows up in the supposedly dispassionate, rational evaluations of corporate strategy, leadership, and execution. Firms that are successful are consistently rated as having visionary strategies, strong leadership, and sound execution, while firms that are performing badly are described as suffering from some combination of misguided strategy, poor leadership, or shoddy execution. But as Rosenzweig shows, firms that exhibit large swings in performance over time attract equally divergent ratings, even when they have pursued exactly the same strategy, executed the same way, under the same leadership all along. Remember that Cisco Systems went from the poster child of the Internet era to a cautionary tale in a matter of a few years. Likewise, for six years before its spectacular implosion in 2001, Enron was billed by *Fortune* magazine as "America's most innovative company," while Steve & Barry's—a now-defunct low-cost clothing retailer—was heralded by the *New York Times* as a game-changing business only months before it declared bankruptcy. Rosenzweig's conclusion is that in all these cases, the way firms are rated has more to do with whether they are perceived as succeeding than what they are actually doing.[5]

To be fair, Enron's appearance of success was driven in part by outright deception. If more had been known about what was really going on, it's possible that outsiders would have been more circumspect. Better information might also have tipped people off to lurking problems at Steve & Barry's and maybe even at Cisco. But as Rosenzweig shows, better information is not on its own any defense against the Halo Effect. In one early experiment, for example, groups of participants were told to perform a financial analysis of a fictitious firm, after which they were rated on their performance and asked to evaluate how well their team had functioned on a variety of metrics like group cohesion, communication, and motivation. Sure enough, groups that received high performance scores consistently rated themselves as more cohesive, motivated, and so on than groups that received low scores. The only problem with these assessments was that the performance scores were assigned at random by the experimenter—there *was* no difference in performance between the high and low scorers. Rather than highly functioning teams delivering superior results, in other words, the appearance of superior results drove the illusion of high functionality. And remember, these were not assessments made by external observers who might have lacked inside information—they were by the very members of the teams themselves. The Halo Effect, in other words, turns conventional wisdom about performance on its head. Rather than the evaluation of the outcome being determined by the quality of the process that led to it, it is the observed nature of the outcome that determines how we evaluate the process.[6]

Negating the Halo Effect is difficult, because if one cannot rely on the outcome to evaluate a process then it is no longer clear what to use. The problem, in fact, is not that there is anything wrong with evaluating processes in terms of outcomes—just that it is unreliable to evaluate them in terms of any *single* outcome. If we're lucky enough to get to try out different plans many times each, for example, then by keeping track of all their successes and failures, we can indeed hope to determine their quality directly. But in cases where we only get to try out a plan once, the best way to avoid the Halo Effect is to focus our energies on evaluating and improving what we are doing while we are doing it. Planning techniques like scenario analysis and strategic flexibility, which I discussed earlier, can help organizations expose questionable assumptions and avoid obvious mistakes, while prediction markets and polls can exploit the collective intelligence of their employees to evaluate the quality of plans before their outcome is known. Alternatively, crowdsourcing, field experiments, and bootstrapping—discussed in the last chapter—can help organizations learn what is working and what isn't and then adjust on the fly. By improving the way we make plans and implement them, all these methods are designed to increase the likelihood of success. But they can't, and should not, guarantee success. In any one instance, therefore, we need to bear in mind that a good plan can fail while a bad plan can succeed—just by random chance—and therefore try to judge the plan on its own merits as well as on the known outcome.[7]

TALENT VERSUS LUCK

Even when it comes to measuring individual performance, it's easy to get tripped up by the Halo Effect—as the current outrage over compensation in the financial industry exemplifies. The source of the outrage, remember, isn't that bankers got paid lots of money—because we always knew that—but rather that they got paid lots of money for what now seems like disastrously bad performance. Without doubt there is something particularly galling about so-called pay for failure. But really it is just a symptom of a deeper problem with the whole notion of pay for performance—a problem that revolves around the Halo Effect. Consider, for example, all the financial-sector workers who qualified for large bonuses in 2009—the year *after* the crisis hit—because they made money for their employers. Did they deserve to be paid bonuses? After all, it wasn't *them* who screwed up, so why should they be penalized for the foolish actions of other people? As one recipient of the AIG bonuses put it, "I earned that money, and I had nothing to do with all of the bad things that happened at AIG."[8] From a pragmatic perspective, moreover, it's also entirely possible that if profit-generating employees aren't compensated accordingly, they will leave for other firms, just as their bosses kept saying. As the same AIG employee pointed out, "They needed us to stay, because we were still making them lots of money, and we had the kind of business we could take to any competitor or, if they wanted, that we could wind down profitably." This all sounds reasonable, but it could just be the Halo Effect again. Even as the media and the public revile one group of bankers—those who booked "bad" profits in the past—it still seems reasonable that bankers who make "good" profits deserve to be rewarded with bonuses. Yet for all we know, these two groups of bankers may be playing precisely the same game.

Imagine for a second the following thought experiment. Every year you flip a coin: If it comes up heads, you have a "good" year; and if it comes up tails, you have a "bad" year. Let's assume that your bad years are really bad, meaning that you lose a ton of money for your employer, but that in your good years you earn an equally outsized profit. We'll also adopt a fairly strict pay-for-performance model in which you get paid nothing in your bad years—no cheating, like guaranteed bonuses or repriced stock options allowed—but you receive a very generous bonus, say $10 million, in your good years. At first glance this arrangement seems fair—because you only get paid when you perform. But a second glance reveals that over the long run, the gains that you make for your employer are essentially canceled out by your losses; yet your compensation averages out at a very handsome $5 million per year. Presumably our friend at AIG doesn't think that he's flipping coins, and that my analogy is therefore fundamentally misconceived. He feels that his success is based on his skill, experience, and hard work, not luck, and that his colleagues committed errors of judgment that he has avoided. But of course, that's precisely what his colleagues were saying a year or two earlier when they were booking those huge profits that turned out to be illusory. So why should we believe him now any more than we should have believed them? More to the point, is there a way to structure pay-for-performance schemes that only reward real performance?

One increasingly popular approach is to pay bonuses that are effectively withheld by the employer for a number of years. The idea is that if outcomes are really random in the sense of a simple coin toss, then basing compensation on multiyear performance ought to average out some of that randomness. For example, if I take a risky position in some asset whose value booms this year and tanks a year from now, and my bonus is based on my performance over a three-year period, I won't receive any bonus at all. It's a reasonable idea, but as the recent real estate bubble demonstrated, faulty assumptions can appear valid for years at a time. So although stretching out the vesting period diminishes the role of luck in determining outcomes, it certainly doesn't eliminate it. In addition to averaging performance over an extended period, therefore, another way to try to differentiate individual talent from luck is to index performance relative to a peer group, meaning that a trader working in a particular asset class— say, interest rate swaps—should receive a bonus only for outperforming an index of all traders in that asset class. Put another way, if everybody in a particular market or industry makes money at the same time—as all the major investment banks did in the first quarter of 2010—we ought to suspect that performance is being driven by a secular trend, not individual talent.

Delaying bonuses and indexing performance to peers are worthy ideas, but they may still not solve the deeper problem of differentiating luck from talent. Consider, for example, the case of Bill Miller, the legendary mutual fund manager whose Value Trust beat the S&P 500 fifteen years straight—something no other mutual fund manager has ever accomplished. Over this period, Miller's success seems like a textbook case of talent trumping luck. He really did outperform his peers, year after year, for fifteen years—a winning streak that, as the investment strategist Michael Mauboussin has shown, would be extremely unlikely to have occurred in the historical population of fund managers if everyone were tossing proverbial coins.[9] At the end of his streak, therefore, it would have been hard to dispute that Miller was doing something special. But then, in the three-year period from 2006 to 2008, right after his record streak ended, Miller's performance was bad enough to reverse a large chunk of his previous gains, dragging his ten-year average below that of the S&P. So was he a brilliant investor who simply had some bad luck, or was he instead the opposite: a relatively ordinary investor whose ultimately flawed strategy just happened to work for a long time? The problem is that judging from his investing record alone, it's probably not possible to say. Just as Michael Raynor explained for business strategies, like Sony versus Matsushita in the video war described in Chapter 7, investing strategies can be successful or unsuccessful for several years in a row for reasons that have nothing to do with skill, and everything to do with luck. Naturally, it won't seem like luck, but there is no way to know that whatever story is concocted to explain that success isn't simply another manifestation of the Halo Effect.

To be sure that we are not just falling for the Halo Effect, we really need a different measure of performance altogether—one that assesses individual skill directly rather than by inferring it from outcomes that might be determined by forces beyond the individual's control. At the end of his streak, Miller was compared a lot with Joe DiMaggio, who had a famous hitting streak of fifty-six consecutive games during the 1941 baseball season. Superficially, the streaks are analogous, but in DiMaggio's case, we also know that his career batting average was 0.3246, which is the 44th highest in baseball history, and that during the time of the streak it was an astonishing .409.[10] So although there was still an element of luck in DiMaggio's streak, his skill ensured that he was more likely to be "lucky" than most other players.[11]

Ideally then, we would like to have the equivalent of a batting average to measure performance in different professions. But outside of sports, unfortunately, such statistics are not so easy to put together.[12] The reason is that outcomes in sports are generally repeated many times under close-to-identical conditions. A baseball player may have six hundred at-bats in a single season, and many thousands throughout his career, each one of which is, roughly speaking, an independent test of individual skill. Even for more ephemeral skills, like outstanding positional play in professional basketball, that are harder to measure directly but still help the team win, we have almost one hundred NBA games each season that we can watch to observe a player's effect on his team and on the outcome.[13] At first, it seems that an accomplishment like beating the S&P 500 for the year is a pretty good equivalent of a batting average for fund managers—and indeed fund managers with long streaks do tend to beat the S&P 500 more often than average, just like baseball players with high batting averages. By this measure, however, in a forty-year career a fund manager will get only forty "at-bats" total—simply not enough data to estimate the true value with any confidence.[14]

THE MATTHEW EFFECT

And finance is in many respects an easy case—because the existence of indices like the S&P 500 at least provide agreed-upon benchmarks against which an individual investor's performance can be measured. In business or politics or entertainment, however, there is much less agreement about how to measure individual skill, and even fewer independent trials over which to measure it. Most important of all, serial accomplishments are usually not *independent* demonstrations of skill in the way that, say, each of Roger Federer's grand slam victories in tennis are independent. One could argue that Federer's reputation can intimidate opponents, thereby giving him a psychological edge, or that tournament draws are organized in such a way that the top seeds don't play each other until the later rounds—all of which could be seen as an advantage deriving from his previous success. Nevertheless, every time Federer walks out on the court he has to win under more or less the same circumstances as the very first time he played professional tennis. No one would think it fair to give him, say, an extra serve, or the ability to overrule the referee, or any other advantage over his opponent, just because he's won so often in the past. Likewise, it would be outrageous to give the team that wins the first of seven games in an NBA playoff series ten extra points at the start of the second game. In sports, that is, we place tremendous importance on making the playing field as level as possible and every test of skill independent from every other.

Much of life, however, is characterized by what the sociologist Robert Merton called the Matthew Effect, named after a sentence from the book of Matthew in the Bible, which laments "For to all those who have, more will be given, and they will have an abundance; but from those who have nothing, even what they have will be taken away." Matthew was referring specifically to wealth (hence the phrase "the rich get richer and the poor get poorer"), but Merton argued that the same rule applied to success more generally. Success early on in an individual's career, that is, confers on them certain structural advantages that make subsequent successes much more likely, regardless of their intrinsic aptitude. In science, for example, junior scientists who land jobs at top research universities tend to experience lighter teaching loads, attract better graduate students, and have an easier time getting grants or publishing papers than their peers who end up at second- or third-tier universities. As a result, two individuals in the same field who may have been roughly comparable at the beginning of their careers may experience dramatically different levels of success five or ten years down the road on no more grounds than that they were hired at different institutions. And from there, it just gets more unequal still. Successful scientists also tend to receive a disproportionate share of the credit for anything with which they are associated, as when they write papers with unknown graduate students, who may have actually done most of the work or had the key ideas. Once someone is perceived as a star, in other words, not only can he attract more resources and better collaborators—thus producing far more than he would otherwise have been able to—he also tends to get more than his fair share of the credit for the resulting work.[15]

Merton was writing about scientific careers, but as the sociologist Daniel Rigney argues in his recent book *The Matthew Effect*, the same forces apply to most other careers as well. Success leads to prominence and recognition, which leads in turn to more opportunities to succeed, more resources with which to achieve success, and more likelihood of your subsequent successes being noticed and attributed to you. Isolating the effects of this accumulated advantage from differences in innate talent or hard work is difficult, but a number of studies have found that no matter how carefully one tries to select a pool of people with similar potential, their fortunes will diverge wildly over time, consistent with Merton's theory. For example, it is known that college students who graduate during a weak economy earn less, on average, than students who graduate in a strong economy. On its own, that doesn't sound too surprising, but the kicker is that this difference applies not just to the years of the recession itself, but continues to accumulate over decades. Because the timing of one's graduation obviously has nothing to do with one's innate talent, the persistence of these effects is strong evidence that the Matthew Effect is present everywhere.[16]

Typically we don't like to think that the world works this way. In a meritocratic society, we want to believe that successful people must be more talented or must have worked harder than their less-successful counterparts—at the very least they must have taken better advantage of their opportunities. Just as when we try to understand why some book became a bestseller, when we try to explain why some individual is rich or successful common sense insists that the outcome arises from some intrinsic quality of the object or person in question. A best-selling book must be good *somehow* or else people wouldn't have bought it. A wealthy man must be smart in *some* manner or else he wouldn't be rich. But what the Halo Effect and the Matthew Effect should teach us is that these commonsense explanations are deeply misleading. It may be true that abjectly incompetent people rarely do well, or that amazingly talented individuals rarely end up as total failures, but few of us fall into those extremes. For most of us, the combination of randomness and cumulative advantage means that relatively ordinary individuals can do very well, or very poorly, or anywhere in between. But because every individual's story is unique, we can always persuade ourselves that the outcome we have witnessed was somehow a product of their unique attributes.

None of this is to say, of course, that people, products, ideas, and companies don't have different qualities or abilities. Nor does it suggest that we should stop believing that quality *should* lead to success. What it does suggest, however, is that talent ought to be evaluated on its own terms. One doesn't have to know Roger Federer's ranking to appreciate that he is a great tennis player—you can tell that simply by watching him. In the same way, if everyone who knows Bill Miller agrees that he is an exceptionally smart and thoughtful investor, then he probably is. As Miller himself has emphasized, statistics like his fifteen-year streak are as much artifacts of the calendar as indicators of his talent.[17] Nor is it even the case that his talent ought to be judged by his cumulative career success—because that too could be undone by a single unlucky stroke. As unsatisfying as it may sound, therefore, our best bet for evaluating his talent may be simply to observe his investing process itself.[18] What we conclude may or may not correlate with his track record, and it is almost certainly a more difficult evaluation to perform. But whenever we find ourselves describing someone's ability in terms of societal measures of success—prizes, wealth, fancy titles—rather than in terms of what they are capable of doing, we ought to worry that we are deceiving ourselves. Put another way, the cynic's question, if you're so smart, why aren't you rich? is misguided not only for the obvious reason that at least some smart people care about rewards other than material wealth, but also because talent is talent, and success is success, and the latter does not always reflect the former.[19]

THE MYTH OF THE CORPORATE SAVIOR

If separating talent from success seems difficult, it is especially hard when performance is measured not in terms of individual actions, like an investment banker's portfolio, but rather the actions of an entire organization. To illustrate this problem, let's step away from bankers for a moment and ask a less-fashionable question: To what extent should Steve Jobs, founder and CEO of Apple Inc., be credited with Apple's recent success? Conventional wisdom holds that he is largely responsible for it, and not without reason. Since Jobs returned in the late 1990s to lead the company that he founded in 1976 with Steve Wozniak in a Silicon Valley garage, its fortunes have undergone a dramatic resurgence, producing a string of hit products like the iMac, the iPod, and the iPhone. As of the end of 2009, Apple had outperformed the overall stock market and its industry peers by about 150 percent over the previous six years, and in May 2010 Apple overtook Microsoft to become the most valuable technology company in the world. During all this time, Jobs has reportedly received neither a salary nor a cash bonus—his entire compensation has been in Apple stock.[20]

It's a compelling story, and the list of Apple's successes is long enough that it's hard to believe it's all due to chance. Nevertheless, because Apple's history can only be run once, we can't be sure that we aren't simply succumbing to the Halo Effect. For example, as, I discussed in Chapter 7, the iPod strategy had a number of elements that could easily have led it to fail, as did the iPhone. Microsoft CEO Steve Ballmer looks silly now for scoffing at the idea that consumers would pay $500 for a phone that locked consumers into a two-year contract with AT&T and didn't have a keyboard, but it was actually quite a reasonable objection. Both products now seem like strokes of genius, but only because they succeeded. Had they instead bombed, we would not be talking about Jobs's brilliant strategy and leadership that simply didn't work. Rather, we would be talking about his arrogance and unwillingness to pay attention to what the market wanted. As with all explanations that depend on the known outcome to account for why a particular strategy was good or bad, the conventional wisdom regarding Apple's recent success is vulnerable to the Halo Effect.

Quite aside from the Halo Effect, however, there is another potential problem with the conventional wisdom about Apple. And that is our tendency to attribute the lion's share of the success of an entire corporation, employing tens of thousands of talented engineers, designers, and managers to one individual. As with all commonsense explanations, the argument that Steve Jobs is the irreplaceable architect of Apple's success is entirely plausible. Not only did Apple's turnaround begin with Jobs's return, after a decade of exile, from 1986 to 1996, but his reputation as a fiercely demanding manager with a relentless focus on innovation, design, and engineering excellence would seem to draw a direct line between his approach to leadership and Apple's success. Finally, large companies like Apple need a way to coordinate the activities of many individuals on a common goal, and a strong leader seems required to accomplish this coordination feat. Because this *role* of leader is by definition unique, the leader seems unique also, and therefore justified in receiving the lion's share of the credit for the company's success.

Steve Jobs may in fact be such an individual—the sine qua non of Apple. But if he is, he is the exception rather than the rule in corporate life. As sociologist and Harvard Business School professor Rakesh Khurana argues in *Searching for a Corporate Savior,* corporate performance is generally determined less by the actions of CEOs than by outside factors, like the performance of the overall industry or the economy as a whole, over which individual leaders have no control.[21] Just as with the hubs and influencers that I discussed in Chapter 4, Khurana concludes that conventional explanations of success invoke the power of inspirational leaders not because the evidence supports that conclusion, but rather because without such a figure we do not have any intuitive understanding how a large, complex entity functions. Our need to see a company's success through the lens of a single powerful individual, Khurana explains, is the result of a combination of psychological biases and cultural beliefs—particularly in cultures like the United States, where individual achievement is so celebrated. The media, too, prefers simple, human-centered narratives to abstract explanations based on social, economic, and political forces. Thus we both gravitate to, and are also disproportionately exposed to, explanations that emphasize the influence of special individuals in directing the course of incredibly complex organizations and events.[22]

Reinforcing this mentality is the peculiar way in which corporate leaders are selected. Unlike regular markets, which are characterized by large numbers of buyers and sellers, publicly visible prices, and a high degree of substitutability, the labor market for CEOs is characterized by a small number of participants, many of whom are already socially or professionally connected, and operates almost entirely out of public scrutiny. The result is something like a self-fulfilling prophecy. Corporate boards, analysts, and the media all believe that only certain key people can make the "right" decisions; thus only a few such people are considered for the job in the first place. This artificial scarcity of candidates in turn empowers the winners to extract enormously generous compensation packages, which are then presented as evidence that "the market" has valued the candidate rather than a small group of like-minded individuals. Finally, the firm is then either successful, in which case obviously the "right" leader was chosen, or it is not successful, in which case the board made a mistake and a new leader is sought out. Sometimes "failed" CEOs walk away with huge severance packages, and it is these instances that tend to get all the attention. In Khurana's view, however, the outrage that is often expressed over these instances nevertheless perpetuates the mistaken belief that a firm's performance can be attributed to any one individual— even the CEO—in the first place. If boards were more willing to question the very idea of the irreplaceable CEO, and if searches for CEOs were then opened to a wider pool of candidates, it would be more difficult for candidates to negotiate such extravagant packages at the outset.[23]

THE INDIVIDUAL AND SOCIETY

Whether we can answer them or not, questions about how to differentiate luck from talent and individual contributions from collective performance can also inform our thinking about fairness and justice in society as a whole. This issue was raised in somewhat different language in a famous argument between the political philosophers Robert Nozick and John Rawls over what constitutes a just society. Nozick was a libertarian who believed that people, in essence, got what they had worked for, and therefore no one was entitled to take it from them, even if that meant putting up with large inequalities in society. Rawls, by contrast, asked what kind of society each of us would choose to live in if we didn't know beforehand where in the socioeconomic hierarchy we would end up. Rawls reasoned that any rational person would prefer an egalitarian society—one in which the worst off were as well off as possible—over one in which a few people were very rich and many were very poor, because the odds of being one of the very rich was so small.[24]

Nozick found Rawls's argument deeply disturbing, in large part because it attributed at least part of what an individual accomplishes to society rather than to his or her own efforts. If an individual cannot keep the output of his talent and hard work, Nozick's reasoning went, he is effectively being forced to work for someone else against his free will, and therefore does not fully "own" himself. Taxation, it follows, along with all other attempts to redistribute wealth, is the moral equivalent of slavery, and therefore unacceptable no matter what benefits it might confer on others. Nozick's argument was appealing to many people, and not only because it provided a philosophical rationale for low taxes. By reasoning about what would be considered fair in a hypothetical "state of nature," Nozick's arguments also played well to common-sense notions of individual success and failure. In a state of nature, that is, if one man invests the time and effort to build, say, a canoe for fishing, no one else is entitled to take it from him, even if it means that the man lacking the canoe will suffer or perish. Individual outcomes, in other words, are solely the product of individual efforts and skill.

And in a state of nature, Nozick might well be right. But the whole point of Rawls's argument was that we do not live in such a world. Rather, we live in a highly developed society in which disproportionately large rewards can accrue to individuals who happen to possess particular attributes and who experience the right opportunities. In the United States, for example, two equally skilled and disciplined athletes—one a world-class gymnast and the other a world-class basketball player—are likely to enjoy wildly different degrees of fame and fortune through no fault or merit of their own. Likewise, two children with indistinguishable genetic endowments—one of whom is born into a wealthy, highly educated, socially prestigious family, and the other who is born into a poor, socially isolated family with no history of educational achievement—have dramatically different prospects for lifetime success.[25] Finally, even random differences in opportunities that arise early in one's career can accumulate, via the Matthew Effect, to generate large differences in outcomes over the course of a lifetime. Rawls's claim was that because the mechanisms of inequality are essentially accidents—whether of birth, or of talent, or of opportunity—a just society is one in which the adverse effects of these accidents is minimized.

Rawls's claim is often misunderstood to mean that inequality of any kind is undesirable, but this is not at all what he was saying. Allowing for the possibility that through hard work and application of one's talents one can do better than one's peers is no doubt beneficial for society as a whole—just as libertarians believe. In a Rawlsian world, therefore, people are free to do whatever they want, and are perfectly within their rights to take whatever they can according to the rules of the game. And if the rules of the game have it that basketball players earn more than gymnasts, or investment bankers earn more than teachers, so be it. Rawls's point was just that the rules of the game themselves should be chosen to satisfy social, not individual, ends. Bankers, in other words, are entitled to whatever they are able to negotiate with their employers, but they are not entitled to an economic system in which the financial industry is so much more profitable than any other.

The counterintuitive consequence of this argument is that debates over individual compensation should not be conducted at the level of individuals. If it's true that bankers are paid too much, in other words, the solution is not to get into the messy business of regulating individual pay—as indeed the financial industry itself has argued. Instead, it is to make banking less profitable overall, say by limiting how much banks and hedge funds can leverage their portfolios with borrowed money, or by forcing so-called over-the-counter derivatives to be traded on public exchanges. The financial industry could argue, of course, that leverage and customization offer benefits to their customers and to the broader economy as well as to themselves. And these claims, although self-serving, may have merit. But if the purported benefits are outweighed by the economic costs of increased risk to the economic system as a whole, then there is nothing inherently unjust about society changing the rules. We can argue about whether making banking a less profitable industry would, on balance, be a good or a bad thing for society, but that's what the debate should be about—not about whether particular individuals deserve their $10-million bonuses. Libertarian arguments about what would or would not be fair in a state of nature are simply irrelevant, because in a state of nature nobody would be getting a $10-million bonus.

For much the same reasons, arguments about the so-called redistribution of wealth are mistaken in assuming that the existing distribution is somehow the natural state of things, from which any deviation is unnatural, and hence morally undesirable. In reality, *every* distribution of wealth reflects a particular set of choices that a society has made: to value some skills over others; to tax or prohibit some activities while subsidizing or encouraging other activities; and to enforce some rules while allowing other rules to sit on the books, or to be violated in spirit. All these choices can have considerable ramifications for who gets rich and who doesn't—as recent revelations about explicit and implicit government subsidies to student lenders and multinational oil companies exemplify.[26] But there is nothing "natural" about any of these choices, which are every bit as much the product of historical accident, political expediency, and corporate lobbying as they are of economic rationality or social desirability. If some political actor, say the president or Congress, attempts to alter some of these choices, say by shifting the tax burden from the working class to the superrich, or by taxing consumption rather than income, or by eliminating subsidies to various industries, then it is certainly valid to argue about whether the proposed changes make sense on their merits. But it is not valid to oppose them simply on the grounds that altering the distribution of wealth itself is wrong in principle.

PRIVATIZE THE GAINS, SOCIALIZE THE LOSSES

Arguments about the claims that society can justly make on its members are also relevant to questions of accountability. For example, a great deal has been written recently about whether the banks and other financial firms that pose a serious systemic risk should be allowed to exist in the first place.[27] Much of this discussion has revolved around whether it is the size or interconnectedness or some other attribute of a financial institution that determines how much risk its failure might create for the rest of the economy. Addressing these questions is important, if only to understand better how to measure systemic risk, and hopefully to limit it through thoughtful regulation. But it is also possible that there is no way to eliminate systemic risk in financial systems, or to guarantee the robustness and stability of any complex interconnected system. Power-transmission grids are generally able to withstand the failure of individual transmission lines and generators, but occasionally a seemingly innocuous failure can cascade throughout the entire system, knocking out hundreds of power stations and affecting millions of consumers—as has happened several times in recent years in the United States, Europe, and Brazil.[28] Likewise, our most sophisticated engineering creations, such as nuclear reactors, commercial aircraft, and space shuttles, all of which are designed to maximize safety, occasionally suffer catastrophic failures. Even the Internet, which is extremely robust to physical failures of all kinds, turns out to be highly vulnerable to a whole range of nonphysical threats, including chronic spam, Internet worms, botnets, and denial-of-service attacks. It may be, in fact, that once a system has attained a certain level of complexity, there is no way to rule out the possibility of fail-ure.[29] If so, we need not only better tools for thinking about systemic risk, but also a better way of thinking about how to respond to systemic failures when they inevitably occur.

To illustrate, consider the response of the banking commu-nity to the Obama administration's proposal to tax certain trading profits as a way to recoup taxpayer bailout money. In the bankers' view, they had already paid back their bailout money—with interest—and therefore nothing more could le-gitimately be asked of them. But imagine for a moment what the banking industry profits *would have* been in 2009 absent the several hundred billion dollars of government funds from which they benefited both directly and indirectly. We can never know for sure, of course, because we didn't run that experiment, but we can make some educated guesses. AIG, for one, would probably not exist and its various counterpar-ties, including Goldman Sachs, would be short several tens of billions of dollars that were funneled to them through AIG. Citigroup might well have collapsed, and Merrill Lynch, Bear Stearns, and Lehman Brothers might all have been dissolved rather than merged with other banks.

All told, the banking industry might have lost tens of bil-lions of dollars in 2009—quite the opposite of the tens of billions they actually made—and many thousands of bank-ers who in reality received bonuses would instead have been out of work. Now imagine that in the fall of 2008 the lead-ers of Goldman Sachs, J.P. Morgan, Citigroup, and the like were offered a choice between the "systemic support" world in which they were guaranteed government support and the "libertarian" world in which they would be left hung out to dry. Forget for a moment the devastation that would have been wreaked on the rest of the economy, and ask how much of their future compensation the banks would have been willing to concede in order to not be allowed to fail? Again, it's a hypothetical question, but with their very survival in the balance it seems safe to assume that they would have agreed to commit more than the face value of their direct loans.

That the banks and their allies have instead managed to portray themselves as victims of stifling government intervention and political populism run amok is therefore disingenuous, and not only for the obvious reason that the banks benefited from considerable government largess other than direct loans.[30] The real reason is philosophical consistency. When times are good, banks wish to be perceived as independent risk-taking entities, entitled to the full fruits of their hard-won labors. But during a crisis they wish to be treated as critical elements in a larger system to which their failure would pose an existential threat. Whether this latter claim is true because they are too big or too interconnected, or for any other reason, is actually not so important. The real point is that either they are libertarians, who should bear the full weight of their own failures as well as their successes, or else they are Rawlsians, paying their dues to the system that takes care of them. They should not be able to switch philosophies at their convenience.

BEARING EACH OTHER'S BURDENS

In his recent book *Justice*, the philosopher Michael Sandel makes a similar point, arguing that all questions of fairness and justice have to be adjudicated in light of how dependent we are on each other—most obviously, on our networks of friends, family, colleagues, and classmates, but also on our communities, on our national and ethnic identities, and even on our distant ancestors. We are proud of what "our" people have accomplished, we protect them against outsiders, and we come to their aid when necessary. We feel that we owe them our loyalty for no reason other than that we are connected to them, and we expect them to reciprocate. It should come as no surprise, therefore, that social networks play a critical role in our lives, connecting us with resources, providing information and support, and facilitating transactions on the basis of mutual trust and assumed respect. So embedded are we in networks of social relations that it would be hard to imagine ourselves outside of them.[31]

So far, this view seems uncontroversial. Even Margaret Thatcher, who claimed that "there is no such thing as society," conceded that families mattered as well as individuals. But Sandel argues that the importance of social networks has a counterintuitive consequence for the notion of individual freedom. Whatever we might like to think, we are never entirely free, nor would we want to be. The very ties that give our lives meaning also constrain us, and it is precisely *by* constraining us that they give us meaning. From Sandel's perspective, it makes no more sense to reason about fairness or justice exclusively from the perspective of individual freedom than it does to reason about what is fair exclusively by analogy with some imaginary state of nature. Neither is an accurate representation of the world in which we actually live. Like it or not, our notions of justice must deal with this tension between the individual and society as a whole. Yet this can be easier said than done. For example, Sandel argues that one ought not to feel proud of one's heritage as an American without also feeling shame about the country's history of slavery. Libertarians might argue that it was their ancestors, not them, who carried out such reprehensible deeds and therefore they have nothing to apologize for. But surely these same people are also proud of their ancestry, and would rather live in this country than in any other. In Sandel's view, one cannot simply decide at one's convenience when to identify with one's ancestors and when to absolve oneself of them. Either you're a part of that extended community, in which case you must share the costs as well as the benefits, or you're not, in which case you get neither.

Sandel's argument that our individual actions are inextricably embedded in networks of social relations has consequences not only for arguments about fairness and justice, but also for morality and virtue. In fact, Sandel argues that one cannot determine what is fair without also evaluating the moral status of competing claims. And that in turn requires us to resolve the moral purpose of social institutions. We cannot decide whether gay marriage is right or just, for example, without first deciding what the point of marriage is. We cannot determine whether a particular university's admission criteria are fair or unfair until we have first determined what the purpose of a university is. And we cannot decide if the way bankers are compensated is appropriate without first establishing what it is that banking should accomplish for society. In this respect, Sandel's view harks back to the ancient philosophy of Aristotle, who also believed that questions of justice require reasoning about the purpose of things. Unlike Aristotle, however, Sandel does not espouse a view of purpose that is determined outside of the social system itself—say by divine decree. Rather, purpose is something that the members of a society must decide collectively. Sandel therefore concludes that a just society is not one that seeks to adjudicate disputes between individuals from a morally neutral perspective, but one that facilitates debate about what the appropriate moral perspective ought to be. As Sandel acknowledges, this is likely to be a messy affair and always a work in progress, but he does not see any way around it.

What's particularly interesting about Sandel's arguments—at least to a sociologist—is how sociological they are. Sociologists, for example, have long believed that the meaning of individual action can only be properly understood in the context of interlocking networks of relationships—a concept that is called embeddedness.[32] Even more so, Sandel's claim that the values by which we judge fairness are necessarily the product of society reflects the idea, first advanced by sociologists in the 1960s, that social reality is a construction of society itself—not something that is handed to us by some external world.[33] An important implication of Sandel's argument, therefore, is that the fundamental questions of political philosophy are sociological questions as well.

How are we to answer these questions then? Certainly thinking about them in the way that Sandel does is one approach, and that has generally been the way that sociologists have approached them as well. But relying on unaided intuition to reason through these sorts of questions can also be limiting. It's fine to argue, as many people have argued recently, that banks whose actions result in systemic risk ought to be held accountable for that risk, say by purchasing "systemic risk" insurance or being required to increase their capital reserves. But without a sound understanding of systemic risk, it is impossible to measure how much systemic risk a particular action creates, and therefore how much of a penalty ought to be imposed for taking it. Likewise, it is one thing to point out that we place too much emphasis on outcomes when evaluating processes, or attribute too much importance to "special people" in determining those outcomes. But it is quite another to come up with better measures of performance and a better sense of how complex social systems like companies, markets, and societies actually work. As important as it is to think through these issues, in other words, it is also important to do more than simply argue about them. And on this point it is worth asking what, if anything, social science might be able to offer.

CHAPTER 10

The Proper Study of Mankind

Know then thyself, presume not God to scan,
The proper study of mankind is Man.
—Alexander Pope, "An Essay on Man"

When Alexander Pope published his "Essay on Man" in 1732 our understanding of the world was very different from what it is today. Written just decades after Isaac Newton's masterpiece, *Principia,* had laid out the mathematical principles of planetary motion, Pope's essay arrived when intellectuals were still wrapping their heads around a concept that must have been staggering at the time—that the laws governing the motion of everyday objects here on Earth were exactly the same laws as those governing the heavenly spheres. In fact, they were still grappling with the idea that physical "laws" of any kind could be written down in terms of mathematical equations, and that these equations could then be used to predict with uncanny precision the future behavior of everything ranging from tomorrow's high tide to the return of distant comets. It must have been a magical time to be alive when the universe, so long an enigma, seemed suddenly to have been conquered by the mind of a single man. As Pope himself said,

Nature and Nature's laws lay hid in night:
God said, Let Newton be! and all was light.[1]

For the next three centuries, the knowledge of mankind would swell inexorably, sweeping before it the mysteries of the world. The results have been impressive. We have theories of the universe that go all the way back to the big bang, and telescopes that peer across galaxies. We have sent space probes out of the solar system and put men on the moon. We have built bombs that can level an entire city, and missiles that can fly through a window. We have measured the earth to great precision and understood its inner workings. We have engineered immense buildings and bridges, and changed the shape of rivers, mountains, even coastlines. We have clocks that can measure time in billionths of a second, and computers that can search through every word ever written in less time than it takes to write just one. In science, it seems, we can make the angels dance on the head of a pin.

It's pretty obvious that social science has not kept up, but it's easy to infer the wrong lesson from this observation. I was reminded of this problem recently by a physicist colleague of mine who complained to me that he'd been reading a lot of sociology, and that in his opinion the problem with the discipline was that it hadn't discovered any laws of human behavior that were anywhere near as general or accurate as those he was accustomed to in physics. Instead, it seemed to him, sociology was just an endless conglomeration of special cases, when someone did something for some reason one time, and someone else did something else for some other reason at another time. As a physicist, he found this lack of lawlike behavior particularly frustrating. After all, it is hard to imagine how any of the remarkable progress in physics could have occurred in the absence of laws like Newton's that apply generally across time and space. So integral to the success of science have these laws been, in fact, that they have come to be associated with the very idea of science itself. Surely, he felt, the inability of sociologists to come up with anything remotely comparable meant that social science didn't really deserve to be thought of as science at all.

PHYSICS ENVY

As it turns out, this tendency to judge sociology by the standards of physics is an old one, going all the way back to Auguste Comte, the nineteenth-century philosopher who is often credited as the founding father of sociology. Comte imagined that sociology, which he even called social physics, would take its place alongside mathematics, astronomy, physics, chemistry, and biology as one of the six fundamental sciences describing all of reality. Sociology in Comte's view would be a "total theory" of all human experience, encompassing all the other sciences and extending them to account for cultures, institutions, economies, politics, everything—exactly the kind of general theory that my physicist friend was looking for. Comte never got around to articulating this theory in any detail, but his philosophy of positivism—the idea that social entities and forces can be described and analyzed in the same way as physical entities and forces—set the stage for all the grand theories that followed.

One of the first such theories was proposed shortly after Comte by the philosopher Herbert Spencer, a contemporary of Darwin's. Spencer advanced the notion that societies could be understood as organisms, where individual humans could be thought of as cells, institutions played the role of organs, and development was driven by some loose analog of natural selection. It was Spencer, in fact, not Darwin, who coined the phrase "survival of the fittest." Spencer's specific ideas were quickly rejected as naïve, but his basic philosophical claim that societies are organized the way they are in order to serve some holistic function persisted alongside Comte's positivism, and informed the thinking of sociologists such as Émile Durkheim, who is still considered one of the giant figures of the discipline.

The apotheosis of grand theorizing, however, didn't arrive until the mid-twentieth century in the work of Harvard sociologist Talcott Parsons, who advanced a brand of theory that became known as structural functionalism. According to Parsons, social institutions were made up of networks of interlocking roles, which in turn were played by individuals who were motivated by rational ends. At the same time, however, individual action was constrained by social norms, laws, and other mechanisms of control that were encoded in the institutions of which the individuals were a part.[2] By exhaustively classifying all the various functions that different sorts of behavior could satisfy, along with the different social and cultural structures in which they took place, Parsons attempted nothing less than to describe all of society. It was a grand edifice indeed, and Parsons's name is generally listed among the great social theorists of the ages. But as with Spencer and Comte before him, the ink was scarcely dry on Parsons's "general theory" before the critics tore it apart: it said little more than that "people do things because they want to," it was not really a theory at all, but just a "set of concepts and definitions," and it was so complicated that nobody could understand it.[3]

Looking back on the wreckage of Parsons's theory some years later, Robert Merton—the sociologist whose work on the Matthew Effect I discussed in the previous chapter—

concluded that social theorists had been too quick to try to emulate the theoretical successes of their physicist colleagues. It wasn't that Merton didn't sympathize with the envy that physicists could inspire in others. As he put it, "Many sociologists take the achievements of physics as the standard for self-appraisal. They want to compare biceps with their bigger brothers. They, too, want to *count*. And when it becomes evident that they neither have the rugged physique nor pack the murderous wallop of their big brothers, some sociologists despair. They begin to ask: is a science of society really possible unless we institute a total system of sociology?" Although sympathetic, Merton cautioned that "this perspective ignores the fact that between twentieth century physics and twentieth century sociology stand billions of hours of sustained, disciplined, and cumulative research." In physics, it was only after Copernicus and Brahe and a host of others had conducted centuries' worth of painstaking observations that astronomers like Kepler sought out mathematical regularities that could account for the data they had inherited. And *only then* was a singular genius like Newton in a position to reduce these regularities to bona fide laws. By contrast, the social theorists Merton was describing had gone about it the other way around, proposing whole systems of thought at the outset and only then worrying about what it was that they needed to measure.[4] "Perhaps," Merton lamented, "sociology is not yet ready for its Einstein because it has not yet found its Kepler—to say nothing of its Newton, Laplace, Gibbs, Maxwell, or Planck."[5]

Rather than questing after grand theories or universal laws of human behavior, therefore, Merton instead advocated that sociologists should focus on developing "theories of the middle range," meaning theories that are broad enough to account for more than isolated phenomena but specific enough to say something concrete and useful. For example, the "theory of relative deprivation" states that people feel distressed by circumstances only inasmuch as their hardship exceeds that of the people around them. Thus if your house burns down in a freak fire, you're devastated, but if your whole city is wiped out in an earthquake and hundreds of your neighbors die, you feel lucky to be alive. It's not a completely general theory, claiming only to predict how people respond to adversity, but it also aims to apply to perceptions of adversity quite broadly. Likewise, the "theory of the role set" stresses that each individual plays not only multiple roles—a teacher at school, a father at home, a catcher on the weekend softball team—but also that each of these roles is itself a collection of relationships: between a teacher and his students, between him and his colleagues, and between him and his principal. Again, the theory is somewhat specific—saying nothing about markets or governments, or other important features of the social world—but also somewhat general, applying to people of all kinds.[6]

Merton's call for middle-range theories is generally regarded as sensible, but it didn't quell the ardor for theories of a grander nature. Barely a year after Merton published his critique, in fact, the economist John Harsanyi, who shared the 1994 Nobel memorial Prize in Economics for his work on game theory, proposed that rational choice theory—the theory of human decision making that I discussed in Chapter 2—was ready to provide precisely the kind of general theory that Merton has just concluded was wildly premature. And so another cycle began, with rational choice theorists drawing parallels between their efforts and Newtonian mechanics, while critics increasingly leveled the same complaints against it that the rational choice theorists themselves had made about the previous round of theories like Parsons's.[7] Nor has the growing realization that rational choice theory cannot provide a universal theory of human behavior any more than its predecessors could yet delivered social science from the green-eyed monster of physics envy.[8] Quite to the contrary, if the complaint of my physicist colleague is anything to go by, even if sociologists have finally gotten tired of grand theories of everything, there is a whole generation of physicists waiting to step into the breach.[9]

When you think about the sheer complexity of human behavior, this approach to doing social science seems kind of implausible. As I discussed in Chapter 2, individual behavior is complicated by dozens of psychological biases, many of which operate outside of our conscious awareness and interact in as-yet-unknown ways. And as I discussed in Chapter 3, when individuals interact with one another, their collective behavior may simply not be derivable from their individual attributes and incentives, no matter how much you know about them. Given that the real complexity of the social world—involving not just people and groups, but also a bewildering array of markets, governments, firms, and other institutions that we have created for ourselves—is so much greater than I have even begun to describe here, why on earth would any one person even *think* that they could write down a set of rules that could explain it all?

My answer is that social theorists are people too, and so they make the same mistake that planners, politicians, marketers, and business strategists make, which is to dramatically underestimate the difficulty of what they are trying to do. And just like planners, politicians, and so on, no matter how many times such grand theories fail, there is always someone new who thinks that it can't be that difficult—because, after all, "it's not rocket science." If much of what sociology has to offer seems like common sense, in other words, it is not just because everything about human behavior seems obvious once you know the answer. Part of the problem is also that social scientists, like everyone else, participate in social life and so feel as if they can understand why people do what they do simply by thinking about it. It is not surprising, therefore, that many social scientific explanations suffer from the same weaknesses—ex post facto assertions of rationality, representative individuals, special people, and correlation substituting for causation—that pervade our commonsense explanations as well.

MEASURING THE UNMEASURABLE

One response to this problem, as Lazarsfeld's colleague Samuel Stouffer noted more than sixty years ago, is for sociologists to depend *less* on their common sense, not more, and instead try to cultivate uncommon sense.[10] But getting away from commonsense reasoning in sociology is easier said than done. In large part the difficulty is that for most of the history of social science, it simply hasn't been possible to *measure* the elements of social phenomena the way we measure the elements of physical and biological phenomena. Social phenomena, as I have already noted, consist of large populations of people interacting with and influencing one another as well as with the organizations and governments they create—none of which is easy to observe directly, let alone put in a lab.[11]

Recently, however, the world has begun to change in ways that may lift some of these historical limitations on social science. Communication technologies, like e-mail, cell phones, and instant messaging now implicitly trace out social networks among billions of individuals, along with the flow of information among them. Online communities such as Facebook, Twitter, Wikipedia, and World of Warcraft facilitate interactions among people in ways that both promote new kinds of social activity and also record it. Crowdsourcing sites like Amazon's Mechanical Turk are increasingly being used as "virtual labs" in which researchers can run psychological and behavioral experiments.[12] And Web search, online media, and electronic commerce are generating ever-increasing insight into the intentions and actions of people everywhere. The capability to observe the actions and interactions of potentially billions of people presents some serious issues about the rights and privacy of individuals, and so we must proceed with caution.[13] Nevertheless, these technologies also exhibit enormous scientific potential, allowing us for the first time in history to observe, in high fidelity, the real-time behavior of large groups, and even societies as a whole.

For example, the Music Lab experiments that I discussed in Chapter 3, which showed the importance of social influence in determining success, involved nearly thirty thousand participants. One could have dreamed up this experiment fifty years ago—back when social psychologists were first pioneering experimental studies of influence and group decision making—but it would have been impossible to conduct it until recently for the simple reason that you can't fit that many people in a physical lab. Likewise, the "influencers" study on Twitter that I discussed in Chapter 4 was designed to answer a question—about whether or not special individuals cause information to spread—that has been around for decades. Answering it, however, required us to track the diffusion of more than 70 million URLs over the entire Twitter network for a two-month period. Prior to social networking services like Twitter and Facebook, which, remember, are just a few years old, that level of scale and resolution would have been impossible.[14]

Other experiments that I have described, like the Small World experiment from Chapter 4, were certainly possible in the pre-Internet era, but not on the scale at which they can now be conducted. Milgram's original experiment, for example, used physical letters and relied on just three hundred individuals attempting to reach a single person in Boston. The e-mail–based experiment that my colleagues and I conducted back in 2002 involved more than sixty thousand people directing messages to one of eighteen targets, who in turn were located in thirteen countries. In the course of being delivered, the message chains passed through more than 160 different countries; thus for all its limitations, the experiment was at least a crude test of the small-world hypothesis on a truly global scale. Likewise, David Reiley and Randall Lewis's field experiment on ad effectiveness, described in Chapter 8, was similar in design to experiments that had been conducted in the past, but with 1.6 million participants, it was many times larger. The sheer scale of the exercise is impressive simply on the grounds that it can be done at all, but it's also important scientifically—because it's possible that the effects, while real, can be small, in which case one needs very large numbers to tease them out of the noise.[15]

BIRDS OF A FEATHER

Another kind of study that would have been impossible to conduct until recently concerns one of the most widely observed patterns in social life, known in sociology as the homophily principle—the idea that "birds of a feather flock together." For several decades now, wherever sociologists have looked they have found that friends, spouses, coworkers, and social acquaintances are more similar than strangers with respect to a whole range of attributes—like race, age, gender, income, education—and also attitudes. But where does all this similarity come from? At first, the answer seems obvious: People are likely to form ties with others who are similar because, rightly or wrongly, that's whom they'd prefer to spend their time with. But what this commonsense explanation overlooks is that people can only choose their friends from among the people they actually meet, which is determined to a large extent by the people they work with, or who belong to the same organizations, or to whom they are introduced by mutual acquaintances. And as sociologists have also shown, many of these social environments tend to be highly homogeneous in terms of race, gender, age, and education. As a result, it is entirely possible that the similarity we see around us has less to do with our own psychological preferences than the restricted opportunities that the world presents to us.[16]

Resolving problems like this one is important because it has implications for how we go about dealing with controversial issues like racial segregation and affirmative action. Settling the matter with data, however, is extremely difficult because disentangling the various cause-and-effect relationships requires one to keep track of individuals, networks, and groups over extended intervals of time.[17] And historically, that sort of data just hasn't been available. Communication technologies like e-mail, however, have the potential to change all that. Because reciprocated e-mails for the most part represent real relationships, it is possible to use e-mail exchanges as a way to observe underlying social networks. And because e-mail servers can easily log the interactions among thousands or even millions of individuals over long periods of time, it is possible to reconstruct the evolution of even very large networks in great detail. Combine this sort of information with other data that is routinely collected by firms, universities, and other organizations about their members, and a rough approximation of the more complete picture starts to emerge.

Recently my former graduate student Gueorgi Kossinets and I used exactly this kind of approach to study the origins of homophily within the students, faculty, and staff of a university community. As with previous studies, we found that acquaintances—meaning people who exchanged e-mail on a regular basis—were considerably more similar on a range of attributes such as age, gender, academic major, and so on than strangers. We also found that similar people who were not acquainted were more likely than dissimilar people to connect to each other over time—just as common sense would contend. Finally, however, we found that individuals who were already "close" to each other, either because they shared mutual friends or belonged to the same groups, were more similar than distant pairs, and that most of the bias toward connecting similar individuals disappeared once we accounted for the effects of proximity. Our conclusion was that although the individuals in our community did exhibit some preference for others who were similar, it was a relatively weak preference that had been amplified over time, by successive "rounds" of choices, to generate the appearance of a much stronger preference in the observed network.[18]

Another problem to do with homophily that the Internet may help to answer is one that political scientists and sociologists have long worried about—namely, that Americans, whether by choice or by circumstance, are increasingly associating with like-minded neighbors and acquaintances. If true, the trend is thought to be problematic, as homogeneous social circles can also lead to a more balkanized society in which differences of opinion lead to political conflict rather than exchanges of ideas among equals. But is there actually any such trend? Political scientists generally agree that Congress is indeed more polarized now than at almost any point in history, and that the media is not much better. However, studies of polarization among ordinary citizens have tended to reach conflicting conclusions: Some find that it has increased dramatically while others point to levels of agreement that have changed little in decades.[19] One possible explanation for these contradictory results is that people think that they agree with their friends much more than they actually do; thus much of the polarization may be perceived rather than real. But testing this hypothesis, although simple in theory, is difficult in practice. The reason is that in order to measure whether friends agree as much as they think they do, one would need to ask, for every issue of interest, and for every pair of friends A and B, what A thinks about the issue, what B thinks about the issue, and what A thinks B thinks about it. Do this for lots of issues and many pairs of individuals, and you have a tremendously laborious survey exercise, especially if you also have to get each respondent to name friends and then go track them down.[20]

On Facebook, however, it's relatively straightforward. Everyone has already declared who their friends are, and it's even possible to differentiate different strengths of friendships, by counting how many mutual friends they share.[21] Equally important, in 2007 Facebook launched their third-party developer "platform," which allowed outside programmers to write their own applications that would then "run" on Facebook's underlying network. The result was *Friend Sense*, an application that my Yahoo! colleagues Sharad Goel and Winter Mason built over the course of a few weeks in early 2008 that asked people what they thought about a range of social and economic issues, and also what they thought their friends thought about them. By Facebook standards, Friend

Sense was a modest success—about 1,500 people signed up to use it, generating nearly 100,000 responses. But by network survey standards it was quite large. Using traditional interview methods, a study of this scale would have taken a couple of years to plan, fund, and run, and would have cost a couple of hundred thousand dollars (mostly to pay interviewers). On Facebook, we spent a few thousand dollars for ads and had our data in a matter of weeks.

What we found was that friends are indeed more similar than strangers, and that close friends and friends who say they talk about politics are more similar than casual acquaintances—just as the homophily principle would predict. But friends, whether close or not, also consistently believe themselves to be more similar than they actually are. In particular, our respondents were very bad at guessing when one of their friends—even a close friend with whom they discussed politics—disagreed with them. Here, the numbers were borne out by a series of anecdotal reports we received from people who had participated in Friend Sense, and who were frequently dismayed by how their friends and loved ones perceived them: "How could they think that I thought that?" was a frequent refrain. Many of our participants also reported having the experience of being asked a question about someone they thought they knew well, only to realize that they didn't know the answer—even though it seemed like a subject that educated, politically engaged friends ought to be talking about.[22]

So if talking about politics only slightly improves our ability to detect when our friends disagree with us, then what exactly are we talking about? More to the point, in the absence of specific information about what our friends really think about particular issues, what information are we using to guess what they think? By conducting a series of additional analyses, we concluded that when in doubt, which is more often than we'd like to admit, we guess at our friends' views in part by using simple stereotypes—for example, "my friends are mostly left-wing liberal types, and so probably espouse typical left-wing liberal views"—and in part by "projecting" our own views onto them.[23] This last finding is potentially important, because, going back to Lazarsfeld, social and marketing scientists alike have long thought that changes in political opinions are determined more by word-of-mouth influence than by what people hear or see in the mass media. But if it turns out that when thinking about their friends' beliefs people are really just seeing their own beliefs reflected back at them, one has to wonder how much they can really be influenced. Friend Sense, unfortunately, wasn't designed to answer questions about social influence, but other researchers have already begun to run experimental studies of influence on Facebook, so hopefully we will have better answers soon.[24]

Of course, there are all sorts of problems associated with using electronic records, whether they are derived from e-mail exchanges or Facebook friends, as substitutes for "real" social connections. How do we know, for example, what kind of relationship is implied by a connection on Facebook, or how much of all the communication between two people is captured by their e-mail exchanges? I may e-mail my coworkers many times a day and my mother only once or twice a week, but this observation alone says little about the nature and relative importance of these relationships. I may use e-mail to conduct some interactions while preferring text messages, Facebook, or face-to-face meetings to conduct others. And even where I do use the same medium to communicate with different people, some acts of communication may simply be more meaningful than others. From communication frequency alone, therefore, there is only so much one can infer about a given relationship. Nor is it even clear exactly which relationships we ought to care about in the first place. For some purposes, like understanding the efficiency of work-related teams, ties between coworkers might be the only ones that matter, whereas for other purposes, like understanding religious or political beliefs, work relationships might be far less relevant. To discover how a fast-moving rumor spreads, it may matter only with whom you have communicated in the past few days, whereas for information that can spread only through networks of trust, the ties that matter may be those that have persisted for years.[25]

There are many unresolved issues like these that currently limit our ability to draw meaningful sociological inferences from electronic data, no matter how much of it we can acquire. Sheer quantity on its own is certainly not a panacea. Nevertheless, the rapidly increasing availability of observational data, along with the ability to conduct experiments on a previously unimaginable scale, is allowing social scientists to imagine a world where at least some forms of collective human behavior can be measured and understood, possibly even predicted, in the way in which scientists in other fields have long been accustomed.

MESSY MATTERS

It isn't clear where these new capabilities will lead social science, but it probably won't be to the kind of simple universal laws that social theorists like Comte and Parsons dreamt of. Nor should it, for the simple reason that the social world probably isn't governed by any such laws. Unlike gravity, which works the same way at all times and in all places, homophily originates partly out of psychological preferences and partly out of structural constraints. Unlike mass and acceleration, which are defined unambiguously, influence is sometimes concentrated and sometimes distributed, while success derives from a complicated mix of individual choices, social constraints, and random chance. Unlike physical forces, which can be neatly summed to determine their action on a mass, performance is driven by some complicated interaction between extrinsic incentives and intrinsic motivation. And unlike physical reality, which operates with or without us, there is no dissociating social "reality" from our perception of it, where perceptions are driven as much by our own psychological biases as by externally observable attributes.

The social world, in other words, is far messier than the physical world, and the more we learn about it, the messier it is likely to seem. The result is that we will probably never have a science of sociology that will resemble physics. But that's OK. Just because physics has experienced such great success on the strength of a small number of very general laws doesn't mean that that's the only way for science to proceed. Biology doesn't really have universal laws either, and yet biologists still manage to make progress. Surely the real nature of science is not to exhibit any particular form at all, but rather to follow scientific procedures—of theory, observation, and experiment—that incrementally and iteratively chip away at the mysteries of the world. And surely the point of these procedures is not to discover laws of any particular kind, but rather to figure things out—to solve problems. So the less we worry about looking for general laws in social science, and the more we worry about solving actual problems, the more progress we are likely to make.

But what kinds of problems can we hope to solve? More to the point—to return to the question that I raised in the Preface—what can social scientists hope to discover that an ordinary intelligent person couldn't figure out on his or her own? Surely any thoughtful person could figure out just by introspection that we are all influenced by the opinions of our family and friends, that context matters, and that all things are relative. Surely such a person could know without the aid of social science that perceptions matter, or that people care about more than just money. Likewise, a moment's introspection would suggest that success is at least partly luck, that prophecies can be self-fulfilling, and that even the best-laid plans tend to suffer from the law of unintended consequences. Any thoughtful person knows, of course, that the future is unpredictable, and that past performance is no guarantee of future returns. He or she would also know that humans are biased and sometimes irrational, that political systems are rife with inefficiencies and contradictions, that spin sometimes trumps substance, and that simple stories can obscure complicated truths. He or she may even know—or at least have heard it enough to believe it—that everyone is connected to everyone else by just "six degrees of separation." When the subject is human behavior, in other words, it is actually hard to imagine anything that social scientists could possibly discover that wouldn't sound obvious to a thoughtful person, no matter how difficult it might have been to figure it out.

What isn't obvious, however, is how all these "obvious" things fit together. We know, for example, that people influence each other, and we know that hit movies, books, and songs are many times more successful than the average. But what we don't know is how—or even if—the forces of social influence operating at the level of the individual drive inequality and unpredictability at the scale of entire markets. Likewise, we know that people in social networks tend to cluster together in relatively homogeneous groups. But what we can't infer from our own observations of the world is whether these patterns are driven by psychological preferences or structural constraints. Nor is it obvious that it is because of this local clustering, rather than in spite of it, that individuals can navigate through very large networks to reach distant strangers in only a small number of steps. At some level, we accept that the future is unpredictable, but we do not know how much of that unpredictability could be eliminated simply by thinking through the possibilities more carefully, and how much is inherently random in the way that a roll of the dice is random. Even less clear to us is how this balance between predictability and unpredictability ought to change the kinds of strategies we deploy to prepare for future contingencies, or the kinds of explanations we come up with for the outcomes we observed.

It is in resolving these sorts of puzzles that social science can hope to advance well beyond where we can get on the strength of common sense and intuition alone. Better yet, as more such puzzles get resolved, it may turn out that similar sorts of mechanisms come into play in many of them, leading us, perhaps, to the kind of "middle-range" theories that Robert Merton had in mind back in the 1960s. What can we learn by studying social influence in cultural markets that can also tell us something useful about the relationship between financial incentives and individual performance? How, for example, can we connect our findings about the difference between real and perceived similarity in political attitudes with our findings about the origins of similarity in social networks? What can these findings in turn tell us about social influence and collective behavior? And how can we connect network search and social influence, decision making, incentives and performance, perceptions and polarization with the "big" questions of social science—like inequality, social justice, and economic policy?

It isn't clear that we can. Almost certainly, some of the

problems that sociologists and other social scientists find interesting will lie forever beyond the reach of precise measurement. No matter how much the Internet and other new technologies affect their field, therefore, the traditional tools of social scientists—archival research, fieldwork, theoretical models, and deep introspection—will continue to play important roles. Nor is it necessarily the case that the most complicated and pressing real-world problems—such as achieving consensus around matters of social justice or designing institutions that cope with uncertainty—can ever be "solved" in an engineering sense, no matter how much basic science we acquire. For problems like these, we can still discover that some solutions work better than others—using, for example the kind of bootstrapping and experimental approaches outlined in Chapter 8 or the deliberative approach to democracy that political philosophers such as John Rawls and Michael Sandel have long advocated. But the exact cause-and-effect mechanisms may remain forever elusive.

Ultimately, we will probably need to pursue all these approaches simultaneously, attempting to converge on an understanding of how people behave and how the world works both from above and from below, bringing to bear every method and resource that we have at our disposal. It sounds like a lot of work, and it will be. But as Merton noted four decades ago, we have done this kind of thing before, first in physics and then in biology and then again in medical science. Most recently, the genomics revolution that began more than fifty years ago with the discovery of DNA has long promised more in the way of medical treatments than it has been able to deliver; yet that hasn't stopped us from devoting enormous resources to the pursuit of science.[26] Why should the science required to understand social problems such as urban poverty or economic development or public education deserve less attention? It should not. Nor can we claim anymore that the necessary instruments don't exist. Rather, just as the invention of the telescope revolutionized the study of the heavens, so too by rendering the unmeasurable measurable, the technological revolution in mobile, Web, and Internet communications has the potential to revolutionize our understanding of ourselves and how we interact. Merton was right: Social science has still not found its Kepler. But three hundred years after Alexander Pope argued that the proper study of mankind should lie not in the heavens but in ourselves, we have finally found our telescope.[27] Let the revolution begin....

ACKNOWLEDGMENTS

This book has been in the writing for more than three years, and on my mind for twice as long as that. During that time, I've been fortunate to work at some incredible institutions and with many equally impressive people. I'm grateful to all of them, but a few deserve special mention.

First of all, I'm deeply grateful to Yahoo! for providing such a stimulating and supportive research environment over the past three years. It is surprising to many people that a major US corporation in this day and age would choose to invest in a research organization that is dedicated to producing and publishing basic science, and yet that is precisely the mission of Yahoo! Research. Not that our more than 100 research scientists don't make a significant contribution to the corporate bottom line (note to shareholders—we do). Nevertheless, the freedom and flexibility that we experience—including to write books like this one—is remarkable, and a tribute to the leadership of Prabhakar Raghavan, the founding director. I'm also grateful to Preston McAfee and Ron Brachman for their support and encouragement, and to my colleagues Sharad Goel, Dan Goldstein, Jake Hofman, Sebastien Lahaei, Winter Mason, Dave Pennock, David Reiley, Dan Reeves, and Sid Suri, from whom I have learned so much. I've yet to meet a group of people who can be so argumentative and yet so enjoyable to work with.

Prior to joining Yahoo!, I spent several formative years in the sociology department at Columbia University and remain indebted to them for hiring me in the first place (without a sociology degree), as well as for patiently tolerating my ignorance of sociology and educating me in the discipline. I can't claim to have become a "real" sociologist, but I'm certainly far more of one than I would have been otherwise. In particular, I'm grateful to Peter Bearman, Jonathan Cole, Michael Crow, Jeffrey Sachs, David Stark, and Harrison White for their support and advice over the years; and to my students and collaborators, Peter Dodds, Gueorgi Kossinets, Roby Muhamad, and Matt Salganik. I'm also grateful to the late Robert K. Merton—a towering figure in the history of Columbia sociology—whose encouragement at an early stage of my career was as inspiring to me as the work he left behind.

During my Columbia years, my research was supported by grants from the National Science Foundation (SES-0094162 and SES-0339023), the James S. McDonnell Foundation, and Legg Mason Funds, while the Institute for Social and Economic Research and Policy, directed by Peter Bearman, provided valuable administrative support and office space. Without these organizations, much of the research described in this book would have been impossible. Subsequently, I've also benefited from visiting appointments at Nuffield College, Oxford, which generously hosted me for a two-month sabbatical in 2007, and the Santa Fe Institute—my intellectual home away from home—where I spent a few weeks per summer in 2008 and 2009. Without these critical breaks from my usual routine, it's unlikely I would have been able to complete such a long writing project, and I'm grateful to Peter Hedstrom at Nuffield and Geoffrey West and Chris Wood at SFI for their support in arranging these visits.

Finally, I'm grateful to a number of people who have helped me realize this book directly. Roger Scholl, my editor at Crown, proved equally adept both as a cheerleader and a coach, frequently restoring my enthusiasm during the long slog of editing while also steering me clear of numerous traps of my own making. Suzanne Gluck and Eric Lupfer, my agents at William Morris Endeavor, helped immensely in putting together the original proposal and provided valuable input throughout the writing process. Sharad Goel, Dan Goldstein, Victoria Johnson, Michael Mauboussin, Tom McCarthy, Scott Page, Jonah Peretti, and Chuck Sabel were all generous enough to read early drafts of the book, correcting numerous errors and oversights in the process. And to my friends and family, who tolerated years of whining about "the book," thanks for your forbearance. I know I haven't been the best at explaining what all the fuss has been about, but I hope it will be clear now. Maybe even obvious...

APPENDIX

KEY POINTS IN THE BOOK

CHAPTER 1: THE MYTH OF COMMON SENSE

Common sense is great for everyday problem solving, but "problems" to do with government planning, policy, business, and marketing are not like everyday problems. Whereas everyday problems involve making decisions about the immediate here and now, decisions about planning, policy, etc., all involve large numbers of people over extended periods of time. Common sense is simply not designed to solve these sorts of problems, but its limitations are rarely apparent to us. The rest of the book will explain both these claims.

CHAPTER 2: THINKING ABOUT THINKING

The first problem with common sense is that when trying to explain someone's behavior, or to anticipate it, we focus on certain conscious motives and incentives that are most obviously relevant. In doing so, however, we ignore a multitude of other possibly relevant factors, many of which operate below the level of consciousness. Thus, while it is true that people respond to incentives—somehow—this insight tells us little more than that "people have reasons for what they do." It doesn't tell us either what they will do or what reasons they will have for doing it. Once we have observed their behavior, the explanation for it will seem obvious, but this ex–post obviousness is deeply misleading.

CHAPTER 3: THE WISDOM (AND MADNESS) OF CROWDS

The second problem with common sense is that when we try to explain the behavior of groups—crowds, firms, political parties, markets, etc.— we instinctively invoke the language and logic of individual behavior. Yet this sort of explanation ignores a critical component of collective social behavior—namely that it is driven as much by the networks of interactions between individuals as by the attributes of the individuals themselves. Combined with the observation from the previous chapter—that once we observe an individual's action, we can always reconcile it with something we think we know about human behavior—our explanations of collective social behavior are not explanations at all, but really just descriptions of what happened. For example, conventional explanations of success—like the popularity of the *Mona Lisa,* the success of Facebook or *Harry Potter*—are circular, saying little more than "X succeeded because it was more like X than anything else." True, maybe, but also vacuous. The result is that although we always convince ourselves that we understand why certain products or companies or strategies have succeeded or failed in the past, predicting the next hit product or hot company or successful policy is notoriously difficult even for experienced professionals.

CHAPTER 4: SPECIAL PEOPLE

A related problem is that when we do try to understand social networks, we are intuitively drawn to the idea that social networks—and, by extension, social trends—are dominated by certain influential people. Yet these "influencers" also turn out to be a product of circular reasoning. Explanations that invoke influencers, that is, are effectively claiming "X happened because the influencers made it happen and we know they were the influencers because they made it happen." Again this explanation is possibly true, but again it is vacuous, and of little predictive value. Thus although marketers and the like are good at identifying influencers after the fact, they are unable to reliably identify them in advance, which of course is what matters.

CHAPTER 5: HISTORY, THE FICKLE TEACHER

The difference between what we feel we can explain about the past and what we are able to predict about the future seems like it also ought to be obvious. Yet the way we learn from history prevents us from seeing this difference. After the fact, it seems to us as if our predictions would have been right if only we had known something else at the time—something that now seems obvious. But because we are always explaining events after they have happened, at which point we know what it is that we are trying to account for, our explanations dramatically overstate the probability of the sequence of events that actually took place, thus failing to account for all the outcomes that might have happened but didn't. Even worse, a deep result of the philosophy of history shows that knowing what is "relevant" in the historian's sense may not be possible at the time it is happening, even given infinite knowledge of the present and the past, and infinite information processing capabilities. The reason is that what will be deemed relevant in the future depends on events that haven't yet happened; thus knowing the true importance of events as they are happening requires more than prediction—it requires a form of prophecy, meaning the ability to observe the present as if looking back on it from the future. And finally, because the future continues to unfold, the nature of the explanation we give for the past may change continually—what seems like a smart move one day may seem dumb the next, depending on other events that haven't happened yet. For all these reasons, the past is far less deterministic—and far less informative—than it seems.

CHAPTER 6: THE DREAM OF PREDICTION

Our tendency to see the past as more deterministic, and hence more predictable, than it really was in turn distorts our perception of the future. Rather than seeing the future as something that is fundamentally probabilistic, meaning that the best we can hope for is to be able to predict probabilities of particular outcomes, we act instead as if the future has in some sense already been determined and simply hasn't been revealed to us yet. In this way we persuade ourselves that we ought to be able to predict things that we simply can't predict, even in principle. It is this difference between what we can predict and what we think we ought to be able to predict that causes all the problems with common sense, and also makes it so hard for us to appreciate these problems.

CHAPTER 7: THE BEST-LAID PLANS

Just because we can't predict some things, doesn't mean we can't predict anything. When the probability of future events is consistent with the frequency of similar events in the past, statistical models based on historical data, and other methods that exploit the wisdom of crowds, can all generate relatively reliable—albeit still probabilistic—predictions. The main mistake to avoid is to trust any one single opinion, even that of an expert (and especially your own), and the main objective is to keep track of the predictions that you make (or that anyone else makes), thereby learning over time which predictions can be made reliably and which cannot. Almost surely, however, some outcomes—including outcomes such as the next financial crisis or the next disruptive technology—that we would much like to be able to predict cannot be reliably predicted at all. And in these cases, we need to build uncertainty into our strategic planning, devising strategies that are robust to different versions of the future.

CHAPTER 8: THE MEASURE OF ALL THINGS

Another response to uncertainty about the future is to avoid relying on predictions altogether and instead adopt a "measure and react" approach; that is, to become very good at measuring the state of the world in real time and reacting quickly. A variety of methods, such as crowd sourcing, field experiments, and bootstrapping, can be deployed both in business and in policy setting, in some cases to improve performance, and in other cases to avoid disasters.

CHAPTER 9: FAIRNESS AND JUSTICE

Moving from business applications to broader questions of social justice, our overly deterministic view of cause and effect leads us to overweight outcomes when trying to evaluate behavior (hence "all's well that ends well"). In particular, the combination of the Halo Effect (attributing success to talent) and the Matthew Effect (the rich get richer) systematically distorts our perception of merit, often leading us to attribute to individual performance, both good and bad, what is really a consequence of environmental conditions or simply luck. Compounding this problem, the instinct to attribute collective success to the genius of a great leader leads us to overstate the importance of CEOs, which in turn distorts the market for CEO compensation. Finally, the libertarian view that individuals owe nothing to society for their success is fundamentally at odds with the interdependent nature of social and economic systems.

CHAPTER 10: THE PROPER STUDY OF MANKIND

Evaluating the success of the social sciences by comparing them to the physical sciences is deeply misleading, in part because social scientists historically have lacked the accurate measurements of the physical sciences, and in part because human and social phenomena are inherently messier than physical phenomena. The technological revolution of the Internet, however, may herald a new era in social science—one that is equal in magnitude to that ushered in by the invention of the telescope. The result will still not look like physics, nor should it, but it will lead to new ways of thinking about social problems, and possibly better solutions.

BIBLIOGRAPHY

Abe, Sumiyoshi, and Norikuzu Suzuki. 2004. "Scale-free Network of Earthquakes." *Europhysics Letters* 65 (4):581–86.

Abraham, Magid M., and Leonard M. Lodish. 1990. "Getting the Most out of Advertising and Promotion." *Harvard Business Review* 68 (3):50.

Abraham, Magid. 2008. "The Off-line Impact of Online Ads." *Harvard Business Review* (April):28.

Abramowitz, Alan, and Kyle L. Saunders. 2008. "Is Polarization a Myth?" *Journal of Politics* 70 (2):542–55.

Adamic, Lada A., and Eytan Adar. 2005. "How to Search a Social Network." *Social Networks* 27 (3):187–203.

Adar, Eytan, and Lada A. Adamic, 2005. "Tracking Information Epidemics in Blogspace." Paper read at 2005 IEEE/WIC/ACM International Conference on Web Intelligence, Sept. 19–22, at Compiègne University of Technology, France.

Adler, Moshe. 1985. "Stardom and Talent." *American Economic Review* 75 (1):208–12.

Alicke, Mark D., and Olesya Govorun. 2005. "The Better-Than-Average Effect." In *The Self in Social Judgment*, ed. M. D. Alicke, D. A. Dunning, and J. I. Krueger. 85–106.

Alterman, Eric. 2008. "Out of Print: The Death and Life of the American Newspaper." *The New Yorker*, March 31.

Anagnostopoulos, A. R. Kumar, and M. Mahdian. 2008. "Influence and correlation in social networks." Pp. 7–15 in *Proceedings of the 14th ACM SIGKDD international conference on Knowledge discovery and data mining*. Las Vegas: ACM.

Anderson, Philip W. 1972. "More Is Different." *Science* 177 (4047):393–96.

Andreozzi, Luciano. 2004. "A Note on Paradoxes in Economics." *Kyklos* 57 (1):3–20.

Aral, Sinan, Lev Muchnik, and Arun Sundararajan. 2009. "Distinguishing Influence-Based Contagion from Homophily-Driven Diffusion in Dynamic Networks." *Proceedings of the National Academy of Sciences* 106 (51):21544–21549.

Arango, Tim. 2010. "How the AOL-Time Warner Merger Went So Wrong." *New York Times*, Jan. 10.

Arbesman, Sam, and Steven H. Strogatz. 2008. "A Monte Carlo Approach to Joe DiMaggio and Streaks in Baseball." In http://arxiv. org/abs/0807.5082 [2008].

Arceneaux, Kevin, and David Nickerson. 2009. "Who Is Mobilized to Vote? A Re-Analysis of 11 Field Experiments." *American Journal of Political Science* 53 (1):1–16.

Ariely, Dan. 2008. *Predictably Irrational*. New York: HarperCollins.

Ariely, Dan, George Loewenstein, and Drazen Prelec. 2003. "Coherent Arbitrariness: Stable Demand Curves Without Stable Preferences." *Quarterly Journal of Economics* 118 (1):73–105.

Ariely, Dan, Uri Gneezy, George Lowenstein, and Nina Mazar. 2009. "Large Stakes and Big Mistakes." *Review of Economic Studies*, 76(2): 451–469.

Armstrong, J. Scott. 1985. Long-Range Forecasting: From Crystal Ball to Computer. *New York:* John Wiley.

Arrow, Kenneth J., Robert Forsythe, Michael Gorham, et al. 2008. "The Promise of Prediction Markets." *Science* 320 (5878):877–78.

Arthur, W. Brian. 1989. "Competing Technologies, Increasing Returns, and Lock-in by Historical Events." *Economic Journal* 99 (394):116–31.

Asch, Solomon E. 1953. "Effects of Group Pressure Upon the Modification and Distortion of Judgments." In *Group Dynamics: Research and Theory,* ed. D. Cartwright and A. Zander. Evanston, IL: Row, Peterson and Co.

Ayres, Ian. 2008. *Super Crunchers: Why Thinking-by-Numbers Is the New Way to Be Smart*. New York: Bantam.

Baker, George P. 1992. "Incentive Contracts and Performance Measurement." *Journal of Political Economy* 100 (3):598–614.

Baker, Stephen. 2009. *The Numerati*. Boston, MA: Mariner Books.

Bakshy, E., J. M. Hofman, W. A. Mason, and D. J. Watts. 2011. "Everyone's an influencer: quantifying influence on twitter." Pp. 65–74 in *Proceedings of the fourth ACM international conference on Web search and data mining*. Hong Kong: ACM.

Bakshy, Eytan, Brian Karrer, and Lada A. Adamic. 2009. "Social Influence and the Diffusion of User-Created Content." Paper read at 10th ACM Conference on Electronic Commerce, July 6–10, Stanford, California.

Baldassari, Delia, and Peter S. Bearman. 2007. "Dynamics of Political Polarization." *American Sociological Review* 72 (5):784–811.

Baldassari, Delia, and Andrew Gelman. 2008. "Partisans Without Constraint: Political Polarization and Trends in American Public Opinion." *American Journal of Sociology* 114 (2):408–46.

Bandiera, Oriana, Iwan Barankay, and Imran Rasul. 2009. "Team Incentives: Evidence from a Field Experiment." Unpublished manuscript.

Barbera, Robert 2009. *The Cost of Capitalism: Understanding Market Mayhem and Stabilizing Our Economic Future*. New York: McGraw-Hill.

Bargh, John A., and Tanya L. Chartrand. 1999. "The Unbearable Automaticity of Being." *American Psychologist* 54 (7):462–79.

Bargh, John A., Mark Chen, and Lara Burrows. 1996. "Automaticity of Social Behavior: Direct Effects of Trait Construct and Stereotype Activation on Action." *Journal of Personality and Social Psychology* 71:230–44.

Barnes, Brooks. 2009. "Audiences Laughed to Forget Troubles." *New York Times*, Dec. 29.

Bass, Frank M. 1969. "A New Product Growth for Model Consumer Durables." *Management Science* 15 (5):215–27.

Bassetti, Stefano, Werner E. Bischoff, and Robert J. Sherertz. 2005. "Are SARS Superspreaders Cloud Adults." *Emerging Infectious Diseases (serial on the Internet).*

Beck, P. W. 1983. *Forecasts: Opiates for Decision Makers.* UK: Shell.

Becker, Gary S. 1976. *The Economic Approach to Human Behavior.* Chicago: University of Chicago Press.

Becker, Gary S., and Kevin M. Murphy. 2000. *Social Economics: Market Behavior in a Social Environment.* Cambridge, MA: The Belknap Press of Harvard University Press.

Becker, Howard. 1945. "Interpretive Sociology and Constructive Typology." In *Twentieth-Century Sociology*, ed. G. Gurvitch and W. E. Moore. New York: Philosophical Library.

Becker, Howard S. 1998. *Tricks of the Trade: How to Think About Your Research While You're Doing it.* Chicago: University of Chicago Press.

Bengston, William F., and John W. Hazzard. 1990. "The Assimilation of Sociology in Common Sense: Some Implications for Teaching." *Teaching Sociology* 18 (1):39–45.

Berger, Jonah, and Grinne Fitzsimons. 2008. "Dogs on the Street, Pumas on Your Feet: How Cues in the Environment Influence Product Evaluation and Choice." *Journal of Marketing Research (JMR)* 45 (1):1–14.

Berger, Jonah, and Chip Heath. 2007. "Where Consumers Diverge from Others: Identity Signaling and Product Domains." *Journal of Consumer Research* 34 (2):121–34.

Berger, Peter L., and Thomas Luckman. 1966. *The Social Construction of Reality.* New York: Anchor Books.

Berlin, Isaiah. 1960. "History and Theory: The Concept of Scientific History." *History and Theory* 1 (1):1–31.

Berlin, Isaiah. 1997. *The Proper Study of Mankind: An Anthology of Essays.* London: Chatto and Windus.

Berman, Eli. 2009. *Radical, Religious, and Violent: The New Economics of Terrorism.* Cambridge, MA: MIT Press.

Bernard, H. Russell, Eugene C. Johnsen, Peter D. Killworth, and Scott Robinson. 1989. "Estimating the size of an average personal network and of an event population." In *The Small World*, ed. Manfred Kochen. Norwood, NJ: Ablex Publishing.

———. 1991. "Estimating the Size of an Average Personal Network and of an Event Population: Some Empirical Results." *Social Science Research* 20:109–21.

Bernard, H. Russell, Peter D. Killworth, David Kronenfeld, and Lee Sailer. 1984. "The Problem of Informant Accuracy: The Validity of Retrospective Data." *Annual Review of Anthropology* 13:495–517.

Bernard, Tara S. 2010. "A Toolkit for Women Seeking a Raise." *New York Times*, May 14.

Berndt, Ernst R. 1991. *The Practice of Econometrics: Classic and Contemporary*. Reading, MA: Addison Wesley.

Bertrand, Marianne, Dean S. Karlan, Sendhil Mullainathan, et al. 2010. "What's Advertising Content Worth? Evidence from a Consumer Credit Marketing Field Experiment." *Quarterly Journal of Economics*. 119(2): 353–402.

Bettman, James R., Mary Frances Luce, and John W. Payne. 1998. "Constructive Consumer Choice Processes." *Journal of Consumer Research* 25 (3):187–217.

Bielby, William T., and Denise D. Bielby. 1994. "'All Hits Are Flukes': Institutionalized Decision Making and the Rhetoric of Network Prime-Time Program Development." *American Journal of Sociology* 99 (5):1287–313.

Bishop, Bill. 2008. *The Big Sort: Why the Clustering of Like-Minded America Is Tearing Us Apart*. New York: Houghton Mifflin.

Bishop, Christopher M. 2006. *Pattern Recognition and Machine Learning*. New York: Springer.

Black, Donald. 1979. "Common Sense in the Sociology of Law." *American Sociological Review* 44 (1):18–27.

Blass, Thomas. 2009. *The Man Who Shocked the World: The Life and Legacy of Stanley Milgram*. New York: PublicAffairs Books.

Bohman, J. 1998. "Survey article: The coming of age of deliberative democracy." *Journal of Political Philosophy* 6 (4):400–25.

Bohman, James, and William Rehg (Eds.). 1997. *Deliberative Democracy: Essays on Reason and Politics*. Cambridge, MA: MIT Press.

Bollen, Johan, Alberto Pepe, and Huina Mao. 2009. "Modeling Public Mood and Emotion: Twitter Sentiment and Socio-economic Phenomena." Arxiv preprint arXiv:0911.1583.

Bond, Sumuel D., Kurt A. Carlson, Margaret G. Meloy, et al. 2007. "Information Distortion in the Evaluation of a Single Option." *Organizational Behavior and Human Decision Processes* 102 (2):240–54.

Booher-Jennings, Jennifer. 2005. "Below the Bubble: 'Educational Triage' and the Texas Accountability System." *American Educational Research Journal* 42 (2):231–68.

———. 2006. "Rationing Education." *Washington Post*, Oct. 5.

Boudon, Raymond. 1988a. "Common Sense and the Human Sciences." *International Sociology* 3 (1):1–22.

———. 1988b. "Will Sociology Ever Be a 'Normal Science?'" *Theory and Society* 17 (5):747–71.

———. 1998. "Limitations of Rational Choice Theory." *American Journal of Sociology* 104 (3):817–28.

Bowles, Samuel, Ernst Fehr, and Herbert Gintis. 2003. "Strong Reciprocity May Evolve With or Without Group Selection." *Theoretical Primatology Project Newsletter*, Dec. 11.

Brauers, Jutta, and Martin Weber. 1988. "A New Method of Scenario Analysis for Strategic Planning." *Journal of Forecasting* 7 (1):31–47.

Brill, Steven. 2009. "What's a Bailed-Out Banker Really Worth?" *New York Times Magazine*, Dec. 29.

———. 2010. "The Teachers' Unions' Last Stand." *New York Times Magazine* (May 23): 32–47.

Brooker, Katrina. 2010. "Citi's Creator, Alone with His Regrets "*New York Times*, Jan. 2.

Brown, Bernice B. 1968. "Delphi Process: A Methodology Used for the Elicitation of Opinions of Experts." Santa Monica, CA: RAND Corporation.

Brynjolfsson, Erik, and Michael Schrage. 2009. "The New, Faster Face of Innovation." *MIT Sloan Management Review*, August.

Buchanan, James. 1989. "Rational Choice Models in the Social Sciences." In *Explorations into Constitutional Economics*, ed. R. D. Tollison and V. J. Vanberg. College Station, TX: Texas A&M University Press.

Bumiller, Elisabeth. 2010. "Top Defense Officials Seek to End 'Don't Ask, Don't Tell.'" *New York Times*, Feb. 2.

Burson-Marsteller. 2001. "The E-fluentials." New York: Burson-Marsteller.

Cairns, Huntington. 1945. "Sociology and the Social Science." In *Twentieth-Century Sociology*, ed. G. Gurvitch and W. E. Moore. New York: Philosophical Library.

Camerer, Colin F., George Loewenstein, and Matthew Rabin. 2003. *Advances in Behavioral Economics*. Princeton, NJ: Princeton University Press.

Carlson, Jean M., and John Doyle. 2002. "Complexity and Robustness." *Proceedings of the National Academy of Sciences* 99:2538.

Carter, Bill. 2006. *Desperate Networks*. New York: Doubleday.

Cassidy, John. 2009. *How Markets Fail: The Logic of Economic Calamities*. New York: Farrar, Straus and Giroux.

Caves, Richard E. 2000. *Creative Industries: Contracts Between Art and Commerce*. Cambridge, MA: Harvard University Press.

Chapman, Gretchen B., and Eric J. Johnson. 1994. "The Limits of Anchoring." *Journal of Behavioral Decision Making* 7 (4):223–42.

Choi, Hyunyoung, and Hal Varian. 2008. *Predicting the Present with Google Trends*. Available from http://www. google. com/googleblogs/ pdfs/google_predicting_the_present. pdf.

Christakis, Nicholas A., and James H. Fowler. 2009. *Connected: The Surprising Power of Social Networks and How They Shape Our Lives.* New York: Little, Brown.

Cialdini, Robert B. 2001. *Influence: Science and Practice,* 4th ed. Needham Heights, MA: Allyn and Bacon.

Cialdini, Robert B., and Noah Goldstein, J. 2004. "Social Influence: Compliance and Conformity." *Annual Review of Psychology* 55:591–621.

Clark, Kenneth. 1973. "Mona Lisa." *The Burlington Magazine* 115 (840):144–51.

Clauset, Aaron, and Nathan Eagle. 2007. Persistence and Periodicity in a Dynamic Proximity Network in *DIMACS Workshop on Computational Methods for Dynamic Interaction Networks.*

Clifford, Stephanie. 2009. "Put Ad on Web. Count Clicks. Revise." *New York Times,* May 30.

———. 2010. "We'll Make You a Star (if the Web Agrees)." *New York Times,* June 4.

Cohen-Cole, Ethan, and Jason M. Fletcher. 2008a. "Are All Health Outcomes 'Contagious'? Detecting Implausible Social Network Effects in Acne, Height, and Headaches." Available at SSRN: ssrn.count/abstract=133901.

———. 2008b. "Is Obesity Contagious? Social Networks vs. Environmental Factors in the Obesity Epidemic." *Journal of Health Economics* 27 (5):1382–7.

Cohn, Jonathan. 2007. *Sick: The Untold Story of America's Health Care Crisis—and the People Who Pay the Price.* New York: HarperCollins.

Coleman, James S. 1986. *Individual Interests and Collective Action.* Cambridge, UK: Cambridge University Press.

Coleman, James S., and Thomas J. Fararo. 1992. *Rational Choice Theory: Advocacy and Critique.* Thousand Oaks, CA: Sage.

Coleman, James Samuel. 1993. "The Impact of Gary Becker's Work on Sociology." *Acta Sociologica* 36:169–78.

Collins, Harry. 2007. "Bicycling on the Moon: Collective Tacit Knowledge and Somatic-Limit Tacit Knowledge." *Organization Studies* 28 (2):257.

Cook, Karen S., Richard M. Emerson, Mary R. Gillmore, and Toshio Yamagishi. 1983. "The Distribution of Power in Exchange Networks: Theory and Experimental Results." *American Journal of Sociology* 89:275–305.

Cook, Karen S., Linda D. Molm, and Toshio Yamagishi. 1993. "Exchange Relations and Exchange Networks: Recent Developments in Social Exchange Theory." In *Theoretical Research Programs: Studies in Theory Growth,* ed. J. Berger and M. Zelditch. Palo Alto, CA: Stanford University Press.

Cooper, William H. 1981. "Ubiquitous Halo." *Psychological Bulletin* 90 (2):218–44.

Corbusier, Le. 1923. "Towards a New Architecture." Trans. F. Etchells. New York: Dover. First published as Vers une Architecture.

Cortes, Corinna, Daryl Pregibon, and Chris Volinsky. 2003. "Computational Methods for Dynamic Graphs." *Journal of Computational and Graphical Statistics* 12 (4):950–70.

Cox, Gary W. 1999. "The Empirical Content of Rational Choice Theory: A Reply to Green and Shapiro." *Journal of Theoretical Politics* 11 (2):147–69.

Cutting, James E. 2003. "Gustave Caillebotte, French Impressionism, and Mere Exposure." *Psychonomic Bulletin & Review* 10 (2):319.

Danto, Arthur C. 1965. *Analytical Philosophy of History*. Cambridge, UK: Cambridge University Press.

Dawes, R. M. 1999. "A message from psychologists to economists: Mere predictability doesn't matter like it should (without a good story appended to it)." *Journal of Economic Behavior and Organization* 39 (1):29–40.

Dawes, Robyn M. 2002. *Everyday Irrationality: How Pseudo-Scientists, Lunatics, and the Rest of Us Systematically Fail to Think Rationally*. Boulder, CO: Westview Press.

Dawes, Robyn. 1979. "The Robust Beauty of Improper Linear Models in Decision Making." *American Psychologist* 34 (7):571–82.

De Choudhury, Munmun, Jake M. Hofman, Winter A. Mason, and Duncan J. Watts. 2010. "Inferring Relevant Social Networks from Interpersonal Communication." Paper read at 19th International World Wide Web Conference at Raleigh, NC.

de Mesquita, Bruce B. 2009. *The Predictioneer's Game: Using the Logic of Brazen Self-Interest to See and Shape the Future*. New York: Random House.

Dennett, Daniel C. 1984. "Cognitive Wheels: The Frame Problem of AI." In *Minds, Machines and Evolution*, ed. C. Hookaway. Cambridge, UK: Cambridge University Press.

De Vany, Arthur. 2004. *Hollywood Economics: How Extreme Uncertainty Shapes the Film Industry*. London: Routledge.

De Vany, Arthur, and W. David Walls. 1996. "Bose-Einstein Dynamics and Adaptive Contracting in the Motion Picture Industry." *The Economic Journal* 106 (439):1493–1514.

Denrell, Jerker. 2004. "Random Walks and Sustained Competitive Advantage." *Management Science* 50 (7):922–34.

Dholakia, Utpal M., and Silvia Vianello. 2009. "The Fans Know Best." *MIT Sloan Management Review*, August 17.

Diermeier, Daniel. 1996. "Rational Choice and the Role of Theory in Political Science." In *The Rational Choice Controversy: Economic Models of Politics Reconsidered*, ed. J. Friedman. New Haven, CT: Yale University Press.

DiMaggio, Paul, John Evans, and Bethany Bryson. 1996. "Have American's Social Attitudes Become More Polarized?" *American Journal of Sociology* 102 (3):690–755.

DiMaggio, Paul, and W. W. Powell. 1983. "The Iron Cage Revisited: Institutional Isomorphism and Collective Rationality in Organizational Fields." *American Sociological Review*:147–60.

DiPrete, Thomas A. 2002. "Life Course Risks, Mobility Regimes, and Mobility Consequences: A Comparison of Sweden, Germany, and the United States." *American Journal of Sociology* 108 (2):267–309.

DiPrete, Thomas A., and Gregory M. Eirich. 2006. "Cumulative Advantage as a Mechanism for Inequality: A Review of Theoretical and Empirical Developments." *Annual Review of Sociology* 32 (1):271–97.

Dobbin, Frank. 1994. "Cultural Models of Organization: The Social Construction of Rational Organizing Principles." In *The Sociology of Culture: Emerging Theoretical Perspectives*, ed. D. Crane. Oxford: Basil Blackwell.

Dodds, Peter S., and Christopher M. Danforth. 2009. "Measuring the Happiness of Large-Scale Written Expression: Songs, Blogs, and Presidents." *Journal of Happiness Studies* 11(4): 44–56.

Dodds, Peter S., Roby Muhamad, and Duncan J. Watts. 2003. "An Experimental Study of Search in Global Social Networks." *Science* 301 (5634):827–29.

Duesenberry, James. 1960. "Comment on 'An Economic Analysis of Fertility.'" In *Demographic and Economic Change in Developed Countries: A Conference of the Universities*, ed. National Bureau of Economic Research. Princeton, NJ: Princeton University Press.

Dunning, David, Judith A. Meyerowitz, and Amy D. Holzberg. 1989. "Ambiguity and Self-Evaluation: The Role of Idiosyncratic Trait Definitions in Self-Serving Assessments of Ability." *Journal of Personality and Social Psychology* 57 (6):1082–90.

Eagle, Nathan, Alex Pentland, and David Lazer. 2009. "Inferring Social Network Structure Using Mobile Phone Data." *Proceedings of the National Academy of Sciences* 106(36): 15274–15278.

Easterly, William. 2006. *The White Man's Burden: Why the West's Efforts to Aid the Rest Have Done So Much Ill and So Little Good*. New York: Penguin.

Elster, Jon. 1993. "Some Unresolved Problems in the Theory of Rational Behavior." *Acta Sociologica* 36:179–90.

———. 2009. *Reason and Rationality*. Princeton, NJ: Princeton University Press.

Erikson, Robert S., and Christopher Wlezien. 2008. "Are Political Markets Really Superior to Polls as Election Predictors?" *Public Opinion Quarterly* 72 (2):190–215.

Farmer, Mary K. 1992. "On the Need to Make a Better Job of Justifying Rational Choice Theory." *Rationality and Society* 4 (4):411–20.

Fehr, Ernst, and Urs Fischbacher. 2003. "The Nature of Human Altruism." *Nature* 425:785–91.

Fehr, Ernst, and Simon Gachter. 2000. "Cooperation and Punishment in Public Goods Experiments." *American Economic Review* 90 (4): 980–94.

———. 2002. "Altruistic Punishment in Humans." *Nature* 415:137–40.

Feld, Scott L. 1981. "The Focused Organization of Social Ties." *American Journal of Sociology* 86 (5):1015–35.

Ferdows, Kasra, Michael A. Lewis, and Jose A. D. Machuca. 2004. "Rapid-Fire Fulfillment." *Harvard Business Review* 82 (11).

Festinger, Leon. 1957. *A Theory of Cognitive Dissonance*. Palo Alto, CA: Stanford University Press.

Fiorina, Morris P., Samuel J. Abrams, and Jeremy C. Pope. 2005. *Culture Wars? The Myth of a Polarized America*. New York: Pearson Longman.

Fischhoff, Baruch. 1982. "For Those Condemned to Study the Past: Heuristics and Biases in Hindsight." In *Judgment Under Uncertainty: Heuristics and Biases*, ed. D. Kahneman, P. Slovic, and A. Tversky. New York: Cambridge University Press.

Fisher, Marshall. 2009. "Rocket Science Retailing: The 2006 Philip McCord Morse Lecture." *Operations Research* 57 (3):527–40.

Fodor, Jerry. 2006. "How the Mind Works: What We Still Don't Know." *Daedalus* 135 (3):86–94.

Frank, Robert H. 2007. *The Economic Naturalist: In Search of Explanations for Everyday Enigmas*. New York: Perseus Books Group.

Freeman, Linton C. 2004. *The Development of Social Network Analysis*. Vancouver, British Columbia: Empirical Press.

Friedman, Jeffrey, ed. 1996. *The Rational Choice Controversy: Economic Models of Politics Reconsidered*. New Haven, CT: Yale University Press.

Frist, Bill, Mark McCellan, James P. Pinkerton, et al. 2010. "How the G.O.P. Can Fix Health Care." *New York Times*, Feb. 21.

Gabel, Jon R. 2009. "Congress's Health Care Numbers Don't Add Up "*New York Times*, Aug. 25.

Gaddis, John Lewis. 2002. *The Landscape of History: How Historians Map the Past*. Oxford, UK: Oxford University Press.

Gawande, Atul. 2008. *Better: A Surgeon's Notes on Performance*. London: Profile Books.

Geertz, Clifford. 1975. "Common Sense as a Cultural System." *The Antioch Review* 33 (1):5–26.

Gelb, Leslie. 2009. *Power Rules: How Common Sense Can Rescue American Foreign Policy*. New York: Harper Collins.

Gelman, Andrew, David Park, Boris Shor, et al. 2008. *Red State, Blue State, Rich State, Poor State: Why Americans Vote the Way They Do*. Princeton, NJ: Princeton University Press.

Gerber, Alan S., Dean Karlan, and Daniel Bergan. 2009. "Does the Media Matter? A Field Experiment Measuring the Effect of Newspapers on Voting Behavior and Political Opinions." *American Economic Journal: Applied Economics* 1 (2):35–52.

Gigerenzer, Gerd. 2007. *Gut Feelings: The Intelligence of the Unconscious.* New York: Viking.

Gigerenzer, Gerd, Peter M. Todd, and ABC Research Group. 1999. *Simple Heuristics That Make Us Smart,* ed. S. Rich. New York: Oxford University Press.

Gilbert, Daniel. 2006. *Stumbling on Happiness.* New York: Alfred A. Knopf.

Gilovich, Thomas, Dale Griffin, and Daniel Kahneman, eds. 2002. *Heuristics and Biases: The Psychology of Intuitive Judgment.* Cambridge, UK: Cambridge University Press.

Ginsberg, Jeremy, Matthew H. Mohebbi, Rajan S. Patel, et al. 2008. "Detecting Influenza Epidemics Using Search Engine Query Data." *Nature* 457 (7232):1012–14.

Giuliani, Elisa, Roberta Rabellotti, and Meine P. van Dijk. 2005. *Clusters Facing Competition: The Importance of External Linkages.* Farnham, UK: Ashgate Publishing Co.

Gladwell, Malcolm 1999. "Six Degrees of Lois Weisberg." *New Yorker* 11: 52–63.

Gladwell, Malcolm. 2000. *The Tipping Point: How Little Things Can Make a Big Difference.* New York: Little, Brown.

Gelman, Andrew, Jeffery Lax, and Justin Phillips. 2010. "Over Time, a Gay Marriage Groundswell." *New York Times,* August 21.

Gleick, James. 1987. "Chaos: Making a New Science." *New York: Viking Penguin.*

Glenn, David. 2009. "Senator Proposes an End to Federal Support for Political Science." *Chronicle of Higher Education,* Oct. 7.

Gneezy, U., G. Loewenstein, and N. Mazar. 2009. "Large Stakes and Big Mistakes." *Review of Economic Studies* 76 (2):451–69.

Goel, Sharad, Sebastien Lahaie, Jake Hofman, et al. 2010. "Predicting Consumer Behavior with Web Search". *Proceedings of the National Academy of Sciences* (DOI: 10.1073/pnas.1005962107).

Goel, Sharad, Winter Mason, and Duncan J. Watts. 2010. "Perceived and Real Attitude Similarity in Social Networks." *Journal of Personality and Social Psychology,* 99(4): 611-621.

Goel, Sharad, Roby Muhamad, and Duncan J. Watts. 2009. "Social Search in 'Small-World' Experiments." In *Proceedings of the 18th International Conference on World Wide Web.* Madrid, Spain: Association of Computing Machinery.

Goel, Sharad, Daniel Reeves, David M. Pennock, and Duncan J. Watts. 2010c. "Prediction Without Markets." In *11th ACM Conference on*

Electronic Commerce. Harvard University, Cambridge, MA: Association of Computing Machinery, pp. 357–366.

Goldstein, Daniel G., Eric J. Johnson, Andreas Herrmann, and Mark Heitmann. 2008. "Nudge Your Customers Toward Better Choices." *Harvard Business Review* 86 (12):99–105.

Goldthorpe, John H. 1998. "Rational Action Theory for Sociology." *British Journal of Sociology* 49 (2):167–92.

Goodman, Peter S. 2009. "Reluctance to Spend May Be Legacy of Recession." *New York Times,* August 28.

Granovetter, Mark. 1978. "Threshold Models of Collective Behavior." *American Journal of Sociology,* 83(6):1420–1443.

———. 1985. "Economic Action and Social Structure: The Problem of Embeddedness." *American Journal of Sociology,* 91 (3):481–510.

Green, Donald P., and Ian Shapiro. 1994. *Pathologies of Rational Choice Theory.* New Haven, CT: Yale University Press.

———. 2005. "Revisiting the Pathologies of Rational Choice." In *The Flight from Reality in the Human Sciences,* ed. I. Shapiro. Princeton, NJ: Princeton University Press.

Gribbin, John. 1998. "Review: How Not to Do It." *New Scientist,* January 10.

Griffin, Dale, Wendy Liu, and Uzma Khan. 2005. "A New Look at Constructed Choice Processes." *Marketing Letters* 16 (3):321.

Gurerk, Ozgur, Bernd Irlenbusch, and Bettina Rockenbach. 2006. "The Competitive Advantage of Sanctioning Institutions." *Science* 312 (5770):108–11.

Hall, Brian, and Jeffrey B. Liebman. 1998. "Are CEOs Really Paid Like Bureaucrats?" *The Quarterly Journal of Economics* 113(3) 653–691.

Harding, David J., Cybelle Fox, and Jal D. Mehta. 2002. "Studying Rare Events Through Qualitative Case Studies: Lessons from a Study of Rampage School Shootings." *Sociological Methods & Research* 31 (2):174.

Harford, Timothy. 2006. *The Undercover Economist.* New York: Oxford University Press.

Harmon-Jones, Eddie, and Judson Mills, eds. 1999. *Cognitive Dissonance: Progress on a Pivotal Theory in Social Psychology.* Washington, DC: American Psychological Association.

Harsanyi, John C. 1969. "Rational-Choice Models of Political Behavior vs. Functionalist and Conformist Theories." *World Politics* 21 (4):513–38.

Hayek, Friedrich A. 1945. "The Use of Knowledge in Society." *American Economic Review* 35(4):519–530.

Heath, Chip, and Dan Heath. 2010. *Switch: How to Change Things When Change Is Hard.* New York: Broadway Business.

Helft, Miguel. 2008. "Changing That Home Page? Take Baby Steps." *New York Times,* October 17.

Helper, Susan, John Paul MacDuffie, and Charles F. Sabel. 2000. "Pragmatic Collaborations: Advancing Knowledge While Controlling Opportunism." *Industrial and Corporate Change* 9:443–83.

Henrich, Joseph, Robert Boyd, Samuel Bowles, et al. 2001. "In Search of Homo Economicus: Behavioral Experiments in 15 Small-Scale Societies." *American Economic Review* 91 (2):73–78.

Herszenhorn, David M. 2009. "Plan to Change Student Lending Sets Up a Fight. "*New York Times,* April 12.

Herzberg, Frederick. 1987. "One More Time: How Do You Motivate Employees?" *Harvard Business Review* 65(5):109–120.

Higginbotham, Don. 2001. *George Washington Reconsidered.* University of Virginia Press.

Hodgson, Geoffrey M. 2007. "Institutions and Individuals: Interaction and Evolution." *Organization Studies* 28 (1):95–116.

Holmstrom, Bengt, and Paul Milgrom. 1991. "Multitask Principal-Agent Analyses: Incentive Contracts, Asset Ownership, and Job Design." *Journal of Law, Economics & Organization* 7:24–52.

Hoorens, Vera. 1993. "Self-Enhancement and Superiority Biases in Social Comparison." *European Review of Social Psychology* 4 (1):113–39.

Howard, Philip K. 1997. *The Death of Common Sense.* New York: Warner Books.

Howe, Jeff. 2006. "The Rise of Crowdsourcing." *Wired Magazine* 14 (6):1–4.

———. 2008. *Crowdsourcing: Why the Power of the Crowd Is Driving the Future of Business.* New York: Crown Business.

Hu, Ye, Leonard M. Lodish, and Abba M. Krieger. 2007. "An Analysis of Real World TV Advertising Tests: A 15-year Update." *Journal of Advertising Research* 47 (3):341.

Huckfeldt, Robert, Paul E. Johnson, and John Sprague. 2004. *Political Disagreement: The Survival of Disagreement with Communication Networks.* Cambridge, UK: Cambridge University Press.

Huckfeldt, Robert, and John Sprague. 1987. "Networks in Context: The Social Flow of Political Information." *American Political Science Review* 81 (4):1197–1216.

Ijiri, Yuji, and Herbert A. Simon. 1975. "Some Distributions Associated with Bose-Einstein Statistics." *Proceedings of the National Academy of Sciences of the United States of America* 72 (5):1654–57.

Jackson, Matthew O. 2008. *Social and Economic Networks.* Princeton, NJ: Princeton University Press.

Jacobs, Jane. 1961. *The Life and Death of Great American Cities.* New York: Random House.

James, William. 1909. *Pragmatism.* New York: Longmans, Green and Co.

Janiak, Andrew, ed. 2004. *Newton: Philosophical Writings.* Cambridge, UK: Cambridge University Press.

Johnson, Eric J., and Daniel Goldstein. 2003. "Do Defaults Save Lives?" *Science,* 302:1538–39.

Kadlec, Dan. 2010. "Attack of the Math Brats." *Time* June 28:36–39.

Kahn, Lisa B. 2010. "The Long-Term Labor Market Consequences of Graduating from College in a Bad Economy." *Labour Economics* 17 (2):303–16.

Katz, Elihu, and Paul Felix Lazarsfeld. 1955. *Personal Influence: the Part Played by People in the Flow of Mass Communications.* Glencoe, IL: Free Press.

Keay, Douglas. 1987. "Aids, Education and the Year 2000!" *Woman's Own.* October 31.

Keller, Ed, and Jon Berry. 2003. *The Influentials: One American in Ten Tells the Other Nine How to Vote, Where to Eat, and What to Buy.* New York: Free Press.

Khurana, Rakesh. 2002. *Searching for a Corporate Savior: The Irrational Quest of Charismatic CEOs.* Princeton, NJ: Princeton University Press.

Kindleberger, Charles. 1978. *Manias, Panics, and Crashes: A History of Financial Crises.* New York: Basic Books.

Kirman, Alan D. 1992. "Whom or What Does the Representative Individual Represent?" *Journal of Economic Perspectives* 6 (2):117–36.

Kiser, Edgar, and Michael Hechter. 1998. "The Debate on Historical Sociology: Rational Choice Theory and Its Critics." *American Journal of Sociology* 104 (3):785–816.

Kittur, Aniket, Ed H. Chi, and Bongwon Suh. 2008. "Crowdsourcing User Studies with Mechanical Turk." *Proceedings of the Twenty-sixth Annual SIGCHI Conference on Human Factors in Computing Systems.* Florence, Italy, pp. 453–56.

Klar, Yechiel, and Eilath E. Giladi. 1999. "Are Most People Happier Than Their Peers, or Are They Just Happy?" *Personality and Social Psychology Bulletin* 25 (5):586.

Klein, Lisl. 2006. "Applied Social Science: Is It Just Common Sense?" *Human Relations* 59 (8):1155–72.

Kleinberg, Jon M. 2000a. "Navigation in a Small World—It Is Easier to Find Short Chains Between Points in Some Networks Than Others." *Nature* 406 (6798):845.

Kleinberg, Jon M. 2000b. "The Small-World Phenomenon: An Algorithmic Perspective." Paper read at Proceedings of the 32nd Annual ACM Symposium on Theory of Computing, at New York.

Kleinberg, Jon, and David Easley. 2010. *Networks, Crowds, and Markets: Reasoning About a Highly Connected World.* Cambridge, UK: Cambridge University Press.

Kleinfeld, Judith S. 2002. "The Small World Problem." *Society* 39 (2):61–66.

Knee, Jonathan A., Bruce C. Greenwald, and Ava Seave. 2009. *The Curse of the Mogul: What's Wrong with the World's Leading Media Companies.* New York: Portfolio.

Kocieniewski, David. 2010. "As Oil Industry Fights a Tax, It Reaps Subsidies." *New York Times,* July 3.

Kohavi, Ron, Roger Longbotham, and Toby Walker. 2010. "Online Experiments: Practical Lessons." *Computer,* 82–85.

Kohn, Alfie. 1993. "Why Incentive Plans Cannot Work." *Harvard Business Review* 71(5):54–63.

Kossinets, Gueorgi, and Duncan J. Watts. 2006. "Empirical Analysis of an Evolving Social Network." *Science* 311 (5757):88–90.

Kramer, Adam D. I. 2010. "An Unobtrusive Model of 'Gross National Happiness'" *Proceedings of CHI.* ACM Press. 287–290.

Krueger, Joachim, and Russell W. Clement. 1994. "The Truly False Consensus Effect: An Ineradicable and Egocentric Bias in Social Perception." *Journal of Personality and Social Psychology* 67:596–610.

Krueger, Joachim I. 2007. "From Social Projection to Social Behaviour." *European Review of Social Psychology* 18 (1):1–35.

Kumar, Nirmalya, and Sophie Linguri. 2006. "Fashion Sense." *Business Strategy Review.* 17(2): 80–84.

Kuran, Timur. 1991. "Now Out of Never: The Element of Surprise in the East European Revolution of 1989." *World Politics* 44 (1):7–48.

Landsburg, Steven E. 1993. *The Armchair Economist: Economics and Everyday Life.* New York: Free Press.

———. 2007. *More Sex Is Safer Sex.* New York: Simon and Schuster.

Laumann, Edward O. 1969. "Friends of Urban Men: An Assessment of Accuracy in Reporting Their Socioeconomic Attributes, Mutual Choice, and Attitude Agreement." *Sociometry* 32 (1):54–69.

Lawless, John. 2005. "The Interview: Nigel Newton: Is There Life After Harry Potter? You Bet Your Hogwarts There Is." *Independent,* July 3.

Layman, Geoffrey C., Thomas M. Carsey, and Juliana M. Horowitz. 2006. "Party Polarization in American Politics: Characteristics, Causes, and Consequences." *Annual Review of Political Science* 9: 83–110.

Lazarsfeld, Paul F. 1949. "The American Soldier—An Expository Review." *Public Opinion Quarterly* 13 (3):377–404.

Lazarsfeld, Paul, and Robert Merton. 1954. "Friendship as Social Process: A Substantive and Methodological Analysis." In *Freedom and Control in Modern Society,* ed. M. Berger, T. Abel and C. Page. New York: Van Nostrand.

Lazear, Edward P. 2000. "Performance Pay and Productivity." *American Economic Review* 90 (5):1346–61.

Lazer, David, Alex Pentland, Lada Adamic, et al. 2009. "Social Science: Computational Social Science." *Science* 323 (5915):721.

Leonhardt, David. 2009. "Medical Malpractice System Breeds More Waste." *New York Times,* Sept. 22.

———. 2010. "Saving Energy, and Its Cost." *New York Times,* June 15.

Lerner, Josh. 2009. *Boulevard of Broken Dreams: Why Public Efforts to*

Boost Entrepreneurship and Venture Capital Have Failed—and What to Do About It: Princeton, NJ: Princeton University Press.

Leskovec, Jure, and Eric Horvitz. 2008. "Planetary-Scale Views on a Large Instant-Messaging Network." 17th International World Wide Web Conference, April 21–25, 2008, at Beijing, China.

Levitt, Steven D., and Stephen J. Dubner. 2005. *Freakonomics: A Rogue Economist Explores the Hidden Side of Everything.* New York: William Morrow & Co.

Lewis, Michael. 2009. "The No-Stats All-Star." *New York Times Magazine*, February 13.

Lewis, Randall, and David Reiley. 2009. "Retail Advertising Works! Measuring the Effects of Advertising on Sales via a Controlled Experiment on Yahoo." Working paper, Yahoo.

Lodish, Leonard M., Magid Abraham, Stuart Kalmenson, et al. 1995a. "How TV Advertising Works: A Meta-analysis of 389 Real World Split Cable TV Advertising Experiments." *Journal of Marketing Research* 32: 125–39.

Lodish, Leonard M., Magid Abraham, Jeanne Livelsberger, et al. 1995b. "A Summary of Fifty-five In-Market Experimental Estimates of the Long-term Effect of TV Advertising." *Marketing Science* 14 (3):133–40.

Lohmann, Susanne. 1994. "The Dynamics of Informational Cascades: The Monday Demonstrations in Leipzig, East Germany, 1989–91." *World Politics* 47 (1):42–101.

Lombrozo, Tania. 2006. "The Structure and Function of Explanations." *Trends in Cognitive Sciences* 10 (10):464–70.

———. 2007. "Simplicity and Probability in Causal Explanation." *Cognitive Psychology* 55 (3):232–57.

Lowenstein, Roger, 2000. *When Genius Failed: The Rise and Fall of Long-Term Capital Management.* New York: Random House.

Lukes, Steven. 1968. "Methodological Individualism Reconsidered." *British Journal of Sociology* 19 (2):119–29.

Luo, Michael. 2004. " 'Excuse Me. May I Have Your Seat?' " *New York Times*, Sept. 14.

Lyons, Russell. 2011. "The Spread of Evidence-Poor Medicine via Flawed Social-Network Analysis." *Statistics, Politics, Policy* 2 (1). Article 2. DOI: 10.2202/2151-7509.1024.

Mackay, Charles. 1932. *Extraordinary Popular Delusions and the Madness of Crowds.* Boston: L.C. Page & Company.

Makridakis, Spyros, and Michele Hibon. 2000. "The M3-Competition: Results, Conclusions and Implications." *International Journal of Forecasting* 16:451–76.

Makridakis, Spyros, Michele Hibon, and Claus Moser. 1979. "Accuracy of Forecasting: An Empirical Investigation." *Journal of the Royal Statistical Society,* Series A 142 (2):97–145.

Makridakis, Spyros, Robin M. Hogarth, and Anil Gaba. 2009a. *Dance with Chance: Making Luck Work for You.* Chino Valley, AZ: One World Press.
———. 2009b. "Forecasting and Uncertainty in the Economic and Business World." *International Journal of Forecasting* 25(4), 794–812.
Malmgren, R. Dean, Jacob M. Hofman, Luis A. N. Amaral, and Duncan J. Watts. 2009. "Characterizing Individual Communication Patterns." 15th ACM SIGKDD Conference on Knowledge Discovery and Data Mining, at Paris, pp. 607–16. ACM Press.
Mandel, Naomi, and Eric J. Johnson. 2002. "When Web Pages Influence Choice: Effects of Visual Primes on Experts and Novices." *Journal of Consumer Research* 29 (2):235–45.
Marcus, Gary. 2008. *Kluge: The Haphazard Construction of the Human Mind.* New York: Houghton Mifflin.
Marra, Alexandre, R. Luciana Reis Guastelli, Carla Manuela Pereira de Araújo. 2010. "Positive Deviance: A New Strategy for Improving Hand Hygiene Compliance." *Infection Control and Hospital Epidemiology* 31 (1):12–20.
Marsh, David R., Dirk G. Schroeder, Kirk A. Dearden, et al. 2004. "The Power of Positive Deviance." *British Medical Journal* 329 (7475):1177.
Mason, Winter A., and Duncan J. Watts. 2009. "Financial Incentives and the Performance of Crowds." *Proceedings of the ACM SIGKDD Workshop on Human Computation,* 77–85.
Masuda, Naoki, Norio Konno, and Kazuyuki Aihara. 2004. "Transmission of Severe Acute Respiratory Syndrome in Dynamical Small-World Networks." *Physical Review E* 69 (3): 03197.
Mathisen, James A. 1989. "A Further Look at 'Common Sense' in Introductory Sociology." *Teaching Sociology* 17 (3):307–15.
Mauboussin, Michael J. 2006. *More Than You Know: Finding Financial Wisdom in Unconventional Places.* New York: Columbia University Press.
———. 2009. *Think Twice: Harnessing the Power of Counterintuition.* Cambridge, MA: Harvard Business School Press.
Mauboussin, Andrew, and Samuel Arbesman. 2011. "Differentiating Skill and Luck in Financial Markets with Streaks." *Available at SSRN* http://ssrn.com/abstract=1664031 or http://dx.doi.org/10.2139/ssrn.1664031.
Mayhew, Bruce H. 1980. "Structuralism Versus Individualism: Part 1, Shadowboxing in the Dark." *Social Forces* 59 (2):335–75.
McCormick, Tyler, Matthew J. Salganik, and Tian Zheng. 2008. "How Many People Do You Know? Efficiently Estimating Personal Network Size." *Journal of the American Statistical Association* 105:59–70.
McCotter, Trent. 2008. "Hitting Streaks Don't Obey Your Rules." *New York Times,* March 30.
McDonald, Ian. 2005. "Bill Miller Dishes on His Streak and His Strategy." *Wall Street Journal,* Jan. 6.
McDonald, Lawrence G., and Patrick Robinson. 2009. *A Colossal Failure*

of Common Sense: The Inside Story of the Collapse of Lehman Brothers. New York: Crown Business.

McFadden, Daniel. 1999. "Rationality for Economists?" *Journal of Risk and Uncertainty* 19 (1–3):73–105.

McPherson, Miller J., and Lynn Smith-Lovin. 1987. "Homophily in Voluntary Organizations: Status Distance and the Composition of Face-to-Face Groups." *American Sociological Review* 52:370–79.

McPherson, Miller, Lynn Smith-Lovin, and James M. Cook. 2001. "Birds of a Feather: Homophily in Social Networks." *Annual Review of Sociology* 27:415–44.

Mearian, Lucas 2009. "CDC Adopts New, Near Real-Time Flu Tracking System." *Computer World*, Nov. 5.

Menand, Luis. 2001. *The Metaphysical Club: A Story of Ideas in America.* New York: Farrar, Straus and Giroux.

Merton, Robert K. 1968. "The Matthew Effect in Science." *Science* 159 (3810):56–63.

Merton, Robert K. 1968a. "On Sociological Theories of the Middle Range." In *Social Theory and Social Structure.* New York: Free Press, pp. 39–72.

Merton, Robert K. 1968b. "Patterns of Influence: Local and Cosmopolitan Influentials." In *Social Theory and Social Structure*, ed. R. K. Merton. New York: Free Press, pp. 441–47.

Mervis, Jeffrey. 2006. "Senate Panel Chair Asks Why NSF Funds Social Sciences." *Science* 312(575): 829.

Meyer, John W., and Brian Rowan. 1977. "Institutionalized Organizations: Formal Structure as Myth and Ceremony." *American Journal of Sociology* 83 (2):340.

Meyer, Marshall W. 2002. *Rethinking Performance Measurement: Beyond the Balanced Scorecard.* Cambridge, UK: Cambridge University Press.

Milgram, Stanley. 1969. *Obedience to Authority.* New York: Harper and Row.

Milgram, Stanley, and John Sabini. 1983. "On Maintaining Social Norms: A Field Experiment in the Subway." In *Advances in Environmental Psychology*, ed. Andrew Baum, Jerome E. Singer, and S. Valins. Hillsdale, NJ: Lawrence Erlbaum Associates.

Milgram, Stanley. 1992. *The Individual in a Social World.* Second ed. New York: McGraw Hill.

Millett, Stephen M. 2003. "The Future of Scenarios: Challenges and Opportunities." *Strategy & Leadership* 31 (2):16–24.

Minsky, Marvin. 2006. *The Emotion Machine.* New York: Simon & Schuster.

Mintzberg, Henry. 2000. *The Rise and Fall of Strategic Planning.* Upper Saddle River, NJ: Pearson Education.

Mitchell, Melanie. 2009. *Complexity: A Guided Tour.* New York: Oxford University Press.

Moyo, Dambias. 2009. *Dead Aid: Why Aid Is Not Working and How There Is Another Way for Africa*. New York: Farrar, Straus and Giroux.

Murphy, Kevin J. 1999. "*Executive Compensation.*" *Handbook of Labour Economics* 3(2) 2485–2563.

Newman, M.E.J. 2003. "The Structure and Function of Complex Networks." *SIAM Review,* 45(2): 167–256.

Nielsen. 2009. "Global Faces and Networked Places: A Neilsen Report on Social Networking's New Global Footprint." Feb. 27.

Nickerson, Raymond S. 1998. "Confirmation Bias: A Ubiquitous Phenomenon in Many Guises." *Review of General Psychology* 2:175–220.

Nishiguchi, Toshihiro, and Alexandre Beaudet. 2000. "Fractal Design: Self-Organizing Links in Supply Chain." In *Knowledge Creation: A New Source of Value,* ed. G. Von Krogh, I. Nonaka and T. Nishiguchi. London: MacMillan.

North, Adrian C., David J. Hargreaves, and Jennifer McKendrick. 1997. "In-Store Music Affects Product Choice." *Nature* 390:132.

Norton, Michael I., Jeana H. Frost, and Dan Ariely. 2007. "Less Is More: The Lure of Ambiguity, or Why Familiarity Breeds Contempt." *Journal of Personality and Social Psychology* 92 (1):97–105.

Nozick, Robert. 1974. *Anarchy, State, and Utopia*. New York: Basic Books.

Onnela, J. P., J. Saramäki, J. Hyvönen, et al. 2007. "Structure and Tie Strengths in Mobile Communication Networks." *Proceedings of the National Academy of Sciences* 104 (18):7332.

Orrell, David. 2007. *The Future of Everything: The Science of Prediction*. New York: Basic Books.

O'Toole, Randal. 2007. *Best-Laid Plans: How Government Planning Harms Your Quality of Life, Your Pocketbook, and Your Future*. Washington, D.C.: Cato Institute.

Ostrom, Elinor. 1999. "Coping with Tragedies of the Commons." *Annual Review of Political Science* 2 (1):493–535.

Paolacci, Gabriele, Jess Chandler, and Panos G. Ipeirotis. 2010. "Running Experiments on Amazon Mechanical Turk." *Judgment and Decision Making* 5 (5):411–19.

Parish, James Robert. 2006. *Fiasco: A History of Hollywood's Iconic Flops*. Hoboken, NJ: John Wiley.

Payne, John W., James R. Bettman, and Eric J. Johnson. 1992. "Behavioral Decision Research: A Constructive Processing Perspective." *Annual Review of Psychology* 43 (1):87–131.

Perrottet, Charles M., 1996. "Scenarios for the Future." *Management Review* 85 (1):43–46.

Perrow, Charles. 1984. *Normal Accidents*. Princeton, NJ: Princeton University Press.

Pink, Daniel. 2009. *Drive: The Surprising Truth About What Motivates Us*. New York: Riverhead.

Plosser, Charles I. 1989. "Understanding Real Business Cycles." *The Journal of Economic Perspectives* 3 (3):51–77.

Polgreen, Philip M. Yiling Chen, David M. Pennock, and Forrest D. Nelson. 2008. "Using Internet Searches for Influenza Surveillance." *Clinical Infectious Diseases* 47 (11):1443–48.

Pollack, Andrew. 2010. "Awaiting the Genome Payoff." *New York Times*, June 14.

Pontin, Jason. 2007. "Artificial Intelligence, with Help from the Humans." *New York Times*, March 25.

Powell, Walter W., and Paul J. DiMaggio (eds). 1991. *The New Institutionalism in Organizational Analysis*. Chicago: University of Chicago Press.

Prendergast, Carice. 1999. "The Provision of Incentives in Firms." *Journal of Economic Literature* 37 (1):7–63.

Quadagno, Jill, and Stan J. Knapp. 1992. "Have Historical Sociologists Forsaken Theory? Thoughts on the History/Theory Relationship." *Sociological Methods & Research* 20 (4):481–507.

Ramirez, Anthony, and Jennifer Medina. 2004. "Seeking a Favor, and Finding It, Among the Strangers on a Train." *New York Times*, Sept. 14.

Rampell, Catherine. 2010. "Stiffening Political Backbones for Fiscal Discipline." *New York Times*, Feb. 12.

Rand, Paul M. 2004. "Identifying and Reaching Influencers." Available online at http://www.marketingpower.com/content20476.php.

Ravitch, Diane. 2010. "The Death and Life of the Great American School System." New York: Basic Books.

Rawls, John. 1993. *Political Liberalism*. New York: Columbia University Press.

Rawls, John. 1971. *A Theory of Justice*. Cambridge, MA: Belknap Press.

Raynor, Michael. 2007. *The Strategy Paradox: Why Committing to Success Leads to Failure*. New York: Doubleday.

Reid, T. R. 2009. "The Healing of America: A Global Quest for Better, Cheaper, and Fairer Health Care." New York: Penguin.

Reinhart, Carmen M., and Kenneth Rogoff. 2009. *This Time Is Different: Eight Centuries of Financial Folly*. Princeton, NJ: Princeton University Press.

Rescher, Nicholas. 2005. *Common-Sense: A New Look at Old Tradition*. Milwaukee, WI: Marquette University Press.

Rice, Andrew. 2010. "Putting a Price on Words." *New York Times Magazine*, May 10.

Riding, Alan. 2005. "In Louvre, New Room with View of 'Mona Lisa.'" *New York Times*, April 6.

Rigney, Daniel. 2010. *The Matthew Effect: How Advantage Begets Further Advantage*. New York: Columbia University Press.

Robbins, Jordan M., and Joachim I. Krueger. 2005. "Social Projection to

Ingroups and Outgroups: A Review and Meta-analysis." *Personality and Social Psychology Review* 9:32–47.

Rogers, Everett M. 1995. *Diffusion of Innovations,* 4th ed. New York: Free Press.

Roese, Neal J., and James M. Olson. 1996. "Counterfactuals, Causal Attributions, and the Hindsight Bias: A Conceptual Integration." *Journal of Experimental Social Psychology* 32 (3):197–227.

Rosen, Emmanuel. 2000. *The Anatomy of Buzz: How to Create Word-of-Mouth Marketing.* New York: Doubleday.

Rosenbloom, Stephanie. 2009. "Retailers See Slowing Sales in Key Season." *New York Times,* Aug. 15.

Rosenzweig, Phil. 2007. *The Halo Effect.* New York: Free Press.

Rothschild, David, and Justin Wolfers. 2008. "Market Manipulation Muddies Election Outlook." *Wall Street Journal,* October 2.

Sabel, Charles F. 2007. "Bootstrapping Development." In *On Capitalism,* ed. V. Nee and R. Swedberg. Palo Alto, CA: Stanford University Press.

Sachs, Jeffrey. 2006. *The End of Poverty: Economic Possibilities for Our Time.* New York: Penguin.

Saldovnik, Alan, Jennifer O'Day, and George Bohrnstedt. 2007. *No Child Left Behind and the Reduction of the Achievement Gap: Sociological Perspectives on Federal Educational Policy.* New York: Routledge.

Salganik, Matthew J., Peter Sheridan Dodds, and Duncan J. Watts. 2006. "Experimental Study of Inequality and Unpredictability in an Artificial Cultural Market." *Science* 311 (5762):854–56.

Salganik, Matthew J., and Duncan J. Watts. 2009a. "Social Influence: The Puzzling Nature of Success in Cultural Markets. "In *The Oxford Handbook of Analytical Sociology,* ed. P. Hedstrom and P. Bearman. Oxford, UK: Oxford University Press, pp. 315–41.

Salganik, Matthew, and Duncan J. Watts. 2009b. "Web-Based Experiments for the Study of Collective Social Dynamics in Cultural Markets." *Topics in Cognitive Science* 1:439–68.

Sandel, Michael J. 2009. *Justice: What's the Right Thing to Do?* New York: Farrar Straus & Giroux.

Santayana, George. 1905. *Reason in Common Sense,* Vol. 1. New York: George Scribner's Sons.

Sassoon, Donald. 2001. *Becoming Mona Lisa: The Making of a Global Icon.* New York: Harcourt, Inc.

Schacter, Daniel L. 2001. *The Seven Sins of Memory: How the Mind Forgets and Remembers.* Boston, MA: Houghton Mifflin.

Schnaars, Steven P. 1989. *Megamistakes: Forecasting and the Myth of Rapid Technological Change.* New York: Free Press.

Schoemaker, Paul J. H. 1991. "When and How to Use Scenario Planning: A Heuristic Approach with Illustration." *Journal of Forecasting* 10 (6):549–64.

Schumpeter, Joseph. 1909. "On the Concept of Social Value." *Quarterly Journal of Economics* 23 (2):213–32.

Schwarz, Norbert. 2004. "Metacognitive Experiences in Consumer Judgment and Decision Making." *Journal of Consumer Psychology* 14 (4):332–48.

Scott, James C. 1998. *Seeing Like a State: How Certain Schemes to Improve the Human Condition Have Failed.* New Haven, CT: Yale University Press.

Seabrook, John. 2000. *Nobrow: The Culture of Marketing, the Marketing of Culture.* New York: Vintage Books.

Segal, David. 2010. "It's Complicated: Making Sense of Complexity." *New York Times*, April 30.

Sethi, Rajiv, and Muhamet Yildiz. 2009. "Public Disagreement." In *MIT Department of Economics Working Paper Series*, Cambridge, MA.

Sewell, William H. 1996. "Historical Events as Transformations of Structures: Inventing Revolution at the Bastille." *Theory and Society* 25 (6):841–81.

Shalizi, Cosma, and Andrew C. Thomas. 2011. "Homophily and Contagion Are Generically Confounded in Observational Social Network Studies." *Sociological Methods Research* 40 (2): 211–39.

Sheng, Victor S., Foster Provost, and Panos G. Ipeirotis. 2008. Get Another Label? Improving Data Quality and Data Mining Using Multiple, Noisy Labelers. 14th ACMSIGKDD International Conference on Knowledge Discovery and Data Mining. Las Vegas, NV. ACM Press.

Sherden, William A. 1998. *The Fortune Sellers: The Big Business of Buying and Selling Predictions.* New York: John Wiley.

Sherif, Muzafer. 1937. "An Experimental Approach to the Study of Attitudes." *Sociometry* 1:90–98.

Shneiderman, Ben. 2008. "Science 2.0." *Science* 319 (5868):1349–50.

Small, Michael, Pengliang L. Shi, and Chi Kong Tse. 2004. "Plausible Models for Propagation of the SARS Virus." *IEICE Transactions on Fundamentals of Electronics Communications and Computer Sciences* E87A (9):2379–86.

Snow, Rion, Brendan O'Connor, Daniel Jurafsky, and Andrew Y. Ng. 2008. "Cheap and Fast—But Is It Good? Evaluating Non-Expert Annotations for Natural Language Tasks." In *Empirical Methods in Natural Language Processing.* Honolulu, Hawaii: Association for Computational Linguistics.

Somers, Margaret R. 1998. " 'We're No Angels': Realism, Rational Choice, and Relationality in Social Science." *American Journal of Sociology* 104 (3):722–84.

Sorkin, Andrew Ross (ed). 2008. "Steve & Barry's Files for Bankruptcy." *New York Times*, July 9.

Sorkin, Andrew Ross. 2009a. *Too Big to Fail: The Inside Story of How Wall Street and Washington Fought to Save the Financial System from Crisis—and Themselves.* New York: Viking Adult.

Sorkin, Andrew Ross (ed). 2009b. "A Friend's Tweet Could Be an Ad." *New York Times*, November 23.

Staw, Barry M. 1975. "Attribution of the " 'Causes' of Performance: A General Alternative Interpretation of Cross-Sectional Research on Organizations." *Organizational Behavior & Human Performance* 13 (3):414–32.

Stephen, Andrew. 2009. "Why Do People Transmit Word-of-Mouth? The Effects of Recipient and Relationship Characteristics on Transmission Behaviors." Marketing Department, Columbia University.

Stouffer, Samuel A. 1947. "Sociology and Common Sense: Discussion." *American Sociological Review* 12 (1):11–12.

Sun, Eric, Itamar Rosenn, Cameron A. Marlow, and Thomas M. Lento. 2009. "Gesundheit! Modeling Contagion Through Facebook News Feed." Third International Conference on Weblogs and Social Media, at San Jose, CA. AAAI Press.

Sunstein, Cass R. 2005. "Group Judgments: Statistical Means, Deliberation, and Information Markets." *New York Law Review* 80 (3):962–1049.

Surowiecki, James. 2004. *The Wisdom of Crowds: Why the Many Are Smarter Than the Few and How Collective Wisdom Shapes Business, Economies, Societies, and Nations.* New York: Doubleday.

Svenson, Ola. 1981. "Are We All Less Risky and More Skillful Than Our Fellow Drivers?" *Acta Psychologica* 47 (2):143–48.

Taibbi, Matt. 2009. "The Real Price of Goldman's Giganto-Profits." July 16 http://trueslant.com/

Taleb, Nassim Nicholas. 2001. *Fooled by Randomness.* New York: W. W. Norton.

———. 2007. *The Black Swan: The Impact of the Highly Improbable.* New York: Random House.

Tang, Diane, Ashish Agarwal, Dierdre O'Brien, and Mike Meyer. 2010. Overlapping Experiment Infrastructure: More, Better, Faster Experimentation. 16th ACMSIGKDD International Conference on Knowledge Discovery abd Data Mining, Washington, DC. ACM Press.

Taylor, Carl C. 1947. "Sociology and Common Sense." *American Sociological Review* 12 (1):1–9.

Tetlock, Philip E. 2005. *Expert Political Judgment: How Good Is It? How Can We Know?* Princeton, NJ: Princeton University Press.

Thaler, Richard H., and Cass R. Sunstein. 2008. *Nudge: Improving Decisions about Health, Wealth, and Happiness.* New Haven, CT: Yale University Press.

Thompson, Clive. 2010. "What Is I.B.M.'s Watson?" *New York Times Magazine* (June 20):30–45.

Thorndike, Edward L. 1920. "A Constant Error on Psychological Rating." *Journal of Applied Psychology* 4:25–9.

Tomlinson, Brian, and Clive Cockram. 2003. "SARS: Experience at Prince of Wales Hospital, Hong Kong." *The Lancet* 361 (9368):1486–87.

Tuchman, Barbara W. 1985. *The March of Folly: From Troy to Vietnam.* New York: Ballantine Books.

Tucker, Nicholas. 1999. "The Rise and Rise of Harry Potter." *Children's Literature in Education* 30 (4):221–34.

Turow, Joseph, Jennifer King, Chris J. Hoofnagle, et al. 2009. "Americans Reject Tailored Advertising and Three Activities That Enable It." Available at SSRN: http://ssrn.com/abstract-1478214

Tversky, Amos, and Daniel Kahneman. 1983. "Extensional Versus Intuitive Reasoning: The Conjunction Fallacy in Probability Judgment." *Psychological Review* 90 (4):293–315.

———. 1974. "Judgment Under Uncertainty: Heuristics and Biases." *Science* 185 (4157):1124–31.

Tyler, Joshua R., Dennis M. Wilkinson, and Bernardo A. Huberman. 2005. "Email as Spectroscopy: Automated Discovery of Community Structure Within Organizations." The Information Society 21(2): 143–153.

Tziralis, George, and Ilias Tatsiopoulos. 2006. "Prediction Markets: An Extended Literature Review." *Journal of Prediction Markets* 1 (1).

Venkatesh, S. A. 2002. *American project: The rise and fall of a modern ghetto:* Harvard Univ Press.

Wack, Pierre. 1985a. "Scenarios: Shooting the Rapids." *Harvard Business Review* 63 (6):139–50.

Wack, Pierre. 1985b. "Scenarios: Uncharted Waters Ahead." *Harvard Business Review,* 63(5).

Wade, Nicholas. 2010. "A Decade Later, Genetic Map Yields Few New Cures." *New York Times,* June 12.

Wadler, Joyce. 2010. "The No Lock People." *New York Times,* Jan. 13.

Wasserman, Noam, Bharat Anand, and Nitin Nohria. 2010. "When Does Leadership Matter?" In *Handbook of Leadership Theory and Practice,* ed. N. Nohria and R. Khurana. Cambridge, MA: Harvard Business Press.

Watts, Duncan J. 1999. *Small Worlds : The Dynamics of Networks Between Order and Randomness.* Princeton, NJ: Princeton University Press.

———. 2003. *Six Degrees: The Science of a Connected Age.* New York: W. W. Norton.

Watts, Duncan J. 2004. "The 'New' Science of Networks." *Annual Review of Sociology,* 30:243–270.

———. 2007. "A 21st Century Science." *Nature* 445:489.

———. 2009. "Too Big to Fail? How About Too Big to Exist?" *Harvard Business Review,* 87(6):16.

Watts, Duncan J., P. S. Dodds, and M. E. J. Newman. 2002. "Identity and Search in Social Networks." *Science* 296 (5571):1302–1305.

Watts, Duncan J., and Peter Sheridan Dodds. 2007. "Influentials, Networks, and Public Opinion Formation." *Journal of Consumer Research* 34:441–58.

Watts, Duncan J., and Steve Hasker. 2006. "Marketing in an Unpredictable World." *Harvard Business Review* 84(9).:25–30.

Watts, Duncan J., and S. H. Strogatz. 1998. "Collective Dynamics of 'Small-World' Networks." *Nature* 393 (6684):440–42.

Weaver, Warren. 1958. "A Quarter Century in the Natural Sciences." *Public Health Reports* 76:57–65.

Weimann, Gabriel. 1994. *The Influentials: People Who Influence People.* Albany, NY: State University of New York Press.

Whitford, Josh. 2002. "Pragmatism and the Untenable Dualism of Means and Ends: Why Rational Choice Theory Does Not Deserve Paradigmatic Privilege." *Theory and Society* 31 (3):325–63.

Wilson, Eric. 2008. "Is This the World's Cheapest Dress?" *New York Times,* May 1.

Wimmer, Andreas, and Kevin Lewis. 2010. "Beyond and Below Racial Homophily: ERG Models of a Friendship Network Documented on Facebook." *American Journal of Sociology* 116 (2):583–642.

Wolfers, Justin, and Eric Zitzewitz. 2004. "Prediction Markets." *Journal of Economic Perspectives* 18 (2):107–26.

Wortman, Jenna. 2010. "Once Just a Site with Funny Cat Pictures, and Now a Web Empire." *New York Times,* June 13.

Wright, George, and Paul Goodwin. 2009. "Decision Making and Planning Under Low Levels of Predictability: Enhancing the Scenario Method." *International Journal of Forecasting* 25 (4):813–25.

Zelditch, Morris. 1969. "Can You Really Study an Army in the Laboratory?" In A. Etzioni and E. N. Lehman (eds) *A Sociological Reader on Complex Organizations.* New York: Holt, Rinehent, and Winston. pp. 528–39.

Zheng, Tian, Matthew J. Salganik, and Andrew Gelman. 2006. "How Many People Do You Know in Prison?: Using Overdispersion in Count Data to Estimate Social Structure in Networks." *Journal-American Statistical Association* 101 (474):409.

Zuckerman, Ezra W., and John T. Jost. 2001. "What Makes You Think You're So Popular? Self-Evaluation Maintenance and the Subjective Side of the 'Friendship Paradox.'" *Social Psychology Quarterly* 64 (3):207–23.

NOTES

PREFACE: A SOCIOLOGIST'S APOLOGY

1. For John Gribbin's review of Becker (1998), see Gribbin (1998).
2. See Watts (1999) for a description of small-world networks.
3. See, for example, a recent story on the complexity of modern finance, war, and policy (Segal 2010).
4. For a report on Bailey-Hutchinson's proposal, see Mervis (2006). For a report on Senator Coburn's remarks, see Glenn (2009).
5. See Lazarsfeld (1949).
6. For an example of the "it's not rocket science" mentality, see Frist et al. (2010).
7. See Svenson (1981) for the result about drivers. See Hoorens (1993), Klar and Giladi (1999), Dunning et al (1989), and Zuckerman and Jost (2001) for other examples of illusory superiority bias. See Alicke and Govorun (2005) for the leadership result.

CHAPTER 1: THE MYTH OF COMMON SENSE

1. See Milgram's *Obedience to Authority* for details (Milgram, 1969). An engaging account of Milgram's life and research is given in Blass (2009).
2. Milgram's reaction was described in a 1974 interview in *Psychology Today*, and is reprinted in Blass (2009). The original report on the subway experiment is Milgram and Sabini (1983) and has been reprinted in Milgram (1992). Three decades later, two *New York Times* reporters set out to repeat Milgram's experiment. They reported almost exactly the same experience: bafflement, even anger, from riders; and extreme discomfort themselves (Luo 2004, Ramirez and Medina 2004).
3. Although the nature and limitations of common sense are discussed in introductory sociology textbooks (according to Mathisen [1989], roughly half of the sociology texts he surveyed contained references to common sense), the topic is rarely discussed in sociology journals. See, however, Taylor (1947), Stouffer (1947), Lazarsfeld (1949), Black (1979), Boudon (1988a), Mathisen (1989), Bengston and Hazzard (1990), Dobbin (1994), and Klein (2006) for a variety of perspectives by sociologists. Economists have been even less concerned with common sense than sociologists, but see Andreozzi (2004) for some interesting remarks on social versus physical intuition.
4. See Geertz (1975, p.6).
5. Taylor (1947, p. 1).

6. Philosophers in particular have wondered about the place of common sense in understanding the world, with the tide of philosophical opinion going back and forth on the matter of how much respect common sense ought to be given. In brief, the argument seems to have been about the fundamental reliability of experience itself; that is, when is it acceptable to take something—an object, an experience, or an observation—for granted, and when must one question the evidence of one's own senses? On one extreme were the radical skeptics, who posited that because all experience was, in effect, filtered through the mind, nothing at all could be taken for granted as representing some kind of objective reality. At the other extreme were philosophers like Thomas Reid, of the Scottish Realist School, who were of the opinion that any philosophy of nature ought to take the world "as it is." Something of a compromise position was outlined in America at the beginning of the ninteenth century by the pragmatist school of philosophy, most prominently William James and Charles Saunders Peirce, who emphasized the need to reconcile abstract knowledge of a scientific kind with that of ordinary experience, but who also held that much of what passes for common sense was to be regarded with suspicion (James 1909, p 193). See Rescher (2005) and Mathisen (1989) for discussions of the history of common sense in philosophy.

7. It should be noted that commonsense reasoning also seems to have backup systems that act like general principles. Thus when some commonsense rule for dealing with some particular situation fails, on account of some previously unencountered contingency, we are not completely lost, but rather simply refer to this more general covering rule for guidance. It should also be noted, however, that attempts to formalize this backup system, most notably in artificial intelligence research, have so far been unsuccessful (Dennett 1984); thus, however it works, it does not resemble the logical structure of science and mathematics.

8. See Minsky (2006) for a discussion of common sense and artificial intelligence.

9. For a description of the cross-cultural Ultimatum game study, see Henrich et al. (2001). For a review of Ultimatum game results in industrial countries, see Camerer, Loewenstein, and Rabin (2003).

10. See Collins (2007). Another consequence of the culturally embedded nature of commonsense knowledge is that what it treats as "facts"—self-evident, unadorned descriptions of an objective reality—often turn out to be value judgments that depend on other seemingly unrelated features of the socio-cultural landscape. Consider, for example, the claim that "police are more likely to respond to serious than non-serious crimes." Empirical research on the matter has found that indeed they do—just as common sense would suggest—yet as the sociologist Donald Black has argued, it is also the case that victims of crimes are more likely to classify them as "serious" when the police respond to them. Viewed this way, the seriousness of a crime is determined not only by its intrinsic nature—robbery, burglary, assault, etc.—but also by the circumstances of the people who are

the most likely to be attended to by the police. And as Black noted, these people tend be highly educated professionals living in wealthy neighborhoods. Thus what seems to be a plain description of reality—serious crime attracts police attention—is, in fact, really a value judgment about what counts as serious; and this in turn depends on other features of the world, like social and economic inequality, that would seem to have nothing to do with the "fact" in question. See Black (1979) for a discussion of the conflation of facts and values. Becker (1998, pp. 133–34) makes a similar point in slightly different language, noting that "factual" statements about individual attributes—height, intelligence, etc.—are invariably relational judgments that in turn depend on social structure (e.g., someone who is "tall" in one context may be short in another; someone who is poor at drawing is not considered "mentally retarded" whereas someone who is poor at math or reading may be). Finally, Berger and Luckman (1966) advance a more general theory of how subjective, possibly arbitrary routines, practices, and beliefs become reified as "facts" via a process of social construction.

11. See Geertz (1975).

12. See Wadler (2010) for the story about the "no lock people."

13. For the Geertz quote, see Geertz (1975, p. 22). For a discussion of how people respond to their differences of opinions, and an intriguing theoretical explanation of their failure to converge on a consensus view, see Sethi and Yildiz (2009).

14. See Gelman, Lax, and Phillips. (2010) for survey results documenting Americans' evolving attitudes toward same-sex marriage.

15. It should be noted that political professionals, like politicians, pundits, and party officials, do tend to hold consistently liberal or conservative positions. Thus, Congress, for example, is much more polarized along a liberal-conservative divide than the general population (Layman et al. 2006). See Baldassari and Gelman (2008) for a detailed discussion of how political beliefs of individuals do and don't correlate with each other. See also Gelman et al. (2008) for a more general discussion of common misunderstanding about political beliefs and voting behavior.

16. Le Corbusier (1923, p. 61).

17. See Scott (1998).

18. For a detailed argument about the failures of planning in economic development, particularly with respect to Africa, see Easterly (2006). For an even more negative viewpoint of the effect of foreign aid in Africa, see Moyo (2009), who argues that it has actually hurt Africa, not helped. For a more hopeful alternative viewpoint see Sachs (2006).

19. See Jacobs (1961, p. 4)

20. See Venkatesh (2002).

21. See Ravitch (2010) for a discussion of how popular, commonsense policies such as increased testing and school choice actually undermined public education. See Cohn (2007) and Reid (2009) for analysis of the cost of health care and possible alternative models. See O'Toole (2007) for a detailed discussion on forestry management, urban planning, and other

failures of government planning and regulation. See Howard (1997) for a discussion and numerous anecdotes of the unintended consequences of government regulations. See Easterly (2006) again for some interesting remarks on nation-building and political interference, and Tuchman (1985) for a scathing and detailed account of US involvement in Vietnam. See Gelb (2009) for an alternate view of American foreign policy.

22. See Barbera (2009) and Cassidy (2009) for discussion of the cost of financial crises. See Mintzberg (2000) and Raynor (2007) for overviews of strategic planning methods and failures. See Knee, Greenwald, and Seave (2009) for a discussion of the fallibility of media moguls; and McDonald and Robinson (2009), and Sorkin (2009) for inside accounts of investment banking leaders whose actions precipitated the recent financial crisis. See also recent news stories recounting the failed AOL–Time Warner merger (Arango 2010), and the rampant, ultimately doomed growth of Citigroup (Brooker 2010).

23. Clearly not all attempts at corporate or even government planning end badly. Looking back over the past few centuries, in fact, overall conditions of living have improved dramatically for a large fraction of the world's populations—evidence that even the largest and most unwieldy political institutions do sometimes get things right. How are we to know, then, that common sense isn't actually quite good at solving complex social problems, failing no more frequently than any other method we might use? Ultimately we cannot know the answer to this question, if only because no systematic attempt to collect data on relative rates of planning successes and failures has ever been attempted—at least, not to my knowledge. Even if such an attempt had been made, moreover, it would still not resolve the matter, because absent some other "uncommon sense" method against which to compare it, the success rate of commonsense-based planning would be meaningless. A more precise way to state my criticism of commonsense reasoning, therefore, is not that it is universally "good" or "bad," but rather that there are sufficiently many examples where commonsense reasoning has led to important planning failures that it is worth contemplating how we might do better.

24. For details of financial crises throughout the ages, see Mackay (1932), Kindleberger (1978), and Reinhart and Rogoff (2009).

25. There are, of course, several overlapping traditions in philosophy that already take a suspicious view of what I am calling common sense as their starting point. One way to understand the entire project of what Rawls called political liberalism (Rawls 1993), along with the closely related idea of deliberative democracy (Bohman 1998; Bohman and Rehg 1997), is, in fact, as an attempt to prescribe a political system that can offer procedural justice to all its members without presupposing that any particular point of view—whether religious, moral, or otherwise—is correct. The whole principle of deliberation, in other words, presupposes that common sense is not to be trusted, thereby shifting the objective from determining what is "right" to designing political institutions that don't privilege any one view

of what is right over any other. Although this tradition is entirely consistent with the critiques of common sense that I raise in this book, my emphasis is somewhat different. Whereas deliberation simply assumes incompatibility of commonsense beliefs and looks to build political institutions that work anyway, I am more concerned with the particular types of errors that arise in commonsense reasoning. Nevertheless, I touch on aspects of this work in chapter 9 when I discuss matters of fairness and justice. A second strand of philosophy that starts with suspicion of common sense is the pragmatism of James and Dewey (see, for example, James 1909, p. 193). Pragmatists see errors embedded in common sense as an important obstruction to effective action in the world, and therefore take willingness to question and revise common sense as a condition for effective problem solving. This kind of pragmatism has in turn influenced efforts to build institutions, some of which I have described in chapter 8, that systematically question and revise their own routines and thus can adapt quickly to changes that cannot be predicted. This tradition, therefore, is also consistent with the critiques of common sense developed here, but as with the deliberation tradition, it can be advanced without explicitly articulating the particular cognitive biases that I identify. Nevertheless, I would contend that a discussion of the biases inherent to commonsense reasoning is a useful complement to both the deliberative and pragmatist agendas, providing in effect an alternative argument for the necessity of institutions and procedures that do not depend on commonsense reasoning in order to function.

CHAPTER 2: THINKING ABOUT THINKING

1. For the original study of organ donor rates, see Johnson and Goldstein (2003). It should be noted that the rates of indicated consent were not the same as the eventual organ-donation rate, which often depends on other factors like family members' approval. The difference in final donation rates was actually much smaller—more like 16 percent—but still dramatic.
2. See Duesenberry (1960) for the original quotation, which is repeated approvingly by Becker himself (Becker and Murphy 2000, p. 22).
3. For more details on the interplay between cooperation and punishment, see Fehr and Fischbacher (2003), Fehr and Gachter (2000 and 2002), Bowles et al. (2003), and Gurerk et al. (2006).
4. Within sociology, the debate over rational choice theory has played out over the past twenty years, beginning with an early volume (Coleman and Fararo 1992) in which perspectives from both sides of the debate are represented, and continued in journals like the *American Journal of Sociology* (Kiser and Hechter 1998; Somers 1998; Boudon 1998) and *Sociological Methods and Research* (Quadagno and Knapp 1992). Over the same period, a similar debate has also played out in political science, sparked by the publication of Green and Shapiro's (1994) polemic, *Pathologies of Rational Choice Theory*. See Friedman (1996) for the responses of a number of rational choice advocates to Green and Shapiro's critique, along with Green

and Shapiro's responses to the responses. Other interesting commentaries are by Elster (1993, 2009), Goldthorpe (1998), McFadden (1999), and Whitford (2002).

5. For accounts of the power of rational choice theory to explain behavior, see Harsanyi (1969), Becker (1976), Buchanan (1989), Farmer (1992) Coleman (1993) Kiser and Hechter (1998), and Cox (1999).

6. See *Freakonomics* for details (Levitt and Dubner 2005). For other similar examples see Landsburg (1993 and 2007), Harford (2006), and Frank (2007).

7. Max Weber, one of the founding fathers of sociology, effectively *defined* rational behavior as behavior that is understandable, while James Coleman, one of the intellectual fathers of rational choice theory, wrote that "The very concept of rational action is a conception of action that is 'understandable' action that we need ask no more questions about" (Coleman 1986, p. 1). Finally, Goldthorpe (1998, pp. 184–85) makes the interesting point that it is not even clear how we should talk about irrational, or nonrational behavior unless we first have a conception of what it means to behave rationally; thus even if it does not explain all behavior, rational action should be accorded what he calls "privilege" over other theories of action.

8. See Berman (2009) for an economic analysis of terrorism. See Leonhardt (2009) for a discussion of incentives in the medical profession.

9. See Goldstein et al. (2008) and Thaler and Sunstein (2008) for more discussion and examples of defaults.

10. For details of the major results of the psychology literature, see Gilovich, Griffin, and Kahneman (2002) and Gigerenzer et al., (1999). For the more recently established behavioral economics see Camerer, Loewenstein, and Rabin (2003). In addition to these academic contributions, a number of popular books have been published recently that cover much of the same ground. See, for example, Gilbert (2006), Ariely (2008), Marcus (2008), and Gigerenzer (2007).

11. See North et al. (1997) for details on the wine study, Berger and Fitzsimons (2008) for the study on Gatorade, and Mandel and Johnson (2002) for the online shopping study. See Bargh et al. (1996) for other examples of priming.

12. For more details and examples of anchoring and adjustment, see Chapman and Johnson (1994), Ariely et al. (2003), and Tversky and Kahneman (1974).

13. See Griffin et al. (2005) and Bettman et al. (1998) for examples of framing effects on consumer behavior. See Payne, Bettman, and Johnson (1992) for a discussion of what they call constructive preferences, including preference reversal.

14. See Tversky and Kahneman (1974) for a discussion of "availability bias." See Gilbert (2006) for a discussion of what he calls "presentism." See Bargh and Chartrand (1999) and Schwarz (2004) for more on the importance of "fluency."

15. See Nickerson (1998) for a review of confirmation bias. See Bond et al. (2007) for an example of confirmation bias in evaluating consumer prod-

ucts. See Marcus (2008, pp. 53–57) for a discussion of motivated reasoning versus confirmation bias. Both biases are also closely to related to the phenomenon of cognitive dissonance (Festinger 1957; Harmon-Jones and Mills 1999) according to which individuals actively seek to reconcile conflicting beliefs ("The car I just bought was more expensive than I can really afford" versus "The car I just bought is awesome") by exposing themselves selectively to information that supports one view or discredits the other.

16. See Dennett (1984).

17. According to the philosopher Jerry Fodor (2006), the crux of the frame problem derives from the "local" nature of computation, which—at least as currently understood—takes some set of parameters and conditions as given, and then applies some sort of operation on these inputs that generates an output. In the case of rational choice theory, for example, the "parameters and conditions" might be captured by the utility function, and the "operation" would be some optimization procedure; but one could imagine other conditions and operations as well, including heuristics, habits, and other nonrational approaches to problem solving. The point is that no matter what kind of computation one tries to write down, one must start from some set of assumptions about what is relevant, and that decision is not one that can be resolved in the same (i.e., local) manner. If one tried to resolve it, for example, by starting with some independent set of assumptions about what is relevant to the computation itself, one would simply end up with a different version of the same problem (what is relevant to that computation?), just one step removed. Of course, one could keep iterating this process and hope that it terminates at some well-defined point. In fact, one can always do this trivially by exhaustively including every item and concept in the known universe in the basket of potentially relevant factors, thereby making what at first seems to be a global problem local by definition. Unfortunately, this approach succeeds only at the expense of rendering the computational procedure intractable.

18. For an introduction to machine learning, see Bishop (2006). See Thompson (2010) for a story about the Jeopardy-playing computer.

19. For a compelling discussion of the many ways in which our brains misrepresent both our memories of past events and our anticipated experience of future events, see Gilbert (2006). As Becker (1998, p. 14) has noted, even social scientists are prone to this error, filling in the motivations, perspectives, and intentions of their subjects whenever they have no direct evidence of them. For related work on memory, see Schacter (2001) and Marcus (2008). See Bernard et al. (1984) for many examples of errors in survey respondents' recollections of their own past behavior and experience. See Ariely (2008) for additional examples of individuals overestimating their anticipated happiness or, alternatively, underestimating their anticipated unhappiness, regarding future events. For the results on online dating, see Norton, Frost, and Ariely (2007).

20. For discussions of performance-based pay, see Hall and Liebman (1997) and Murphy (1998).

21. Mechanical Turk is named for a ninteenth-century chess-playing automaton that was famous for having beaten Napoleon. The original Turk, of course, was a hoax—in reality there was a human inside making all the moves—and that's exactly the point. The tasks that one typically finds on Mechanical Turk are there because they are relatively easy for humans to solve, but difficult for computers—a phenomenon that Amazon founder Jeff Bezos calls "artificial, artificial intelligence. See Howe (2006) for an early report on Amazon's Mechanical Turk, and Pontin (2007) for Bezos's coinage of "artificial, artificial intelligence." See http://behind-the-enemy-lines .blogspot.com for additional information on Mechanical Turk.

22. See Mason and Watts (2009) for details on the financial incentives experiment.

23. Overall, women in fact earn only about 75 percent as much as men, but much of this "pay gap" can be accounted for in terms of different choices that women make—for example, to work in lower-paying professions, or to take time off from work to raise a family, and so on. Accounting for all this variability, and comparing only men and women who work in comparable jobs under comparable conditions, roughly a 9 percent gap remains. See Bernard (2010) and http://www.iwpr.org/pdf/C350.pdf for more details.

24. See Prendergast (1999), Holmstrom and Milgrom (1991), and Baker (1992) for studies of "multitasking." See Gneezy et al. (2009) for a study of the "choking" effect. See Herzberg (1987), Kohn (1993), and Pink (2009) for general critiques of financial rewards.

25. Levitt and Dubner (2005, p. 20)

26. For details on the unintended consequences of the No Child Left Behind Act, see Saldovnik et al. (2007). For a specific discussion of "educational triage" practices that raise pass rates without impacting overall educational quality, see Booher-Jennings (2005, 2006). See Meyer (2002) for a general discussion on the difficulty of measuring and rewarding performance.

27. See Rampell (2010) for the story about politicians.

28. This argument has been made most forcefully by Donald Green and Ian Shapiro, who argue that when "everything from conscious calculation to 'cultural inertia' may be squared with some variant of rational choice the-ory...our disagreement becomes merely semantic, and rational choice the-ory is nothing but an ever-expanding tent in which to house every plausible proposition advanced by anthropology, sociology, or social psychology." (Green and Shapiro, 2005, p. 76).

CHAPTER 3: THE WISDOM (AND MADNESS)
OF CROWDS

1. See Riding (2005) for the statistic about visitors. See http://en.wikipedia. org/wiki/Mona_Lisa for other entertaining details about the *Mona Lisa*.

2. See Clark (1973, p. 150).

3. See Sassoon (2001).

4. See Tucker (1999) for the full article on *Harry Potter*. See (Nielsen 2009)

for details of their Facebook analysis. See Barnes (2009) for the story on movies.

5. For the story about changes in consumer behavior postrecession, see Goodman (2009). Bruce Mayhew (1980) and Frank Dobbin (1994) have both made a similar argument about circular reasoning.

6. This argument was made long ago by the physicist Philip Anderson in a famous paper titled "More Is Different" (Anderson 1972).

7. For Thatcher's original quote, see Keay (1987).

8. The definition of "methodological individualism" is typically traced to the early twentieth century in the writings of the Austrian economist Joseph Schumpeter (1909, p. 231); however, the idea goes back much earlier, at least to the writings of Hobbes, and was popular among the thinkers of the Enlightenment, for whom an individualistic view of action fit perfectly with their emerging theories of rational action. See Lukes (1968) and Hodgson (2007) for a discussion of the intellectual origins of methodological individualism, as well as a scathing critique of its logical foundations.

9. I am oversimplifying here, but not a lot. Although the original models of business cycles did assume a single representative agent, more recent models allow for multiple agents, each of which represents different sectors of the economy (Plosser 1989). Nevertheless, the same essential problem arises in all these models: the agents are not actually real people, or even firms, who pay attention to what other people and firms are doing, but rather are representative agents who make decisions on behalf of a whole population.

10. A number of excellent critiques of the representative individual idea have been written, most notably by the economist Alan Kirman (1992). That the criticism is so well known, however, and yet has had so little influence on the actual practice of social science, should demonstrate how difficult a problem it is to expunge.

11. Even rational choice theorists—who are as much as anyone the inheritors of methodological individualism—are in practice just as comfortable applying the principle of utility maximization to social actors like households, firms, unions, "elites," and government bureaus as to individual people. See Becker (1976), Coleman and Fararo (1992), Kiser and Hechter (1998), and Cox (1999) for numerous examples of representative agents employed in rational choice models.

12. See Granovetter (1978) for details of the "riot model."

13. For more details on the origins of social influence, see Cialdini (2001) and Cialdini and Goldstein (2004)

14. For examples of cumulative advantage models, see Ijiri and Simon (1975), Adler (1985), Arthur (1989), De Vany and Walls (1996), and De Vany (2004).

15. For the "army in a lab" quote, see Zelditch (1969). Experiments, it should be noted, are not entirely foreign to sociology. For example, the field of "network exchange" is one area of sociology in which it is common to run lab experiments, but these networks generally comprise only four or five individuals (Cook et al. 1983; Cook et al. 1993). Cooperation studies

in behavioral economics, political science, and sociology also use experiments, but once again the groups involved are small (Fehr and Fischbacher 2003).

16. See Salganik, Dodds, and Watts (2006) for a detailed description of the original Music Lab experiment.

17. See Salganik and Watts (2009b; 2009a) for more background on Music Lab, and details of follow-up experiments.

CHAPTER 4: SPECIAL PEOPLE

1. The movie *The Social Network*, about the founding of Facebook, was released in 2010. The Fosters beer commercial is available at http://www.youtube.com/watch?v=nPgSa9djYU8.

2. For a history of social network analysis, see Freeman (2004). For summaries of the more recent literature on network science, see Newman (2003), Watts (2004), Jackson (2008), and Kleinberg and Easley (2010). For more popular accounts, see Watts (2003) and Christakis and Fowler (2009).

3. See Leskovec and Horvitz (2008) for details of the Microsoft instant messenger network study.

4. See Jacobs (1961, pp. 134–35).

5. Milgram did not invent the phrase "six degrees of separation," referring only to the "small world problem." Instead, it was the playwright John Guare who wrote a play with that title in 1990. Oddly, Guare has credited the origin of the phrase to Guglielmo Marconi, the Italian inventor and developer of radiotelegraphy, who reportedly said that in a world connected by the telegraph, everyone would be connected to everyone else via only six degrees of separation. According to numerous citations on the web (see, e.g. http://www.megastarmedia.us/mediawiki/index.php/Six_degrees_of_separation), Marconi is supposed to have made this claim during his Nobel Prize lecture in 1909. Unfortunately, the speech itself (http://nobelprize.org/nobel_prizes/physics/laureates/1909/marconi-lecture.html) makes no mention of the concept; nor have I been able to locate the source of Marconi's quote anywhere else. Regardless of the ultimate origin of the phrase, however Milgram deserves the credit for having been the first to put some evidence behind it.

6. As a number of critics have noted, Milgram's results were less conclusive than they have sometimes been portrayed (Kleinfeld 2002). In particular, of the three hundred chains that started out to reach the target, a third began in Boston itself, and another third began with individuals in Omaha who were investors in the stock market—which at the time would have required them to have access to a stockbroker. Seeing as the sole target of the experiment was a Boston stockbroker, it is not so surprising anymore that these chains could reach him. Thus the most compelling evidence for the small-world hypothesis came from the ninety-six chains that began with randomly selected people in Omaha, and only seventeen of these chains actually made it. Given these uncertainties, one has to be careful when plac-

ing too much weight on the role of people like Mr. Jacobs, who could easily have been a statistical fluke. Indeed, Milgram himself noted as much, claiming only that "the convergence of communication chains through common individuals is an important feature of small world nets, and it should be accounted for theoretically."

7. See Gladwell (1999).

8. Naturally, how many friends you count people as having depends a lot on how you define "friendship," a concept that has always been ambiguous, and is even more so now in the era of social networking sites, where you can "friend" someone you don't even know. The result is that what we might call "true" friendship has become difficult to distinguish from mere "acquaintanceship," which in turn has gotten blurred together with the even more ephemeral notion of "one-way acquaintanceship" (i.e., "I've heard of you, but you don't know me from Adam"). Although some people on MySpace have a million "friends," as soon as we apply even the loosest definition of friendship, such as each person knowing the other on a first-name basis, the number immediately drops to the range of a few hundred to a few thousand. Interestingly, this range has remained surprisingly constant since the first studies were conducted in the late 1980s (McCormick et al. 2008; Bernard et al. 1989, 1991; Zheng et al. 2006).

9. There are a number of subtleties to the issue of chain lengths in small-world experiments that have led to a certain amount of confusion regarding what can and cannot be concluded from the evidence. For details about the experiment itself, see Dodds, Muhamad, and Watts (2003), and for a clarifying discussion of the evidence, as well as a detailed analysis of chain lengths, see Goel, Muhamad, and Watts (2009).

10. See Watts and Strogatz (1998); Kleinberg (2000a; 2000b); Watts, Dodds, and Newman (2002); Watts (2003, ch. 5); Dodds, Muhamad, and Watts (2003); and Adamic and Adar (2005) for details on the searchability of social networks.

11. Influencers go by many names. Often they are called opinion leaders or influentials but they are also called e-fluentials, mavens, hubs, connectors, alpha mums, or even passionistas. Not all of these labels are intended to mean exactly the same thing, but they all refer to the same basic idea that a small number of special individuals have an important effect on the opinions, beliefs, and consumption habits of a large number of "ordinary" individuals (see Katz and Lazarsfeld 1955, Merton 1968b, Weimann 1994, Keller and Berry 2003, Rand 2004, Burson-Marsteller 2001, Rosen 2000, and Gladwell 2000 for a range of influentials-related labels). Ed Keller and Michael Berry claim that "One in ten Americans tells the other nine how to vote, where to eat, and what to buy." They conclude, in fact, that "Few important trends reach the mainstream without passing through the Influentials in the early stages, and the Influentials can stop a would-be trend in its tracks" (Keller and Berry 2003, pp. 21–22); and the market-research firm Burson-Marsteller concurs, claiming that "The far-reaching effect of this powerful group of men and women can make or break a brand, marshal

or dissolve support for business and consumer issues, and provide insight into events as they unfold." All one needs to do, it seems, is to find these individuals and influence them. As a result, "Influencers have become the 'holy grail' for today's marketers" (Rand 2004).

12. For the original quote, see Gladwell (2000, pp. 19–21).

13. See Keller and Berry (2003, p. 15).

14. See, for example, Christakis and Fowler (2009), Salganik et al. (2006), and Stephen (2009).

15. In fact, even then you can't be sure. If A and B are friends, they are likely to have similar tastes, or watch similar shows on TV and so be exposed to similar information; thus what looks like influence may really just be homophily. So if every time a friend of A's adopts something that A adopts, we attribute that to A's influence, we are probably overestimating how influential A is. See Aral (2009), Anagostopoulos et al. (2008), Bakshy et al. (2009), Cohen-Cole and Fletcher (2008b, 2008a) Shalizi and Thomas (2011), and Lyons (2011) for more details on the issue of similarity versus influence.

16. See Katz and Lazarsfeld (1955) for a discussion of the difficulty of measuring influence, along with a more general introduction to personal influence and opinion leaders. See Weimann (1994) for a discussion of proxy measures of influence.

17. See Watts (2003) and Christakis and Fowler (2009) for discussions of contagion in social networks.

18. The connection between influentials and contagion is most explicit in Gladwell's analogy of "social epidemics," but a similar connection is implied throughout the literature on influentials. Everett Rogers (1995, p. 281) claims that "The behavior of opinion leaders is important in determining the rate of adoption of an innovation in a system. In fact, the S-shape of the diffusion curve occurs because once opinion leaders adopt and tell others about the innovation, the number of adopters per unit time takes off." Keller and Berry make a similar point when they claim that influentials are "like the central processing units of the nation. Because they know many people and are in contact with many people in the course of a week, they have a powerful multiplier effect, spreading the word quickly across a broad network when they find something they want others to know about" (Keller and Berry 2003, p. 29).

19. For details of the models, see Watts and Dodds (2007).

20. The original Bass model is described by Bass (1969).

21. See Gladwell (2000, p. 19).

22. A number of people interpreted this result as a claim that "influentials don't exist," but that's actually not what we said. To begin with, as I've discussed, there are so many different kinds of influentials that it would be impossible to rule them all out even if that was what we intended to do. But we didn't intend to do that. In fact, the whole point of our models was to assume the existence of influentials and see how much they mattered relative to ordinary individuals. Another misconception regarding our paper was that we had claimed that "influentials don't matter," but that's not what we said

either. Rather, we found only that influentials are unlikely to play the role described by the law of the few. Whether or not influentials, defined somehow, can be reliably identified and exploited in some manner remains an open question.

23. See Adar and Adamic (2005); Sun, Rosenn, Marlow, and Lento (2009); Bakshy, Karrer, and Adamic (2009); and Aral et al. (2009) for details.

24. For details of the Twitter study see Bakshy et al (2010).

25. For the anecdote about Kim Kardashian's $10,000 Tweets, see Sorkin (2009, b).

CHAPTER 5: HISTORY, THE FICKLE TEACHER

1. A number of sociologists have even argued explicitly that history ought to be a scientific discipline with its own laws and methods for extracting them (Kiser and Hechter 1998). Historians, meanwhile, have been more circumspect regarding the scientific status of their discipline but have nonetheless been tempted to draw analogies between their own practices and those of natural scientists (Gaddis 2002).

2. See Scott (1998) for a discussion of what he calls *metis* (the Greek word for "skill"), meaning the collection of formal decision procedures, informal rules of thumb, and trained instinct that characterized the performance of experienced professionals.

3. For more on creeping determinism and hindsight bias, see the classic article by Baruch Fischhoff (1982). Philosophers and psychologists disagree over how strong our psychological bias to think deterministically really is. As Roese and Olson (1996) point out, people frequently do engage in counterfactual thinking—imagining, for example, how things might have worked out "if only" some antecedent event had not taken place—suggesting that commonsense views of causality are more conditional than absolute. A more correct way to state the problem, therefore, is that we systematically overweight the likelihood of what happened relative to the counterfactual outcomes. For the purpose of my argument, however, it is sufficient that we do the latter.

4. See Dawes (2002, Chapter 7) for the full story of Flight 2605 and analysis.

5. See Dawes (2002) and Harding et al. (2002) for more on school shootings.

6. See Gladwell (2000, p. 33)

7. See Tomlinson and Cockram (2003) for details on the SARS outbreaks in the Prince of Wales Hospital and the Amoy Gardens apartment complex. Various theoretical models (Small et al. 2004; Bassetti et al. 2005; Masuda et al. 2004) have subsequently been proposed to explain the SARS epidemic in terms of superspreaders.

8. See Berlin (1997, p. 449).

9. Gaddis (2002), in fact, makes more or less this argument.

10. For the full argument, see Danto (1965).

11. For the full story of Cisco, see Rosenzweig (2007).

12. See Gaddis (2002).

13. See Lombrozo (2007) for details of the study. It should be noted that when told in simple terms the relative probabilities of the different explanations, participants did in fact choose the more complex explanation at a much higher rate. Such explicit information, however, is rarely available in real-world scenarios.

14. See Tversky and Kahneman (1983) for details.

15. For evidence of confidence afforded by stories, see Lombrozo (2006, 2007) and Dawes (2002, p. 114). Dawes (1999), in fact, makes the stronger argument that human "cognitive capacity shuts down in the absence of a story."

16. For example, a preference for simplicity in explanations is deeply embedded in the philosophy of science. The famous Ockham's razor—named for the fourteenth-century English logician William of Ockham—posits that "plurality ought never be posited without necessity," meaning essentially that a complex theory ought never to be adopted where a simpler one would suffice. Most working scientists regard Ockham's razor with something close to reverence—Albert Einstein, for example, once claimed that a theory "ought to be as simple as possible, and no simpler"—and the history of science would seem to justify this reverence, filled as it is with examples of complex and unwieldy ideas being swept away by simpler, more elegant formulations. What is perhaps less appreciated about the history of science is that it is also filled with examples of initially simple and elegant formulations becoming increasingly more complex and inelegant as they struggle to bear the burden of empirical evidence. Arguably, in fact, it is the capacity of the scientific method to pursue explanatory power, even at the cost of theoretical elegance and parsimony, where its real strength lies.

17. For Berlin's full analysis of the differences between science and history, and the impossibility of remaking the latter in the image of the former, see Berlin (1960).

18. See Gaddis (2002) for a warning about the perils of generalizing, and also some examples of doing just that.

19. George Santayana (1905).

CHAPTER 6: THE DREAM OF PREDICTION

1. See Rosenbloom (2009).

2. See Tetlock (2005) for details.

3. See Schnaars (1989, pp. 9–33) for his analysis and lots of entertaining examples. See also Sherden (1998) for additional evidence of the lousy forecasting record of futurologists. See also Kuran (1991) and Lohmann (1994) for discussions of the unpredictability of political revolutions; specifically the 1989 collapse of the East Germany. And see Gabel (2009) for a retrospective look at the Congressional Budget Office's Medicare cost predictions.

4. See Parish (2006) for a litany of intended blockbusters that tanked at the U.S. box office (although some, like *Waterworld*, later became profitable

through foreign box office revenues and video and DVD sales). See Sea-brook (2000) and Carter (2006) for some entertaining stories about some disastrous miscalculations and near-misses inside the media industry. See Lawless (2005) for some interesting background on the publisher Blooms-bury's decision to acquire *Harry Potter* (for £2,500). General information about production in cultural industries is given in Caves (2000) and Bielby and Bielby (1994).

5. In early 2010, the market capitalization of Google was around $160B, but it has fluctuated as high as $220B. See Makridakis, Hogarth, and Gaba (2009a) and Taleb (2007) for lengthier descriptions of these and other missed predictions. See Lowenstein (2000) for the full story of Long-Term Capital Management.

6. Newton's quote is taken from Janiak (2004, p. 41).

7. The Laplace quote is taken from http://en.wikipedia.org/wiki/Laplace's -demon.

8. Lumping all processes into two coarse categories is a vast oversimplifica-tion of reality, as the "complexity" of a process is not a sufficiently well understood property to be assigned anything like a single number. It's also a somewhat arbitrary one, as there's no clear definition of when a pro-cess is complex enough to be called complex. In an elegant essay, Warren Weaver, then vice president of the Rockefeller Foundation, differentiated between what he called disorganized and organized complexity (Weaver 1958), where the former correspond to systems of very large numbers of independent entities, like molecules in a gas. Weaver's point was that disor-ganized complexity can be handled with the same kinds of tools that apply to simple systems, albeit in a statistical rather than deterministic way. By organized complexity, however, he means systems that are neither simple nor subject to the helpful averaging properties of disorganized systems. In my dichotomous classification scheme, in other words, I have effectively lumped together simple systems with disorganized systems. As different as they are, however, they are similar from the perspective of making predic-tions; thus conflation does not affect my argument.

9. See Orrell (2007) for a slightly different take on prediction in simple versus complex systems. See Gleick (1987), Watts (2003), and Mitchell (2009) for more general discussions of complex systems.

10. When I say we can predict only the probability of something happening, I am speaking somewhat loosely. The more correct way to talk about predic-tion for complex systems is that we ought to be able to predict properties of the distribution of outcomes, where this distribution characterizes the probability that a specified class of events will occur. So, for example, we might predict the probability that it will rain on a given day, or that the home team will win, or that a movie will generate more than a certain level of revenue. Equivalently, we might ask questions about the number of points by which we expect the home team to win, or the expected rev-enue of a particular class of movies to earn, or even the variance that we expect to observe around the average. Regardless, all these predictions are

about "average properties" in the sense that they can be expressed as an expectation of some statistic over many draws from the distribution of outcomes.

11. For a die roll, it's even worse: The best possible performance is to be right one time out of six, or less than 17 percent. In real life, therefore, where the range of possible outcomes can be much greater than a die roll—think, for example, of trying to predict the next bestseller—a track record of predicting the right outcome 20 percent of the time might very well be as good as possible. It's just that being "right" 20 percent of the time also means being "wrong" 80 percent of the time; that just doesn't sound very good.

12. See http://www.cimms.ou.edu/~doswell/probability/Probability.html. Orrell (2007) also presents an informative discussion of weather prediction; however, he is mostly concerned with longer-range forecasts, which are considerably less reliable.

13. Specifically, "frequentists" insist that statements about probabilities refer to the relative fraction of particular outcomes being realized, and therefore apply only to events, like flipping a coin, that can in principle be repeated ad infinitum. Conversely, the "evidential" view is that a probability should be interpreted only as the odds one ought to accept for a particular gamble, regardless of whether it is repeated or not.

14. See de Mesquita (2009) for details.

15. As Taleb explains, the term "black swan" derives from the European settlement of Australia: Until the settlers witnessed black swans in what is now Western Australia, conventional wisdom held that all swans must be white.

16. For details of the entire sequence of events surrounding the Bastille, see Sewell (1996, pp. 871–78). It is worth noting, moreover, that other historians of the French Revolution draw the boundaries rather differently from Sewell.

17. Taleb makes a similar point—namely that to have predicted the invention of what we now call the Internet, one would have to have known an awful lot about the applications to which the Internet was put after it had been invented. As Taleb puts it, "to understand the future to the point of being able to predict it, you need to incorporate elements from this future itself. If you know about the discovery you are about to make, then you have almost made it" (Taleb 2007, p. 172).

CHAPTER 7: THE BEST-LAID PLANS

1. Interestingly, a recent story in *Time* magazine (Kadlec 2010) contends that a new breed of poker players is relying on statistical analysis of millions of games played online to win at major tournaments.

2. See Ayres (2008) for details. See also Baker (2009) and Mauboussin (2009) for more examples of supercrunching.

3. For more details on prediction markets, see Arrow et al. (2008), Wolfers and Zitzewitz (2004), Tziralis and Tatsiopoulos (2006), and Sunstein

(2005). See also Surowiecki (2004) for a more general overview of the wisdom of crowds.

4. See Rothschild and Wolfers (2008) for details of the Intrade manipulation story.

5. In a recent blog post, Ian Ayres (author of *Supercrunchers*) calls the relative performance of prediction markets "one of the great unresolved questions of predictive analytics" (http://freakonomics.blogs.nytimes.com/2009/12/23/prediction-markets-vs-super-crunching-which-can-better-predict-how-justice-kennedy-will-vote/).

6. To be precise, we had different amounts of data for each of the methods—for example, our own polls were conducted over only the 2008–2009 season, whereas we had nearly thirty years of Vegas data, and TradeSports predictions ended in November 2008, when it was shut down—so we couldn't compare all six methods over any given time interval. Nevertheless, for any given interval, we were always able to compare multiple methods. See Goel, Reeves, et al. (2010) for details.

7. In this case, the model was based on the number of screens the movie was projected to open on, and the number of people searching for it on Yahoo! the week before it opened. See Goel, Reeves, et al. (2010) for details. See Sunstein (2005) for more details on the Hollywood Stock Exchange and other prediction markets.

8. See Erikson and Wlezien (2008) for details of their comparison between opinion polls and the Iowa Electronic Markets.

9. Ironically, the problem with experts is not that they know too little, but rather that they know too much. As a result, they are better than non-experts at wrapping their guesses in elaborate rationalizations that make them seem more authoritative, but are in fact no more accurate. See Payne, Bettman, and Johnson (1992) for more details of how experts reason. Not knowing anything, however, is also bad, because without a little expertise, one has trouble even knowing what one ought to be making guesses about. For example, while most of the attention paid to Tetlock's study of expert prediction was directed at the surprisingly poor performance of the experts—who, remember, were more accurate when making predictions outside their area of expertise than in it—Tetlock also found that predictions made by naïve subjects (in this case university undergraduates) were significantly worse than those of the experts. The correct message of Tetlock's study, therefore, was not that experts are no better than anyone at making predictions, but rather that someone with only general knowledge of the subject, but not no knowledge at all, can outperform someone with a great deal of knowledge. See Tetlock (2005) for details.

10. Spyros Makridakis and colleagues have shown in a series of studies over the years (Makridakis and Hibon 2000; Makridakis et al. 1979; Makridakis et al. 2009b) that simple models are about as accurate as complex models in forecasting economic time series. Armstrong (1985) also makes this point.

11. See Dawes (1979) for a discussion of simple linear models and their usefulness to decision making.

12. See Mauboussin (2009, Chapters 1 and 3) for an insightful discussion on how to improve predictions, along with traps to be avoided.

13. The simplest case occurs when the distribution of probabilities is what statisticians call stationary, meaning that its properties are constant over time. A more general version of the condition allows the distribution to change as long as changes in the distribution follow a predictable trend, such as average house prices increasing steadily over time. However, in either case, the past is assumed to be a reliable predictor of the future.

14. Possibly if the models had included data from a much longer stretch of time—the past century rather than the past decade or so—they might have captured more accurately the probability of a large, rapid, nationwide downtown. But so many other aspects of the economy also changed over that period of time that it's not clear how relevant much of this data would have been. Presumably, in fact, that's why the banks decided to restrict the time window of their historical data the way they did.

15. See Raynor (2007, Chapter 2) for the full story.

16. Sony did in fact pursue a partnership with Matsushita, but abandoned the plan in light of Matsushita's quality problems. Sony therefore opted for product quality while Matsushita opted for low cost—both reasonable strategies that had a chance of succeeding.

17. As Raynor writes, "Sony's strategies for Betamax and MiniDisc had all the elements of success, but neither succeeded. The cause of these failures was, simply put, bad luck: the strategic choices Sony made were perfectly reasonable; they just turned out to be wrong." (p. 44).

18. For an overview of the history of scenario planning, see Millet (2003). For theoretical discussions, see Brauers and Weber (1988), Schoemaker (1991), Perrottet (1996), and Wright and Goodwin (2009). Scenario planning also closely resembles what Makridakis, Hogarth and Gaba (2009a) call "future perfect thinking."

19. For details of Pierre Wack's work at Royal Dutch/Shell, see Wack (1985a; 1985b).

20. Raynor actually distinguishes three kinds of management: functional management, which is about optimizing daily tasks; operational management, which is focused on executing existing strategies; and strategic management, which is focused on the management of strategic uncertainty. (Raynor 2007, pp. 107–108)

21. For example, a 2010 story about Ford's then CEO claimed that "What Ford won't do is change direction again, at least not under Mr. Mulally's watch. He promises that he—and Ford's 200,000 employees—will not waver from his 'point of view' about the future of the auto industry. 'That is what strategy is all about,' he says. 'It's about a point of view about the future and then making decisions based on that. The worst thing you can do is not have a point of view, and not make decisions.' New York Times, January 9, 2010.

22. This example was originally presented in Beck (1983), but my discussion of it is based on the analysis by Schoemaker (1991).

23. According to Schoemaker (1991, p. 552), "A deeper scenario analysis would have recognized the confluence of special circumstances (e.g. high oil prices, tax incentives for drilling, conducive interest rates, etc.) underlying this temporary peak. Good scenario planning goes beyond just high-low projections."

24. See Raynor (2007, p. 37).

CHAPTER 8: THE MEASURE OF ALL THINGS

1. Some more details about Zara's supply chain management are provided in a *Harvard Business Review* case study of the company (2004, pp. 69–70). Additional details are provided in Kumar and Linguri (2006).

2. Mintzberg, it should be noted, was careful to differentiate strategic planning from "operational" planning, which is concerned with short-term optimization of existing procedures. The kind of planning models that don't work for strategic plans actually do work quite well for operational planning—indeed, it was for operational planning that the models were originally developed, and it was their success in this context that Mintzberg believed had encouraged planners to repurpose them for strategic planning. The problem is therefore not that planning of any kind is impossible, any more than prediction of any kind is impossible, but rather that certain kinds of plans can be made reliably and others can't be, and that planners need to be able to tell the difference.

3. See Helft (2008) for a story about the Yahoo! home page overhoul.

4. See Kohavi et al. (2010) and Tang et al. (2010).

5. See Clifford (2009) for a story about startup companies using quantitative performance metrics to substitute for design instinct.

6. See Alterman (2008) for Peretti's original description of the Mullet Strategy. See Dholakia and Vianello (2009) for a discussion of how the same approach can work for communities built around brands, and the associated tradeoff between control and insight.

7. See Howe (2008, 2006) for a general discussion of crowdsourcing. See Rice (2010) for examples of recent trends in online journalism.

8. See Clifford (2010) for more details on Bravo, and Wortman (2010) for more details on Cheezburger Network. See http://bit.ly/9EAbjR for an interview with Jonah Peretti about contagious media and BuzzFeed, which he founded.

9. See http://blog.doloreslabs.com for many innovative uses of crowd sourcing.

10. See Paolacci et al (2010) for details of turker demographics and motivations. See Kittur et al. (2008) and Snow et al. (2008) for studies of Mechanical Turk reliability. And see Sheng, Provost, and Ipeirotis (2008) for a method for improving turker reliability.

11. See Polgreen et al. (2008) and Ginsberg et al. (2008) for details of the influenza studies. Recently, the CDC has reduced its reporting delay for influenza

caseloads (Mearian 2009), somewhat undermining the time advantages of search-based surveillance.

12. The Facebook happiness index is available at http://apps.facebook.com/usa -gnh. See also Kramer (2010) for more details. A similar approach has been used to extract happiness indices from song lyrics and blog postings (Dodds and Danforth 2009) as well as Twitter updates (Bollen et al. 2009).

13. See http://yearinreview.yahoo.com/2009 for a compilation of most popular searches in 2009. Facebook has a similar service based on status updates, as does Twitter. As some commenters have noted (http://www.collisiond etection.net/mt/archives/2010/01/the_problem_wit.php), these lists often produce rather banal results, and so possibly would be more interesting or useful if constrained to more specific subpopulations of interest to particular individuals—like his or her friends, for example. Fortunately, modifications like this are relatively easy to implement; thus the fact that topics of highest average interest are unsurprising or banal does not imply that the capability to reflect collective interest is itself uninteresting.

14. See Choi and Varian (2008) for more examples of "predicting the present" using search trends.

15. See Goel et al. (2010, Lahaie, Hofman) for details of using web search to make predictions.

16. Steve Hasker and I wrote about this approach to planning in marketing a few years ago in the *Harvard Business Review* (Watts and Hasker 2006).

17. The relationship between sales and advertising is in fact a textbook example of what economists call the endogeneity problem (Berndt 1991).

18. In fact, there was a time when controlled experiments of this kind enjoyed a brief burst of enthusiasm among advertisers, and some marketers, especially in the direct-mail world, still run them. In particular, Leonard Lodish and colleagues conducted a series of advertising experiments, mostly in the early 1990s using split cable TV (Abraham and Lodish 1990; Lodish et al. 1995a; Lodish et al. 1995b; and Hu et al. 2007). Also see Bertrand et al. (2010) for an example of a direct-mail advertising experiment. Curiously, however, the practice of routinely including control groups in advertising campaigns, for TV, word-of-mouth, and even brand advertising, never caught on, and these days it is mostly overlooked in favor of statistical models, often called "marketing mix models" (http://en.wikipedia.org/wiki/Marketing_mix_modeling).

19. See, for example, a recent Harvard Business School article by the president and CEO of comScore (Abraham 2008). Curiously, the author was one of Lodish's colleagues who worked on the split-cable TV experiments.

20. User anonymity was maintained throughout the experiment by using a third-party service to match Yahoo! and retailer IDs without disclosing individual identities to the researchers. See Lewis and Reiley (2009) for details.

21. More effective advertising may even be better for the rest of us. If you only saw ads when there was a chance you might be persuaded by them, you'd

probably see many fewer ads, and possibly wouldn't find them as annoying.

22. See Brynjolfsson and Schrage (2009). Department stores have long experimented with product placement, trying out different locations or prices for the same product in different stores to learn which arrangements sell the most. But now that virtually all physical products are labeled with unique barcodes, and many also contain embedded RFID chips, they have the potential to track inventory and measure variation between stores, regions, times of the day, or times of the year—possibly leading to what Marshall Fisher of the University of Pennsylvania Wharton School has called the era of "Rocket Science" retailing (Fisher 2009). Ariely (2008) has also made a similar point.

23. See http://www.povertyactionlab.org/ for information on the MIT Poverty Action Lab. See Arceneaux and Nickerson (2009) and Gerber et al (2009) for examples of field experiments run by political scientists. See Lazear (2000) and Bandiera, Barankay, and Rasul (2009) for examples of field experiments run by labor economists. See O'Toole (2007, p. 342) for the example of the national parks and Ostrom (1999, p. 497) for a similar attitude to common pool resource governance, in which she argues that "all policy proposals must be considered as experiments." Finally, see Ayers (2007, chapter 3) for other examples of field experiments.

24. Ethical considerations also limit the scope of experimental methods. For example, although the Department of Education could randomly assign students to different schools, and while that would probably be the best way to learn which education strategies really work, doing so would impose hardship on the students who were assigned to the bad schools, and so would be unethical. If you have a reasonable suspicion that something might be harmful, you cannot ethically force people to experience it even if you're not sure; nor can you ethically refuse them something that might be good for them. All of this is as it should be, but it necessarily limits the range of interventions to which aid and development agencies can assign people or regions randomly, even if they could do so practically.

25. For specific quotes, see Scott (1998) pp. 318, 313, and 316, respectively.

26. See Leonhardt (2010) for a discussion of the virtues of cap and trade. See Hayek (1945) for the original argument.

27. See Brill (2010) for an interesting journalistic account of the Race to the Top. See Booher-Jennings (2005) and Ravitch (2010) for critiques of standardized testing as the relevant metric for student performance and teacher quality.

28. See Heath and Heath (2010) for their definition of bright spots. See Marsh et al. (2004) for more details of the positive deviance approach. Examples of positive deviance can be found at http://www.positivedeviance.org/. The hand-washing story is taken from Gawande (2008, pp. 13–28), who describes an initial experiment run in Pittsburgh. Gawande cautions that it is still uncertain how well the initial results will last, or whether they will generalize to other hospitals; however, a recent controlled experiment (Marra et al. 2010) suggests that they might.

29. See Sabel (2007) for a description of bootstrapping. See Watts (2003, Chapter 9) for an account of Toyota's near catastrophe with "just in time" manufacturing, and also their remarkable recovery. See Nishiguchi and Beaudet (2000) for the original account. See Helper, MacDuffie, and Sabel (2000) for a discussion of how the principles of the Toyota production system have been adopted by American firms.

30. See Sabel (2007) for more details on what makes for successful industrial clusters, and Giuliani, Rabellotti, and van Dijk (2005) for a range of case studies. See Lerner (2009) for cautionary lessons in government attempts to stimulate innovation.

31. Of course in attempting to generalize local solutions, one must remain sensitive to the context in which they are used. Just because a particular hand-washing practice works in one hospital does not necessarily mean that it will work in another, where a different set of resources, constraints, problems, patients, and cultural attitudes may prevail. We don't always know when a solution can be applied more broadly—in fact, it is precisely this unpredictability that makes central bureaucrats and administrators unable to solve the problem in the first place. Nevertheless, that should be the focus of the plan.

32. Easterly (2006, p. 6).

CHAPTER 9: FAIRNESS AND JUSTICE

1. Herrera then sued the city, which in 2006 eventually settled for $1.5 million. Three other officers who were involved in the incident were fired, and overall seventeen members of the 72nd precinct, including the commander, were disciplined. Police Commissioner Kerik opened an investigation into the operation of the midnight shift, which was apparently known to suffer from poor supervision and lax routines. Both Mayor Giuliani, and his successor, Michael Bloomberg, weighed in on the case, as did Governor Pataki. The legal status of the unborn baby Ricardo resulted in a fight between the medical examiner, who claimed the baby did not live independently of its mother and was therefore not to be considered a separate death, and the district prosecutor, who claimed the opposite. From the initial reports of the accident through the settlement of the lawsuit, the *New York Times* published nearly forty articles about the tragedy.

2. For a discussion of the relationship between rational organizing principles and the actual functioning of real social organizations, see Meyer and Rowan (1977), DiMaggio and Powell (1983), and Dobbin (1994). For a comprehensive treatment of the "new institutionalist" view of organizational sociology, see Powell and DiMaggio (1991).

3. See Menand (2001, pp. 429–33) for a discussion of Wendell Holmes's reasoning.

4. The psychologist Ed Thorndike was the first to document the Halo Effect in psychological evaluations (cite Thorndike 1920). For a review of the psychological literature on the Halo Effect, see Cooper (1981). For the John Adams quote, see Higginbotham (2001, p. 216).

5. For more examples of the Halo Effect in business, see Rosenzweig (2007). For a glowing story about the success of Steve & Barry's, see Wilson (2008). For a story about their subsequent bankruptcy, see Sorkin (2008).

6. See Rosenzweig (2007, pp. 54–56) for more examples of attribution error, and Staw (1975) for details of the experiment that Rosenzweig discusses.

7. To illustrate, consider a simple thought experiment in which we compare a "good" process, G, with a "bad" process, B, and where, just for the sake of the example, G has a 60 percent chance of success, while B succeeds only 40 percent of the time. If you think this isn't a big difference, imagine two roulette wheels that produced red outcomes 60 percent and 40 percent of the time—betting on red and black, respectively, one could quickly and easily make a fortune. Likewise, a strategy for making money in financial markets by placing many small bets would do very well if it paid out equal amounts of money 60 percent of the time, and lost them 40 percent of the time. But imagine now that instead of spinning a roulette wheel—a process we can repeat many times—our processes correspond to alternative corporate strategies or education policies. This now being an experiment that can be run only once, we observe the following probabilities

> Prob[G succeeds while B fails] = 0.6 * (1 - 0.4) = 0.36
> Prob[B succeeds while G fails] = 0.4 * (1 - 0.6) = 0.16
> Prob[G and B both succeed] = 0.6 * 0.4 = 0.24
> Prob[G and B both fail] = (1 - 0.6) * (1 - 0.4) = 0.24

In other words, it is more likely that G will do at least as well as B than the other way around—just as one would expect. But it is also the case that only one time in three, roughly, will G succeed while B fails. Almost half the time, in fact, both strategies perform equally well—or poorly—and one time out of six, it will even be the case that B will succeed while G fails. With almost two-thirds probability, it follows that when the good and bad processes are run side by side, the outcomes will not accurately reflect their differences.

8. See Brill (2009) for the original quote.

9. The distinction is important because it is often argued that for any sufficiently large population of fund managers, *someone* will be successful for many years in a row, even if success in any given year is determined by a coin toss. But as Mauboussin (2006, 2010) shows, coin tossing is actually a misleading metaphor. Because the performance of managed funds is assessed after fees, and because the overall portfolio of managed funds does not necessarily mirror the S&P 500, there is no reason to think that 50 percent of funds should "beat the market" in any given year. In fact the actual percentage varied from 7.9 percent (in 1997) to 67.1 percent (in 2005) over the fifteen-year interval of Miller's streak. When these empirical success rates are taken into account, the probability of observing a streak like Miller's is closer to one in 2.3 million (Mauboussin 2006, p. 50).

10. For DiMaggio's statistics see http://www.baseball-almanac.com/fur: DiMaggio's Statistics.

11. Arbesman and Strogatz (2008), using simulations, find that the likelihood of a fifty-six-game streak is somewhere between 20 percent and 50 percent. Interestingly, they also find that DiMaggio was not the most likely player to have attained this distinction; thus his streak was some mixture of skill and luck. See also McCotter (2008), who shows that long streaks happen more frequently than they should if batting average is constant, as Arbesman and Strogatz assume, suggesting that batters in the midst of a streak may be more likely to score a subsequent hit than their season average would suggest. Although they disagree with respect to the likelihood of streaks, however, both models are consistent in the idea that the correct measure of performance is the batting average, not the streak itself.

12. Of course, it's not always easy to agree on what constitutes a reliable measure of talent in sports either: whereas for a 100-meter sprinter it is very clear, in baseball it is much less so, and fans argue endlessly over which statistics—batting average, strikeout rate, runs batted in, slugging percentage—ought to count for more. Mauboussin (2010), for example, argues that strikeout rate is a more reliable measure of performance than batting average. Whatever the right measure is, however, the main point is that sports afford relatively large numbers of "trials" that are conducted under relatively comparable conditions.

13. See Lewis (2009) for an example of measuring performance in terms of a player's effect on the team's win-loss record.

14. Of course, we could artificially increase the number of data points by looking at their daily or weekly performance rather than their annual one; but these measures are also correspondingly noisier than annual measures, so it probably wouldn't help.

15. See Merton for the original paper. See also Denrell (2004) for a related argument about how random processes can account for persistent differences in profitability among businesses.

16. See Rigney (2010). See also DiPrete and Eirich (2006) for a more technical review of the cumulative advantage and inequality literature. See Kahn (2010) for detail on college graduates' earnings.

17. See McDonald (2005) for the Miller quote.

18. Mauboussin (2010) makes this point in considerably more detail.

19. Ironically, the further removed a measure of success is from a direct measure of talent, the more powerful the Halo Effect becomes. As long as your claim to talent is based on your personally having performed a particular thing well, someone can always question how well it was actually done, or how worthwhile a thing it was to do in the first place. But as soon as one's accomplishments become abstracted from their substance—as happens, for example, when a person wins important prizes, achieves great recognition, or makes fabulous amounts of money—concrete, individual metrics for assessing performance are gradually displaced by the Halo. A successful person, like a bestselling book or popular idea, is simply assumed to have displayed the appropriate merit, at which point the success effectively becomes a substitute for merit itself. But even more than that, it is merit that

cannot be easily questioned. If one believes that the *Mona Lisa* is a great piece of art because of X, Y, and Z, a knowledgeable disputant can immediately counter with his or her own criteria, or point out other examples that ought to be considered superior. But if one believes instead that the *Mona Lisa* is a great piece of art simply because it is famous, our pesky disputant can come up with all the objections she desires and we can insist quite reasonably that she must be missing the point. No matter how knowledgably she argues that properties of the *Mona Lisa* aren't uniquely special, we cannot help but suspect that something must have been overlooked, because surely if the artwork was not really special, then it wouldn't be, well, special.

20. See http://www.forbes.com/lists/2009/12/best-boss-09_Steven-P-Jobs_HEDB.html.

21. Sometimes even the leaders themselves concede this point—but interestingly they tend to do so only when things are going badly. For example, when the leaders of the four largest investment banks testified before Congress in early 2010, they did not take personal responsibility for the performance of their firms, claiming instead that to have been victims of a "financial tsunami" that had wreaked havoc on the economy. Yet in the years leading up to the crisis, when their firms were making money hand over fist, these same leaders were not turning down their bonuses on the grounds that everyone in their industry was making money, and therefore they shouldn't be credited with doing anything special. See Khurana (2002) for details, and Wasserman, Anand, and Nohira (2010) for the empirical results on when leadership matters.

22. To quote Khurana directly: "strong social, cultural, and psychological forces lead people to believe in cause-and-effect relationships such as that between corporate leadership and corporate performance. In the United States, the cultural bias towards individualism largely discounts the influence of social, economic, and political forces in human affairs so that accounts of complicated events such as wars and economic cycles reduce the forces behind them to personifications....This process of exaggerating the ability of individuals to influence immensely complex events is strongly abetted by the media, which fixate the public's attention on the personal characteristics of leaders at the expense of serious analysis of events" (Khurana 2002, p. 23).

23. As Khurana and other critics are quick to acknowledge, their research does not mean that anyone can be an effective CEO, or that CEO performance is irrelevant. It is certainly possible, for example, for a CEO to destroy tremendous value by making awful or irresponsible decisions. And because avoiding bad decisions can be difficult, even satisfactory performance requires a certain amount of experience, intellect, and leadership ability. Certainly not everyone has the wherewithal to qualify for the job, or the discipline and energy to perform it. Many CEOs are impressive people who work long hours under stressful conditions and carry heavy burdens of responsibility. It's therefore perfectly reasonable for corporate boards to choose candi-

dates selectively and to compensate them appropriately for their talent and their time. The argument is just that they shouldn't be selected or compensated on the grounds that their individual performance will have more than a weak influence on the future performance of their firm.

24. For a summary of Rawls's and Nozick's arguments, see Sandel (2009). For the original arguments, see Rawls (1971) and Nozick (1974).

25. See DiPrete (2002) for empirical evidence on intergenerational social mobility.

26. See, for example, Herszenhorn (2009) and Kocieniewski (2010).

27. See, for example, Watts (2009).

28. See Watts (2003, Chapter 1) for a detailed discussion of one such cascading failure—the 1996 failure in the western United States.

29. See Perrow (1984) for examples of what he calls normal accidents in complex organizations. See also Carlson and Doyle (2002) for a more technical treatment of the "robust yet fragile" nature of complex systems.

30. See Taibbi (2009) for an example of how Goldman Sachs profited from multiple forms of government assistance.

31. See Sandel (2009).

32. See Granovetter (1985).

33. See Berger and Luckman (1966). The deliberative democracy literature mentioned in Chapter 1, note 25, is also relevant to Sandel's argument.

CHAPTER 10: THE PROPER STUDY OF MANKIND

1. The full text of Pope's "Essay on Man" is available online at Project Gutenberg http://www.gutenberg.org/etext/2428.

2. Parsons's notion of rationality was inspired by Max Weber, who interestingly was not a functionalist, or even a positivist, espousing instead what has become known as an interpretive school of sociology, manifest in his claim that rational action was that which was *understandable* (*verstehen*) to an analyst. Nevertheless, Weber's work was quickly seconded by strongly positivistic theories, of which rational choice theory is the most obvious; thus illustrating how deeply the positivistic urge runs in all forms of science, including social science. Parsons also is sometimes cast as an anti-positivist, but once again, his ideas have been incorporated into positivist theories of social action.

3. For critiques of Parsons, see Mayhew (1980, p. 353), Harsanyi (1969, p. 514), and Coleman and Fararo (1992, p. xvii).

4. Many sociologists—both before Merton and since—have been critical of what they have viewed as facile attempts to replicate the success of natural science by imitating its form rather than its methods As early as the 1940s, for example, Parsons's contemporary Huntington Cairns wrote that "We possess no such synoptic view of social sciences which encourages us to believe that we are now at a stage of analysis where we can with any certainty select the basic concepts upon which an integrated structure of knowledge can be erected" (Cairns 1945, p. 13). More recently, a steady drumbeat of

criticism has been directed at rational choice theory, for much the same reasons (Quadagno and Knapp 1992; Somers 1998).

5. Quotes are from Merton (1968a).

6. See Merton (1968a) for his description of theories of the middle range, including the theory of relative deprivation and the theory of the role set.

7. Harsanyi (1969, p. 514) and Diermeier (1996) both reference Newton, while the political scientists Donald Green and Ian Shapiro have called rational choice theory "an ever-expanding tent in which to house every plausible proposition advanced by anthropology, sociology, or social psychology" (Green and Shapiro 2005).

8. The "success" or "failure" of rational choice theory, it should be noted, is highly controversial, with rational choice advocates claiming that it is unfair to evaluate rational choice theory as a "theory" in the first place, when really it should be regarded rather more as a family of theories unified only by their emphasis on purposive action as the cause of social outcomes over accident, blind conformity, or habit (Farmer 1992; Kiser and Hechter 1998; Cox 1999). Perhaps this is an accurate statement of what rational choice theory has become (although interestingly some rational choice theorists include even habit within the gambit of rational incentives [Becker and Murphy 2000]), but it's certainly not what early proponents like Harsanyi intended it to be. Harsanyi in fact criticized Parsons's theory explicitly for not being a "theory" at all, lacking the ability to derive conclusions logically from a set of axioms—or as he put it, "the very concept of social function in a collectivist sense gives rise to insoluble problems of definition and of empirical identification" (1969, p. 533). Whether or not it has subsequently metamorphosed into something more realistic should therefore not distract from the point that its original mission *was* to be a theory, and that in that sense it has been no more successful than any of its predecessors.

9. Indeed, as Becker (1945, p. 84) noted long ago, natural scientists are every bit as prone as social scientists to overestimate their ability to construct predictive models of human behavior.

10. Stouffer (1947).

11. It should be noted that not all sociologists agree that measurement is really the problem that I'm making it out to be. According to at least one school of thought, sociological theories should help us to make sense of the world, and give us a language with which to argue about it; but they shouldn't aim to make predictions or to solve problems, and so shouldn't be judged by the pragmatic test in the first place. If this "interpretive" view of sociology is correct, the whole positivist enterprise that began with Comte is based on a fundamental misunderstanding about the nature of social science, starting with assumption that it ought to be considered a branch of science at all (Boudon, 1988b). Sociologists, therefore, would do better to focus on developing "approaches" and "frameworks"—ways of thinking about the world that allow them to see what they might otherwise miss, and question what other people take for granted—and forget all about trying to build theories of the kind that are familiar to us from physics. It was essentially

this kind of approach to sociology, in fact, that Howard Becker was advocating in his book *Tricks of the Trade*, the review of which I encountered back in 1998, and that John Gribbin—the reviewer, who, remember, is a physicist—evidently found infuriating.

12. See, for example, Paolacci et al. (2010).

13. The privacy debate is an important one, and raises a number of unresolved questions. First, when asked, people say they care deeply about maintaining their privacy (Turow et al. 2009); however, their actions frequently belie their responses to survey questions. Not only do many people post a great deal of highly personal information about themselves in public but they also decline to pay for services that would guarantee them a higher than default level of privacy. Possibly this disconnect between espoused and revealed preferences implies only that people do not understand the consequences of their actions; but it may also imply that abstract questions about "privacy" are less meaningful than concrete tradeoffs in specific situations. A second, more troubling problem is that regardless of how people "really" feel about revealing particular pieces of information about themselves, they are almost certainly unable to appreciate the ability of third parties to construct information profiles about them, and thereby infer *other* information that they would not feel comfortable revealing.

14. See Sherif (1937) and Asch (1953) for details of their pioneering experiments. See Zelditch (1969) for his discussion of small-group versus large-group studies. See Adar and Adamic (2005), Sun et al. (2009), and Bakshy and Adamic (2009) for other examples of tracking information diffusion in online networks.

15. Now that they've proven the concept, Reiley and Lewis are embarking on a whole array of similar experiments—for department stores, phone providers, financial services companies, and so on—with the aim of measuring differences across domains (do ads work differently for phones than for credit cards?), across demographics (are older people more susceptible than younger?), and even across specific ad layouts and designs (blue background versus white?).

16. See Lazarsfeld and Merton (1954) for the original definition of "homophily," and McPherson et al. (2001) for a recent survey of the literature. See Feld (1981) and McPherson and Smith-Lovin (1987) for discussion of the importance of structural opportunities.

17. The reason is that social structure not only shapes our choices but is also shaped by them. It is true, for example, that whom we are likely to meet in the immediate future is determined to some degree by our existing social circles and activities. But on a slightly longer timescale it is also true that we may choose to do certain things over others precisely because of the people we expect to meet in the course of doing them. The whole point of "social networking" events in the business world, for example, is to put yourself in a situation where you might meet interesting people. Likewise, the determination of some parents to get their children into the "right" schools has less to do with the quality of education they will receive than the classmates they

will have. That said, of course, it is not equally easy for everyone to get into Harvard, or to get invited to the most desirable social gatherings. On a longer timescale again, therefore, your position in the social structure constrains not only whom you can get to know now but also the choices that will determine your future position in the social structure. Arguments about the relative importance of individual preferences and social structure invariably get bogged down in this chicken-and-egg tangle, and so tend to get resolved by ideology rather than by data. Those who believe in the power of individual choice can always contend that structure is simply the consequence of choices that individuals have made, while those who believe in the power of structure can always contend that the appearance of choice is illusory.

18. A similar finding has subsequently been reported in another study of homophily using data collected from Facebook (Wimmer and Lewis, 2010).

19. Some studies have found that polarization is increasing (Abramowitz and Saunders 2008; Bishop 2008), whereas others have found that Americans agree more than they disagree, and that views on one issue, say abortion, turn out to be surprisingly uncorrelated with views on other matters, like gun ownership, or immigration (Baldassari and Gelman 2008; Gelman et al. 2008; DiMaggio et al. 1996; Fiorina et al. 2005).

20. See Baldassari and Bearman (2007) for a discussion of real versus perceived agreement. In spite of the practical difficulties, some pioneering studies of precisely this kind have been conducted, first by Laumann (1969) and later by Huckfeldt and colleagues (Huckfeldt et al. 2004; Huckfeldt and Sprague 1987).

21. Clearly Facebook is an imperfect representation of everyone's friendship network: Not everyone is on Facebook, so some close friends may be missing, while many "friends" are barely acquainted in real life. Counting mutual friends can help differentiate between genuine and illusory friendships, but this method is also imperfect, as even casual acquaintances on Facebook may share many mutual friends. A better approach would be to observe how frequently friends communicate or perform other kinds of relational acts (e.g., clicking on a newsfeed item, commenting, liking, etc.); however, this data is not yet available to third-party developers.

22. For details of the Friend Sense study, see Goel, Mason, and Watts (2010).

23. Projection is a well-studied phenomenon in psychology, but it has been difficult to measure in social networks, for much the same reasons that have stymied network research in general. For a review of the projection literature, see Krueger and Clement (1994), Krueger (2007), and Robbins and Krueger (2005).

24. See Aral, Muchnik, and Sundararajan (2009) for a recent study of influence in viral marketing.

25. For other recent work using e-mail data see, Tyler et al. (2005), Cortes et al. (2003), Kossinets and Watts (2006), Malmgren et al. (2009), De Choudhury et al. (2010), and Clauset and Eagle (2007). For related work using cell-phone data, see Eagle et al. (2007) and Onnela et al. (2007); and for work using instant messaging data, see Leskovec and Horvitz (2008).

26. For information on the progress on cancer see an excellent series of articles, "The Forty Years War" published in the *New York Times*. Search "forty years war cancer" or go to http://bit.ly/c4bsc9. For a similar account of the genomics revolution, see recent articles by Wade (2010) and Pollack (2010).

27. I have made a similar argument elsewhere (Watts 2007), as have a number of other authors (Shneiderman 2008; Lazer et al. 2009).

INDEX

Printed in the United States
by Baker & Taylor Publisher Services